Hopkins' Achieved Self

WITHDRAWN

David Anthony Downes

University Press of America, Inc.
Lanham • New York • London

Copyright © 1996 by
University Press of America,® Inc.
4720 Boston Way
Lanham, Maryland 20706

3 Henrietta Street
London, WC2E 8LU England

Library of Congress Cataloging-in-Publication Data

Downes, David Anthony.
Hopkins' achieved self / David Anthony Downes.
p.   cm.
Includes bibliographical references and index.
1. Hopkins, Gerard Manley, 1844-1889--Criticism and interpretation.
2. Modernism (Literature)--England. 3. Consciousness in literature.
4. Self in literature. I. Title.
PR4803.H44Z6218   1996   821'.8--dc20   95-43572 CIP

ISBN 0-7618-0189-8 (cloth: alk: ppr.)
ISBN 0-7618-0190-1 (paper: alk: ppr.)

To Audrey for whose loving friendship
no gratitude is enough . . .

Contents

ALSO BY DAVID ANTHONY DOWNES

THE GREAT SACRIFICE: STUDIES IN HOPKINS

HOPKINS' SANCTIFYING IMAGINATION

THE IGNATIAN PERSONALITY OF
GERARD MANLEY HOPKINS

"Heidegger says somewhere that the poet sees the sacred while the philosopher sees Being, that they reside on the tops of mountains whence their voices echo and respond."

—Ricoeur

Preface

As a student of literary Modernism, I have long felt that much of what is called "Modernist" had its beginnings in the Victorian era. This view is based upon one of the central facets of twentieth century Modernism, the rise of interest in "consciousness" philosophy and esthetics. While Continental philosophers dominated speculation about consciousness theory, British authors from William Wordsworth throughout the nineteenth century concentrated their imaginative efforts on the interior self of consciousness in their literary creations. In their hands much literature became hermeneutic literary forms of positing authorial consciousness.

The term, "Modernism," can de descriptively defined in many ways; however, central to every definition, it seems to me is the notion of "selving" as Denis Donoghue has asserted in his usefull effort to focus the term: "Modernism is concerned with the validity of one's feelings and the practice of converting apparently external images and events into inwardness, personal energy" (*The Old Moderns* xii). This book is an exploration of converting energies that produce the "inwardness" of consciousness. This book is topically at the heart of what we call "Modernism."

The dynamics of the "inwardness" of consciousness, I have come to believe, is the central phenomenological component of Hopkins' writings. Only two studies have concentrated on the "selving" phenomenology in Hopkins. The earliest is J. Hillis Miller's chapter on Hopkins in his *The Disappearance of God* (1963) and Walter Ong's *Hopkins, the Self, and God* (1986). Miller's study is an effort to show the "selving" in Hopkins' writings as the disintegration of the religious self, thereby placing Hopkins in the vogue of secular Modernism which emphasizes in effect the dilemma of the disappearance of the self. Ong's study attempts to reorient the critical understanding of the self in Hopkins by sorting him out as an unique version of Victorian, Christian "selving" in the development of consciousness philosophy. Miller's approach is to read Hopkins against the Christian spiritual grain of all of his writings, and. while Ong's book is a necessary and very effective correction of Miller's study, he never attempts to demonstrate in full ranging detail the facets of a coherent phenomenology of "selving" in Hopkins' writings. In this book, I am attempting to uncover more fully the character and implications of "selving" in Hopkins' writings

In preparing for the writing of this book, I began reading nineteenth and twentieth century consciousness philosophers. I, as have other scholars, have found aspects of their philosophic discussions of selfness to be strikingly interactive with the notion of selfness in the critical and creative writings of Victorian and Modern authors. Moreover, I noticed, especially, highly significant thought parallels between Victorian G.M.Hopkins and the distinguished contemporary, French hermeneutic philosopher, Paul Ricoeur, particularly in their reflections on the phenomenology of "selving" the "I"-consciousness and the dynamics of religious consciousness formation.

Though Hopkins did not write out a systematic exposition of his thinking, his ideas about "selving" are discussed here and there in notebook jottings, spiritual commentaries and retreat notes. Yet when his notions are pulled together, they amount in their essential perspectives to a "selving" phenomenology and a hermeneutic system. To synthesize the notes and short essays wherein he did discuss his ideas required, it seemed to me, the close juxtaposing of Hopkins' texts with a compatible and fully developed modernist hermeneutics of "selving" in order to help elucidate his thoughts on these matters as well as reveal the extent to which his conceptions anticipated twentieth century thinking.

The key conceptual continuities between their writings seemed to me most significant. The notions of selfness and the expressive "selving" process that Hopkins sketched out are surprisingly echoed in Ricoeur's mature hermeneutics system. After much reading of and reflection on contemporary consciousness philosophers, I chose Paul Ricoeur as my modernist critical foil for studying Hopkins because Ricoeur's brilliant studies on "selving" hermeneutics would help reveal how richly suggestive are Hopkins' writings on human personality. I also felt that since there areno extended applications of Ricoeur's hermeneutic philosophy to the writings of a single author, my efforts might exhibit the critical relevance of his hermeneutics to literary criticism. A book on Hopkins and Ricoeur, then, would be a first.

Moreover, when the critical points of Hopkins' speculations are juxtaposed with the key notions of an advanced, fully developed, modernist, hermeneutic philosophy like Ricoeur's, there is such a striking coincidence that it is fair to go further and make an argument that Victorian Hopkins is an authentic instance of pre-modernist tendencies in his thinking about the self and hermeneutic theory so far as it bears upon the modern understanding of the formation of consciousness .

Indeed, in carrying this parallel out, I have come to believe that these anticipations are more than publishing accidents to Hopkins' status as a "Modernist" writer. In studying the hermeneutic philosophy of Paul Ricoeur, especially his mainframe concepts of "selving," the reflective consciousness, imagination, and the role of language in shaping the human personality, I have found astonishingly concomitant understandings of the same subjects in the writings of Hopkins. As a result of my pairing Ricoeur with Hopkins, a part of my argument is that Hopkins is provocatively modern in his hermeneutics of "selving" along with his poetics, a surprising proposition which I hope this book demonstrates.

This bringing together of the writings of Victorian Hopkins with a contemporary philosopher like Ricoeur, then, is a way of discussing new dimensions of literary Modernism by showing fresh evidence of how this movement was rooted in the previous century. However, the leading focus of this book is to study the "selving" hermeneutics in the writings of Gerard Manley Hopkins. No scholar has extensively studied the hermeneutic aspects of what Hopkins called "selving" in examining his expressions of religious testimony in his prose and poetry. Nor have his now famous terms "instress" and "inscape" been fully examined as having hermeneutic implications.

There is an ancillary intention in this study. It is to offer a new way to read the works of G. M. Hopkins. By "new" I mean to read his writings in the contexts of the author's own "selving" process.   If Hopkins and Ricoeur are right in their views that the poet's words represent the "selving" consciousness uncovered in fresh, original expressive modes, then it follows that an author's productions can be examined in "selving" hermeneutic terms Such probing reading into the redescriptions of his authorial subjectivity refocuses literary scholarship so as to look at literature as "selving" documents, an emphasis that some will argue infringes upon the neutral scholarly point of view. Such formal critical juxtapositions between hermeneutics, poetry, and here in Hopkins' case, religious consciousness, I argue, open up to readers a larger critical panorama within which to view the revealed texted consciousness of an author. Such efforts are rewarding clarifications of the synthesis of self, text, and the transformed consciousness that constitute the literary roots of Modernism.

This book begins with a Prologue in which I place Hopkins generally in the historical context of hermeneutic theory. I attempt to fit Hopkins into the flow of hermeneutic theory, showing his relationship to the hermeneutics of St. Augustine, the Medievalists, Luther, and Romanticism. In the first chapters, I then focus particularly on examining Hopkins' notions of "selving the 'I' " in the consciousness, the role of volition in positing of the self in the consciousness, and the correlative implications for his notions of the hermeneutics of the poetic word in transfiguring the consciousness towards transcendent states. The last chapters of the book are a survey of the "selving" phases discernible in Hopkins' poetic canon looked at as a narrative of the poet's own selfness. These chapters attempt to delineate how powerful is the fusion between Hopkins' understanding of selfness and its articulation in his poetry. The book closes with some postscriptive thoughts about Modernism and the hermeneutics of poetry. In this section I suggest that this study amounts to a critique of the secularist tendencies in Modernism. I argue that the central issue of Modernism in the contemporary world is the dilemma of the transcendent consciousness. It is my contention that the center of human "selving" is the prospect of attaining a hopeful state of transcendent consciousness, that essentially human history is a narration of the spiritual aspirations of consciousness, and that serious "reading" of the creative symbols of this religious quest of the consciousness always involves what might be called a "prayerful" reader's response. This focus is especially true of the literary creations of the past two centuries. Yet any careful inventory of the reading responses of critics to these "selving" productions reveals decreasingly the advocacy of "selving" as being essentially transcendent, and thus increasingly, the denigration of the meaningfulness of "selving" one's "I-ness." The affirmations of such "selving" nihilism amounts to a cultural death of the soul, a betrayal of the transcendent aspirations of the basic tendency of the historical cultural traditions of consciousness philosophy—transforming interiority. By contrast Hopkins and Ricoeur come across as the true revolutionaries of Modernism in their efforts to uncover the baseline spiritual factors operating in the "selving" consciousness.

Preface

Gratitude must be expressed to readers who helped significantly to improve this book. I offer special thanks to Joseph Feeney, S.J., Frank Fennell, John Carmody, Cary Plotkin, all generous colleagues along with other anonymous readers for their very useful critiques, encouragement, and affirmations in supporting the completion of this book. Valuable proofing assistance was contributed by Audrey R. Downes, and Dorothy Albritton and L. Pilar Wyman in preparing the text. Additionally much thanks is due to the staff from the Meriam Library at California University, Chico, for general materials support. Special gratitude is here expressed to quote materials from *The Poetical Works of Gerard Manley Hopkins*, 1990, edited by Norman H. Mackenzie, by permission of Oxford University Press and from Paul Ricoeur's *The Conflict of Interpretations: Essays in Hermeneutics*, 1974, edited by Don Ihde, by permission of Northwestern University Press, Evanston, Ill. I also wish to thank the many scholars whose writings I have consulted and cited, as do I wish to express my gratitude to their publishers for the scholarly "fair use" of their publications.

*****

Note to readers: when I began composing this book, I made use of the then definitive Fourth Edition of G.M. Hopkins' poetry (1967 reprinted 1984). During the book's composition, Norman MacKenzie's Clarendon Oxford Edition of *The Poetical Works of Gerard Manley Hopkins* was published (1990). All the citations have been adjusted to the Clarendon Oxford Edition. Citations designate the poem number in the text; if there is a second numerical designation, these listings are page designations by which I refer the reader to the pertinent commentary of the cited poem or passage.

David Anthony Downes

Prologue

Hopkins' Hermeneutical Stages of Consciousness

Hermeneutics is about making sense of some particle of experience. In this effort to make meaning, the consciousness has to adjust to contexts in which the sense of something exists. The hermeneutical context of something consists partly of the impression of a being-structure as a datum of experience, its traditionally associated conventional meanings, and the status of the interpretative consciousness appropriating the datum. Clearly a specific hermeneutic context is very complex, perhaps never fully clarified. Probably the closest we can get to analyze this process of making meaning is to study how texted meaning has been interpreted, though here too contexts, while more accessible as conventional interpretations, are still so complicated that full hermeneutical exegesis remains problematical. We can, however, ascertain the field of hermeneutic focus in studying the appropriations of any one language set in an effort to uncover operative hermeneutic principles.

The hermeneutic field of focus in Hopkins' writings is primarily religious meaning. Most of his writings are attempts to make meaningful utterances of religious states of consciousness. His texts, in their compositional nineteenth century time-frame, exhibit, I believe, three hermeneutic systems, the Classical / Christian, the Romantic, and the Modern traditions. In this prologue, I will attempt to locate and delineate these traditions primarily using his poetic texts.

The Classical / Christian Hermeneutic Self

In beginning with the Christian hermeneutic tradition in Hopkins, I must shortcut any full discussion of the long evolution of the hermeneutic of Christian texts. This discourse has already been done in much detail by many fine scholars, among them Gerald Bruns, whose incisive historical studies of hermeneutics will be my principal guide in sorting out the various historical traditions and conventions I think most pertinent to Hopkins.

Bruns in a chapter on Scripture interpretation in his book, *Hermeneutics, Ancient and Modern* (139-159), discusses the evolution of Christian hermeneutics as it evolved from its earliest tradition through St. Augustine, thence to Medieval Scholastics such as St. Thomas, and finally Luther. It is Bruns' analysis of Augustine and Luther I wish to focus on. He sees Augustine's Scriptural hermeneutics as one centered on the converted consciousness: "Augustine's hermeneutics implies a process in which one reinterprets oneself in order to enter into the conceptual scheme of another. Understanding, in effect, presupposes conversion" (143).

Conversion means a state of consciousness in which one is hermeneutically positioned to appropriate a sacred text. The consciousness must be readied to encounter a sacred text, a process of preparation that involves a fear of being alienated from God, a sincerely pious desire to be united with God, an understanding of the spiritual necessities of faith, strength to pursue one's spiritual destiny, and the need of God's mercy in the making of salvation. These are the attributes of the interpreter's consciousness in preparing for opening up sacred texts. However they are all activated only by what Augustine called the purification of sight, "where [the interpreter] cleanses that eye through which God may be seen insofar as He can be seen by those who die to the world as much as they are able" (Bruns 142-143). Augustine is using sight here as a figure for an in-seeing spiritualizing process by which the aforementioned attributes of the consciousness are activated to transform the self to a horizon of awareness where the ultimate sense of things is grasped. Hopkins expressed conversion as a hermeneutic process as taking in the "news of God." Sacred texts encountered with this "cleansed eye" are able to be appropriated as if they were self-texts. This transfigured state is the basis of the hermeneutics of conversion, a state wherein one is properly spiritually positioned to "see" sacral meanings in one's own life.

Turning to Hopkins' early religious poetry, we find that most of these poems are efforts to appropriate sacred texts in an unreadied state of religious consciousness, unprepared in the sense that while Hopkins was a cradle Christian, he had yet to confirm his commitment to a Christian tradition to satisfy his faith. These early poems are severally trial poems in which the poet is trying to produce in himself the capacity to understand the spiritual sense of things in the context of their traditional biblical texting. A poem like "Pilate" is an instance where young Hopkins explores the pain of inexpiable guilt; he used the Pilate narratives as allegorized in the Christian tradition to interpret what is meant to be exiled by a "sense of sin":

> The pang of Tartarus, Christians hold,
> Is this, from Christ to be shut out.
> This outer cold, my exile of old
> From God and man, is hell no doubt,
> Would I could hear the other Pilates shout.
> But yet they say Christ comes at the last day,
> Then will he keep [me] in this stay? (10 / 228)

What is interesting here is young Hopkins' knowledge of the post-biblical traditions regarding the fate of Pilate. He exhibits in this early poem awareness of the apocryphal Pilate who is overcome by guilt because he has realized that Christ was the Son of God, that Pilate spent the rest of his life in despairing remorse, and that he may have committed suicide. The poem shows direct echoes from the New Testament, perhaps from Hopkins' reading William Smith's *Dictionary of the Bible* (1860-63) and Walter Scott's *Anne of Geierstein*, as Norman MacKenzie suggests (228-229). The important point is that Hopkins was, in this poem, attempting to locate his own growing sense of alienation in his religious situation; he expressed some felt spiritual kinship through his poetic reflection on the agonies of Pilate. Hermeneutically, making some religious sense of the post-biblical Pilate was at the heart of Hopkins' religious dilemmas in understanding Christian history and tradition, a way to affirm the soundness of his own Christian consciousness.

The poem on Pilate seems to have been part of a pattern of poetic efforts for Hopkins to sort out his understanding of the Christian meaning of the Incarnation and the Holy Eucharist. In his preconversion state, just how the Jesus of the New Testament became the Christ of the Eucharist became crucial for Hopkins in founding his Christian faith on

a sound religious conscience. "Barnfloor and Winepress" is the first of
three poems written about the same time before his conversion to
Catholicism. These poems exhibit his deep concern to "see" the Passion
of Jesus as the making of the Holy Eucharist:

> Thou that on sin's wages starvest
> Behold we have the joy in harvest:
> For us was gather'd the first-fruits,
> For us was lifted from the roots,
> Sheaved in cruel hands, bruised sore,
> Scourged upon the threshing-floor;
> Where the upper mill-stone roof'd His head,
> At morn we found the heavenly Bread
> And, in a thousand altars laid,
> Christ our Sacrifice is made! (17 / 236-238)

Another poem composed at this time also attempts to explicate the
biblical Jesus as the Christ of the Eucharist. In "New Readings," (version
b), Hopkins wrote:

> Although the letter said
> On thistles that men look not grapes to gather,
> I read the story rather
> How soldiers platting thorns around CHRIST'S Head
> Grapes grew and drops of wine were sped.
>   (18 / 238-239)

In these poems Hopkins laid out the crucial hermeneutic issue of
Christian consciousness: How is Christian Scripture to be encountered?
The answer to this central understanding for each believer must be
established on the most intimate spiritual basis, as Hopkins wrote in a
poem that can be included in this conversion grouping, "Heaven-Haven":
"I must hunt down the prize / Where my heart lists, / Must see the eagle's
bulk, render'd in mists, / Hang of a treble size" (21 / 240).

We see in these poems a young man distilling his religious
consciousness through a process of reading sacral texts by going beyond
any particular interpretations resolving textual ambiguities. While the
texts form the bases upon which to build understanding, exegesis alone
won't bring about the transport of personal religious meaning. The sacral
texts in these poems must be experienced as altering transformations in

the consciousness in order to effect conversion. It is interesting that Hopkins tried to express the appropriated text as an event yet, at the same time, his lines clearly rest on the testament of literal meanings. The dominating image in these poems is harvest in which the poet draws out the real senses of harvest as the bases for understanding Jesus and the Eucharist as harvest. Hopkins is not playing with the senses of words. He intended to interpret "harvest" as a real thing in human experience that can be opened up to a new meaning. This happens because the thing and the word for it can be construed in the light of faith. This hermeneutic approach to Scripture is very traditional, both Scholastic and Augustinian. "Hunting" the "prize" of meaning in sacral writing begins in the literal and transliterates things and words into Christian meaning through the predispositional hermeneutics of faith conversion.

However, the hermeneutic tradition that was Hopkins' Protestant foundational Christianity was not based on things, but the polysemy of words, namely, the Lutheran tradition. For it was Luther, as Bruns has pointed out (143-148) who originated the idea of the "pneumatic" text, that is, sacral texts become Christian meaning through the activation of the religious consciousness mode of the interpreter / reader. It is the spirit of the reader who, in encountering the text, releases the spiritual meaning of the text as a transforming religious experience. Sacral hermeneutics is not just making sense of a text; rather hermeneutics is a meaning-making state of the reader who inspirits the text into a personal life meaning. If one reads the poems we have looked at in the context of this Lutheran tradition, the words become "religious" because the poet brought to them a particular spiritual state that induces the religious meaning coded in the text. Luther placed his great reform on this self-interpreting principle of Scripture. The Christian poet, in this view, finds his religious consciousness reconstituted in his poetic texts, themselves hermeneutic offshoots from the impact of sacral texts on him. As Bruns explains Luther's tradition of sacral hermeneutics: "In this tradition, taking the text in spirit in which it was written does not mean producing an objective exegetical reading that can be reproduced and tested; it means being informed or consumed or even exalted by the spirit of the text" (147). The texts of Scripture, then, are pneumatic. that is, words are powers exercised on and by the reader rather than just meanings produced by exegetical reflection.

This Reform hermeneutics is precisely the one Hopkins could not wholly accept. To make every reader the center of the Christian Church was, for him, to be opened up to a Babel of religious polysemy. Plainly put in terms of the essence of his Christian conversion, either the Jesus of history who became the Christ is literally present in the Holy Eucharist or He is not. Hopkins' Protestant tradition said to him a predispositional "maybe." In these conversion poems, Hopkins is declaring a "new reading": "He hath abolished the old drouth. / And rivers run were all was dry . . . / We meet together you and I, / Meet in one acre of one land, / And I will turn my looks to you. /And you shall meet me with reply, / We shall be sheaved with one band / In harvest and in garnering, / When heavenly vales so thick shall stand / With corn that they shall laugh and sing" (19 / 239-240). Hopkins wanted the sense of real things in his Christian hermeneutics, not just the senses of words.

For Hopkins, in the Protestant tradition, there being no guarantor of the transparency of the sacral words and their meaning, he turned to the Roman Catholic Church for its apostolic insurance in protecting the letter and spirit of Christian texts. In the most trying letter, perhaps in all of his correspondence wherein he tried to explain the key to his conversion, he wrote to his deeply discomforted Father:

> I shall hold as a Catholic what I have long held as an Anglican, that
> literal truth of our Lord's words by which I learn that the least
> fragment of the consecrated element in the Blessed Sacrament of the
> Altar is the whole Body of Christ born of the Blessed Virgin, before
> which the whole host of saints and angels as it lies on the altar
> trembles with adoration. This belief once got is the life of the soul
> and when I doubted it I shd. become an atheist the next day (*Further
> Letters* (92).

Can it be argued that there is no Lutheran element in this forthright statement about the essential character of Christianity as expressed in its tradition of sacral texts? It is hard to say absolutely no. While Hopkins is asserting positively the need for directly appropriating sacral texts within a tradition of magisterial affirmation, still the poet in him exhibits a kind of Lutheran hermeneutic temper in these conversion poems. Focussing on their depiction of the hermeneutics of the consciousness being transformed in the light of the holy texts, readers can discern Hopkins' "hunting" religious consciousness being opened through his encounters with texts whose conversion powers are partly due to the condition and situation of the interpreter. Part of Hopkins' reader-centered effort to react to Christian texts was conditioned by the situation of his hermeneutical consciousness. This is to say that his Christian religious poetry is at once exegetical and ontological, but to a degree "pneumatic" in its reexpression of sacral texts. Hermeneutically for Hopkins the youthful convert and poet, perhaps, Augustine and Luther were not so far apart as Christian apologetical history makes them. Hopkins would have been troubled by this assessment, but, nevertheless, there is a "pneumatic" aspect to his poetic expressions of his religious imagination.

The Romantic Hermeneutic Self

Hopkins' religious hermeneutic, however, evolved beyond traditional approaches to Christian meaning. When he began to write his mature poetry, the poetry most admired as Christian poetry, he added a hermeneutic element, the literary hermeneutic of Romanticism. We have seen, that in the first phase of Hopkins' efforts to understand the traditions of Christianity, he was concerned with locating what might be called the true and rightful inheritance of Christian meaning. The resolution of this problem, the basis of his conversion, was to accept the Rule of Faith as the Catholic Church. The Church affirms how we are to stand with respect to all that has been handed on as apostolic Christianity. Tradition as an inheritance of meanings has to be preserved and maintained on behalf of the rightful heirs of the Apostolic followers of Christ. Bruns calls this way of making meaning of the past the hermeneutics of Faith (195-199.)

But to discuss the hermeneutics of a poet, one must move beyond general consciousness to the creative consciousness, that is, from the understandings of all that comes down to us from the past to the redescriptions of these meanings in "selving" expressive forms. In a sense, forms of artistic expression are projections of the consciousness attempting to pass from an internal hermeneutic to an external one. The author translates the meanings of hermeneutic experience into a representative or mimetic text. The English Romantic Movement devised a poetic hermeneutic in which meaning is a revelation of the self projected into the encounter with the world outside the consciousness. In this hermeneutic, the self enters into alien experience by attempting through this self-projection to understand this Other as we understand ourselves. The Romantic hermeneutic is a "reexperiencing the lived experience of another, that is, experiencing a thou as an I, understanding the Other the way we understand ourselves, or perhaps better" (Bruns 160). This hermeneutic involves a poetics of the creative consciousness which can enter imaginatively into any situation from any perspective, thereby understand any point of view. Through a kind of hermeneutic suspension, the projective subjectivity can in some meaningful way become its object.

When we look at the phenomenology of Hopkins' notions of "instress" and "inscape," we discover that, while rooted in the concepts of Classical / Christian hermeneutics, these coined terms incorporate the dynamics of Romantic hermeneutics. Taking in ("instressing") an "inscape" or ontic shape of a thing can be seen as a way of projecting the consciousness into an other. Hopkins is insistent on the preservation of the objectivity of this appropriating process, but at the same time, he noted that, in such appropriations, there is often what he called a "prepossession" of the Other, that is a subjective response anticipatory to the "inscaping," a "feeling," a "passion," or an "enthusiasm," in uttering or wording the thing, " a word to oneself," as he put it (*Journals* 125). The relevant point here is that the "word" that reexpresses the Other is a formal projection of the self into the "scapes" of the senses. and while the world outside the consciousness is the basis of meaning, the reexpressing utterance is partially the self projected into the Other as part of its meaning.

In the writing of Romantic poetry, then, the self takes from the experience of the Other its existential whatness, which is its meaning, and recapitulates this quiddity as repeating mimetic words. If the "instressed inscape" reaches into the deeper form of the Other, then the poetic utterance reaches beyond the formalism of ordinary appropriation, taking the esthetic utterance to the level of a "selving" ontological horizon. Thus when Hopkins wrote, "The world is charged with the grandeur of God," he was reexpressing a very deep appropriation of all existence. And in making this utterance, he was expressing the ultimate by way of projecting his self into the Other; in some way, in his utterance he becomes mimetically the creative consciousness of God experienced as the original and continuing creation of all that is. Hermeneutically his self slips into (projects) the mind of God and words the meaning of that mind from this inside capability. Read this way, the sonnet is really about the meaning of self being projected into an awesome deific "Other" at the horizon of reality.

Perhaps the most elaborate instance of Hopkins' employment of Romantic poetic hermeneutic of self-projection is his ode, " The Wreck of the Deutschland" (101). In this poem we see exemplified what might be taken as two differing instances of the Romantic hermeneutic. In Part The First, the poet reexpresses the making of the meaning of Deity in his own consciousness. In stanza after stanza the poet utters his astonishment at the ways God came to his consciousness as new self-meanings. In stanza 1, the astonishment is that of condescension; incomprehensible infinite power comes down into the very mind of the humble poet as a Presence: "and dost thou touch me afresh? / Over again I feel thy finger and find thee" (119-128 / 321-350). And after this acknowledgment in stanza 2, "I did say yes," the poet was willing to risk his selfness ("mastering me") by projecting his self-meaning into the Other of the "Lord of living and dead." The rest of the stanzas in Part The First are utterances of the meaning of this huge election. We are told the dramatic circumstances of this transforming of his selfness, the trauma that his senses underwent, the huge shifts in his emotions, and, most tellingly, the projection of his own self-being towards union with Christ: "I whirled out wings that spell / And fled with a fling of the heart to the heart of the Host."

The fleeing of the self into the meaning of the "Other," here the deific "Other," is an instance of "selving" by becoming the Other through a grand imaginative leap. In a way, this part of the poem is an "inscaping" of God through extraordinary spiritual "instressing." While such is logically impossible on the basis of the ontological levels of finite and infinite being, yet in some way the poet declares, explains, affirms, and discloses that he has "entered" into the mind of God by appropriating divinity through his own "selving" consciousness. From another hermeneutic perspective, that of inspiration, the poet seems to have experienced God as the inspiriting of his selfness, but at the same time, he himself has penetrated into the Deity inspiriting him. In Romantic, hermeneutical texting, Hopkins "read" God inscribing the "selving-texting" of the poet himself. It is also notable that this self-texting is both recollectively historical ("It dates from day / Of his going to Galilee;") and transcendentally apocalyptic ("Oh, / We lash with the best or worst / Word last!"). The narrative is about this wondrous hermeneutical achievement of understanding God's mastery as a temporal totality transforming the self and the self's poetic utterance of its new "selving" meaning. The narrative is a hermeneutic creation which mediates time as motion and time as duration. The self is posited in time and projected throughout time.

There is a similar enactment of the Romantic hermeneutic in Part The Second of "The Wreck," but there are important differences. In "Part The Second" the poet, in his poetic act of his recreating the experience of the wreck, especially that of the nuns, attempted to make meaning of these events using a more straight forward Romantic hermeneutic, what Wordsworth described in his *Preface to Lyrical Ballads*, "So that it will be the wish of the Poet to bring his feelings near

to those of the persons whose feelings he describes, nay, for short spaces
of time, perhaps, to let himself slip into an entire delusion, and even
confound and identify his own feelings with theirs" (quoted by Bruns
159).

The juncture of what might be called the two poetic hermeneutics in
the ode is approached in Stanza 18 wherein the poet reflects on his own
transported consciousness, now struggling to be extended to the meaning
of the arising nun "lioness," and asks for the inspiration of her own self-
texting ("Ah! there was a heart right! / There was a single eye! / Read the
unshapeable shock night / And knew the who and the why; / Wording it
how but by him that present and past, / Heaven and earth are word of,
worded by?" The hermeneutic situation of the poet, in his own self-
texting, slips "for short spaces of time" into that of the tall nun through
an act of poetic recreation, a projection that is at once hermeneutically
thrilling and dangerous ("Ah, touched in your bower of bone, / Are you!
turned, for an exquisite smart, / Have you! make words break from me
here all alone, / Do you!)."

The poet records the passage of this awesome transfer of self-
meaning as he moves to the climax of Part The Second. In Stanza 19,
the poet identifies the Sister, who is the subject of his felt consciousness,
and after four Stanzas in which he "inscapes" her self-identity—woman,
nun, devotee of St. Francis (20-23), he openly discloses the construction
of the meaning he is about to make in his astonishing utterances about
the tall nun. In Stanza 24, he notes the contrasting solitude of his own
poetic selfness ("On a pastoral forehead of Wales"); in Stanza 25 he
begins the mimetic grounding of his hermeneutic imagination to be
inspirited by the nun's heroism, and, at the same time, he projects himself
into her "triumph": "The majesty! what did she mean? / Breathe, arch
and original Breath." And for two more Stanzas (26-27), the poet works
through reflections about the nun's self-defining meaning. And then,
there breaks into his consciousness the parallel meaning to his own
selving: "Thou heardst me, truer than tongue, confess / Thy terror, O
Christ, O God" (Stanza 2).

All in a moment in stanza 28, the poet, confounded, searches for
ways to utter the nun's self-meaning through a projection of his Christed
consciousness: "But how shall I . . . Make me room there; / Reach me
a . . . Fancy, come faster— / Strike you the sight of it?" The poet in the
recreative act of his Romantic imagination is projected into the
consciousness of the nun, and counterwards, her "selving" inspirits the
poet's own wording self-consciousness. The focus is the inhabiting of

God / Christ in two different hermeneutical situations of the consciousness, the one immediate and the other indirect, in which through a kind of sublime sense of mystical union, both selves are understood, poetically worded, as transcendent, Christed self-images.

The poet celebrates the splendor of this felt "selving" union in the remaining stanzas of his ode (stanzas 29-35). What is narrated in these ecstatic passages, parallel to the poet's personal spiritual ecstasy in Part the First, are instances of self-clarifying ascendancy ("Ah! there was a heart right!"), the consciousness of a miraculous rebirth in the guise of the mystery of Mary, ("For so conceive, so to conceive thee is done"), a sense of maternal self-transmission to others ("be a bell to, rings of it, and / Startle the poor sheep back"). Finally, the poet ends his ode in the sublimity of this new meaning by celebrating its hermeneutic uttering powers, both his and the nun's on the one side, and the Lord's on the other (stanzas 32-35). The key poetic action words in these stanzas are hermeneutic acts of appropriation, "grasp," "fetched," "burn," "flash," "easter"—all exhortations to comprehend what is the essential meaning of Creation ("But here was a heart-throe, birth of a brain, / Word, that heard and kept thee and uttered thee outright" (Stanza 30). "The Wreck of the Deutschland" can be read as one of the greatest poetic creations of the hermeneutic act of Christed "selving" reexpressed by the Romantic imagination.

The poems written during the years of 1877-1879 are Hopkins' richest productions about "selving" meaning. In these poems we see that his "instress-inscape" notions are really dynamic hermeneutic principles. The poet, as Hopkins put it, "takes in an inscape," which is to say that he apprehends ("instresses") a thing to the level of its actualized identification, so deep does its meaning penetrate, and then its singular form is poetically metamorphized ("stressed") in the making of utterance, that is, its "inscaped" form is reexpressed in the verbal form of the poem, a new reincarnation of its "inscaped " ontic form. The poetic utterance in its verbal body is the very eidolon of the original "inscape" possessing in its mimetic symbolism the dynamic nature, ideality, and meaning of the thing. It must be added that in this hermeneutic transfer of "inscape" into metaphoric symbol, the poem itself, in its narrative pattern, image variety, thematic components, its elaborated rhythm and sound systems, becomes a new eidetic entity itself, an "inscape" in its own right open to textual appropriation by readers.

Two observations are in order here. The first is that Hopkins' "instress / inscape" as hermeneutic principles possess aspects of both the Christian hermeneutical tradition and the Romantic. We see in the first, "instress," the effort to seize the vital form / sense of a thing and build its meaning through this appropriation. Things precede words in the true Augustinian mode of the "cleansed eye." Hopkins' poetry, as every reader knows, is a splendid demonstration of seeing the thing clearly ("Glory be to God for dappled things"). In this hermeneutic stance, the "inscaper" is in a special interpretative place, that of being open to be "converted" temporarily to the Other, which allows for full reception of the intelligibility of the "inscape" of the thing perceived. In a sense, the thing "seen" reinterprets the perceptivity of the "see-er."

The second observation is that in some sense the "Instress / inscape" hermeneutic is a Romantic making of meaning. The poet through his imagination projects his felt consciousness into the observed thing, into the energy of its naturality, into the energy of its shaping "inscape," in some sense into a kind of coinherence between himself and the thing being what it is. This intersubjectivity of "inscaper" and "inscaped" produces a kind of fusion of feeling awareness which is the seedbed of figurative language needed to express this duality of associated self-meanings. In a way the poeticizing self is transposed into a new identity, a suspension that is brief, but intensely real and self-identifying. The finitude of one self is felt to merge with the finitude of another, and in this way, an other is possessed interiorly, from the inside out.

Let us look briefly at two more poems which illustrate these hermeneutic modes. "Hurrahing in Harvest" (124-149 / 388-390) opens with the poet "inscaping" a fall harvest field. The first four lines of the octave of the sonnet reexpress the "scape" of the scene ("barbarous in beauty"). The next four lines narrate the poet undergoing a kind of self-projection into the ideality, meaning, sensible form of the landscape, the beginnings of a kind of self-suspension into the thing observed: "I walk, I lift up, I lift up heart, eyes, / Down all that glory in the heavens . . . . "The sestet can be read as a kind of colloquium of fusing self-identities ("These things, these things were here"), that produces in the verbal body of the poem a new self, the figure of the presence of a "Spirit" animating Nature in union with the self of the "inscaper": ("which two when they meet, / The heart rears wings bold and bolder / And hurls for him, O half hurls earth for him off under his feet"). The Romantic hermeneutic ideal of giving over one's selfness into another is the imaginative center of this poem, yet there is that hermeneutic Christian aspect wherein landscape is the text that transforms the self into a new "selving" utterance.

In the "The Windhover" (120 / 376-384), we see a more complex expression of the two hermeneutic actions. In the octave we read about the poet "inscaping" the bird ("I caught this morning . . . dapple-dawn-drawn Falcon"). Perhaps in no other poem has Hopkins delineated the process of "selving" appropriation so clearly by the using of a series of figuring images of the bird that stretches into a seventeen-word first line, followed by lines, powerful in their mimetic effect, dramatizing the flight of the kestrel. In a Classic hermeneutic making of meaning, the sense of the thing becomes the sense of the word of the thing. Yet the poet "sees" this bird meaning is open to a fuller apprehension of meaning: "My heart in hiding / Stirred for a bird,—the achieve of, the mastery of thing."

Then we come to the famous lines in the poem, "Brute beauty and valour and act, oh, air pride, plume, here / Buckle!" The poet now literally calls out for a kind of fusion of selves, an inter-subjectification in which the "instressing" energy-scape of the bird, *mutatis mutandus*, becomes that of the "inscaping" poet. Indeed, this hermeneutic happening comes about through the figuration of the poem, for in the verbal body of the poem, the poet becomes the bird in some sense, as the poet declared the buckling on of a second self represents a "selving-charge" with transforming consequences: "AND the fire that breaks from thee then, a billion / Times told lovelier, more dangerous, O my chevalier." The critical word in these famous lines of the sestet is "told," for it is precisely the "inscape" of the bird being "told" that transfigures it and the poet's self into the poetic identity constituted of both, now a new self-form, a new, unique verbal "inscape" able to be contemplated by all readers.

Finally, one question that arises is, to what degree is the poet's self-possession evacuated? Does the poet preserve his "selving I-ness"? Hopkins is as attentive to preserving intact the exclusivity of his own consciousness as he is much concerned with ontic integrity of the self-being thing observed. Yet he understood, as we have seen in these poems bearing signs of a Romantic hermeneutic, that there takes place a self-transformation through imaginative projection as part of the creative act of poetic appropriation and the uttering of a redescription of this state in the form of a verbal "inscape." The character of this poetic hermeneutic process lies in Hopkins' understanding of poetic speech. Basic to his understanding is that language is an acknowledgement of being, an acknowledgment based upon the given that words convey immanently the real meaning of the real order of things however selved by an "inscaper" / utterer: "Real meaning" is the intelligibility of forms whose existence in things is absolute (*Journals* 120).

Skipping the possible applications of Hopkins' notion of the existential unity of forms of language—grammatical, historical, and logical— to that of poetry, we come to Hopkins' general idea of the "inscape of speech," which is his concept of poetry. By this phrase Hopkins meant "speech only employed to carry the inscape of speech for its own sake" (*Journals* 289). There is implied in this statement an independence of form inhering in poetic speech different from that of the poet's ordinary wording consciousness, a form that can be contemplated for its own sake alone. So we see that for Hopkins' poetry is utterance functioning on three levels. Poems express the "inscapes" of Nature; they express their own unique design (the "inscape" of their poetic speech); they also express the poet's own "selving" consciousness.

Serious poetry for Hopkins escalates awareness to the level of the contemplative consciousness wherein the self comes to realize that "selving" is partly a gift calling for a responsive acknowledgement. Hopkins understood all human "selving," especially poetic "selving," as a hermeneutic act wherein the self utterance of being is a giving back, hence a kenosis of self. The hermeneutic of "selving" according to Hopkins is a paradox. The self, in giving back the "inscapes" of being in faithful utterance, is acknowledging the "inscape" foundational to all being, God / Christ: "the world, man, should after its own manner give God being in return for the being he has given or should give him back that being he has given" (*Sermons* 129). Creativity is an affirming gift to be given back as self-creations. All "selving" is some form of speech, a form of verbal gifting affirming being, a form of humbling praise, giving beauty "back to God beauty's self and beauty's giver," yet simultaneously such giving is a kind of self-exaltation in that uttered consignments of being-beauty involve a kind of acknowledged self-transcendence, a self-beauty that "Never fleets more, fastened with tenderest truth / To its own best being and its loveliness of youth: it is an / everlastingness of, O it is an all youth!" (148-170 / 429431). Hopkins wrote of this justifiable "selving"pride, "MEN OF GENIUS ARE SAID TO CREATE [caps his], a painting, a tale, a tune, a policy; not indeed the colours and the canvas, not the words or notes, but the design, the character, the air, the plan. How then?—from themselves, from their own minds" (*Sermons* 239).

Hopkins understood that the making of meaning of the world (his hermeneutics of "instressing inscapes") is to begin to grasp the ordered unity of Creation. The basic reality principle undergirding this unity (Nature, self, idea, word) is Hopkins' hermeneutic notion of God as the maker of the primal utterance known as Creation. It is God who uttered himself as Creation and thereby surcharged all existence as his "texts." His original utterances are foundational to making sense of everything, hence God is the source of all hermeneutical consciousness: "God's utterance of himself in himself is God the Word, outside himself is the world. This world then is word, expression, news of God. Therefore its end, its purpose, its purport, its meaning, is God and its life or work to name and praise him" (*Sermons* 129). It follows that all "selving" utterance is, advertently or inadvertently, in some sense a reselving praise of the Creator, acts of giving back. Hopkins' religious poems, written under the imaginative aegis of a Romantic hermeneutic, attempt to reach the contemplative ecstasy of reuttering God's utterance of himself.

The Modern Hermeneutical Self

In the last poems in Dublin, Hopkins encountered the ultimate boundaries of the hermeneutics of "selving inscape." We have seen that Hopkins' insights into the ways of hermeneutic acts were both Classical / Christian and Romantic. Philosophically, he held to the Classical notion of essential forms in things which are open to appropriations which reveal the continuity of the order of things, ideas, and words. We have seen that he affirmed the existence of a hermeneutical tradition in and through which the history of "inscapes" constitute a temporal account, an intersecting narration of the past as an institution of meanings handed down as normative and compelling— mastered in the hermeneutic of Faith.

We have also seen that Hopkins as poet conceived of and practiced a poetic that added a Romantic aspect to his analysis of Classical hermeneutics. As poet, he created poetic reflections in which he imaginatively projected his selfness into the objects and persons of his reflections so that the artistic dynamics of his poems involve, at times, a kind of self-transference between the "inscaped" object and the "inscaping" subject. This taking and giving of self-identity effects a powerful sense of the coinherence between consciousness and the objects reflected in its contemplative energies, bespeaking horizons of unifying higher meanings.

Hopkins' hermeneutic puts enormous pressures on the energies in the human consciousness in the making of meaning. The hermeneutic mind must be able to take in the "inscapes" of things and translate them into meangingful "texts" in the upper consciousness, "texts" able to be reexpressed as "selving" meanings which locate the self in a world that makes sense. But what if the consciousness for some unknown reasons loses the efficacy of its highest hermeneutic powers? What if the texts of selved experience scramble? What if the I-self finds little or no self-expressions which locate and display the self's unique I-identity, its uttering powers of "selving" realization? Such a state produces a crisis in the consciousness' energies and abilities to be an authentic expresser of the self, to relate interior meaning with exterior reality wherein hope and freedom are disclosed to the self. To put this disconnection In Hopkins' words, what if because of some failure of creative energy, he could not "give beauty back"?

I think that what happened to Hopkins during his last years in Dublin, 1884-1889 was a strange circuit break in his energy to take in "inscapes" and to utter them in apposite "selving" fashion. It is not to our purpose here to discuss the enigmatic biographical causes of this sad debility that afflicted Hopkins during these years. It is to our purpose to look at some of these last poems as possessing a different poetical hermeneutic.

Before analyzing his last hermeneutic, some assumptions often made about this period of Hopkins' predicament must be sorted through. First, Hopkins did not succumb to what Paul Ricoeur calls a "hermeneutics of "suspicion"; Hopkins did not abandon his understanding of the real as real, that is, that there is no meaningful hermeneutic relationship between Nature, self, idea, and word because of some suspicion that there is a kind of undiscovered slippage between and among these vital elements of a reality-based hermeneutic. There is no evidence that he overturned his earlier notions and descriptions of his reality-based "instress / inscape" hermeneutic principles. Moreover, Hopkins did not turn himself away from Classical / Christian hermeneutics to one that confirms that the meanings that come down to us from the past are chimerical. Nor did he succumb to an extreme version of the projective hermeneutic of the Romantics wherein the self, through some kind of displacing, imaginative role-playing, gets lost in the imagined Other, a condition that can become possessive to the point of self-obliteration. I do not think Hopkins faced any of these risks to his hermeneutic consciousness even in these last poems of torment.

What Hopkins was facing, speaking hermeneutically, was a breakdown in his own contemplative energies to utter exalted feelings about his felt presence of God in himself and hence in Creation. Hermeneutics for Hopkins was a poetic mediation between things pathetically perceived, taken in, and contemplatively raised to a horizon level of consciousness. When these poetic energies were producing transforming mediations producing testamentory acts of utterance, a circuit of utterances poetic and prayerful, then "selving" expressive of his own I-ness happened, that is, an "instressing-inscaping" communion through "selving" speech was realized. Creation , Christ, and self were in a discursive colloquy. But when his imagination was not moved by his "instressing" sensibilities leading to creative utterances, then he felt deeply the loss of his contemplating poetic voice. I believe this hermeneutic collapse is the underlying subject of his "dark" sonnets.

Looking at his last writings from both spiritual and poetic perspectives, we see over and over again his declaration that his powers to take in ("instress") "inscapes" had seriously diminished as a result of some combination of spiritual aridity, physical debility, and professional lassitude. These elements, in this time of his life, he experienced as enervations of his "selving" powers. Such losses depressed him, harassed him, and, at times made him fearful that his was going to undergo a kind of total loss of his creative, expressive powers, a poetic death. This crisis in his hermeneutic powers of his consciousness, we must remember, touched deeply into his religious vocation in that "giving beauty back" to God was at the heart of his spirituality. The instress of "inscaped" poetic speech is prayer, the Word worded. Additionally, the more he struggled with the puzzlement over his vacated expressive powers, he began to sense that his "selving" of Christ had become somehow opaquely mysterious. What he had earlier experienced as the creative joy of Christ's energy, "inscaping" in the pied beauty of everything, now had moved out of worded sighting. His eye for such "inscapes" needed cleansing if his voice was to come back. For this to happen, he felt he had to "inscape" not the landscape of Nature, but the "inscape" of his selfness.

We cannot here examine in full depth all of those sonnets written during this period which are often called "terrible." We can, however, scan them to see that they are about the hermeneutic dilemmas in his creative, expressive consciousness. Every one of these poems touch on the "instress" stasis in his poetic consciousness at this time of his life

In the sonnet,"To seem the stranger" (154 / 445-447), Hopkins considers his isolation from his home surroundings in England as a condition of his feelings of creative lassitude: "England, whose honour O all my heart woos, wife / To my creating thought, would neither hear / Me," bringing the poet to a kind of creative banishment: "Only what word / Wisest my heart breeds dark heaven's baffling ban / Bars or hell's spell thwarts. This to hoard unheard, / Heard unheeded, leaves me a lonely began." Looking at these lines as expressive of a hermeneutic frustration by taking the passage, "word / Wisest my heart breeds" as a description of a state wherein the consciousness is disenabled to selve meaning, is a way to read the sonnet, on one level, as about not being able to operate the self as a productive "selving" energy. "Lonely began" intensifies this sense of the poem, for the phrase is a figure of hermeneutic "choke," for a poet of huge imaginative, expressive powers, a terrible frustration.

"I wake and feel the fell of dark, not day" (155 / 447-448), read in the context of hermeneutic disorder, is strikingly ironical. The poet is "inscaping" with great expressive powers the continuing darkening of his night-shaded consciousness. His trenchant "inscaping" of this state of consciousness reveals enormous creative, expressive, selving powers. No "lonely began" here. But his "instressing" has turned inside, towards his own self-scape: "What hours, O what black hours we have spent / This night! what sights you, heart, saw, ways you went!" The spiritual logic of the sonnet is that such contemplative failures as he was experiencing must be his fault. God was still present in Creation; Christ was still the creative energy of every self; so the breakdown in his "instressing" capacities, the selving hermeneutic of uttering "God's news," must be his own failure, a kind of religious betrayal in the consciousness: "I am gall, I am heartburn, God's most deep decree / Bitter would have me taste: my taste was me; / Bones built in me, flesh filled, blood brimmed the curse." "Selving" so powerfully his hermeneutic catastrophe in this way amounted to a form of Romantic narcissism, a "selving" projection for its own sake, hence not a "selving" utterance of Creation and Christ, the self as prayer, but an act of self-interpretation, self-wording unmediated by the Word. For Hopkins such a reduction of his "instressing" poetic powers of speech to mere subjectivity was humiliating, worse, hermeneutically the speech of self-damnation— a "curse."

"No worst, there is none" (157 / 449-452) is another instance of Hopkins spiritual hermeneutics gone awry, only in this speaking of it, Hopkins is plunged into a kind of hermeneutic despair. The sonnet is about poetic speech incarcerated in the consciousness, unable to instress Nature as Creation "news," unable to hear the audibility of Christ in the heart, only able to hear his own cries of desperation over such losses. As is the case in all of these sonnets, there is a situational irony regarding the expressive powers of the poetic "inscapes" in these sonnets; Hopkins, his poetic powers at high pitch, here most trenchantly "inscapes" his selfness from the inside, enacts the subjectivity of Romantic hermeneutic powers, disclosing incisively what is it like to experience the self disenabled to make the self meaningful, unable to find words of "selving" identity truly disclosive of the "self of self," only able to make pitiful, sorrowing sounds of "selving" dislocation, portending profound inexpressibility and hence language / literacy itself hanging in the balance, a descent into hermeneutic madness: "My cries heave, herds-long; huddled in a main, a chief- / Woe, world-sorrow . . . / O the mind, the mind has mountains; cliffs of fall / Frightful, sheer, no-man-fathomed." This sonnet is about the tragedy of the self becoming unworded.

The other three sonnets usually included in the "dark" sonnets grouping, "carrion comfort" (159 / 454-457), "Patience" (162 / 460-461), and "My own heart" (163 / 455-463), are poems in which the poet begins to experience a return of his contemplative energies. This comes about through a renewal of the volitional powers of the consciousness. Hopkins (as we shall see in greater detail in a later chapter) allied the hermeneutic power of the consciousness to will-power. For Hopkins it is the transmission powers of the volitional consciousness which operates the deeper "instressing" perceptions of things and mediates them into "selving" meaning. Understanding has to be desired and chosen. From these choices arises attention that becomes meaning, interpretation that becomes self-speech. Hopkins, in both his artistic and spiritual understanding of the consciousness, emphasized "selving" as expression that is made, constructed, achieved. The self's desire to accord with the will of God occurs through the enacting energies of the will which surcharges the consciousness to mediate sensation and response towards uttering the "news" of God in Nature, the Word selved as the chosen self-word.

We see such "selving" utterance in these last three sonnets. In "Carrion Comfort," Hopkins announces the volitional energy of his renewed determination to reclaim his selfness: "Not, I'll not, carrion comfort, Despair not feast on thee. . . I can; / Can something, hope, wish day come, not choose not to be." His contemplative hermeneutic powers being so nearly totally unraveled, he could only reverse the situation through a terrible struggle, which the sonnet describes. But he won the internal battle. Somehow he was enabled (his "stress" and / or Christ's "Instress"?) to relocate his selfness, reestablish his expressive powers, come again to possession of his powers to selve the world as the self of Christ: "Hand, rather, my heart lo! lapped strength, stole joy, would laugh, cheer." The time-frame within which the poet's struggle is redescribed suggests that this sonnet is not about the "terror" of defeat but rather about the triumph of recovery. To be sure, spiritual mystery and darkness in the self had to be encountered, but the poet has been able to regain that point of self-utterance wherein he is able to sound selfness in response to his frightening "instress" of God as pursuer. His word fought His Word and finally an exchange took place. The broken hermeneutic circle was mended; the verbal energy of the self again finds it possible to express the communion of love and faith.

Once this exchange is opened up again, then, whatever the pains and sufferings, then the self is predisposed to become patient, to wait in caring attention for those "selving" interpretations which acknowledge the self again "talking" with God. Hopkins makes clear that however strong the desire to know and selve God in the self, the ready willingness to choose the words that express prayerful communion with Christ, human volition is powerless on its own to make the spiritual hermeneutic of Faith operate: "Yet the rebellious wills / Of us we do bid God bend to him even so. / And where is he who more and more distills / delicious kindness?— He is patient." Hopkins humbly acknowledges that the contemplative energy of the self is finite, can only word God indirectly, needs his graceful mediation before the hermeneutic of Faith can be spoken. This same awareness is expressed in the sonnet beginning, "My own heart let me more have pity on." Again Hopkins affirmed that the revival of the self's hermeneutic powers, to make meaning at the horizon of God's presence in Creation, depends finally on some "graced" meaning-making power coming from outside the "selving" consciousness. He must be patient, he must be open, he must be attentive, he must desire to exchange, but he must wait for some signaling inscape from on high. Until God's "news" arrives, he must stand at attention: "Soul, self; come, poor Jackself, I do advise? You, jaded, let be; call off thoughts awhile / Elsewhere; leave comfort root-room; let joy size / At God knows when to God knows what." Practically, his self-advice means to be patiently attentive, always ready to try to "instress" the landscapes of Nature and self for Christ's "inscaping" speech, meaning that initiates the poetry of faith.

We have seen that the final poems in Hopkins' canon are able to be read as poems about the formation and maintenance of the hermeneutic consciousness. Placing them in the context of the evolution of Hopkins' phenomenology and hermeneutics, they represent a movement to another stage of hermeneutic development. In these poems he expressed his struggle to awaken his creative consciousness, to energize his capacities to "instress" once again the landscapes of his experience at the horizon of Creation and to give back beauty in his redescriptions of them. To be sure, this crisis in his consciousness was dire in that his "selving" utterances began to risk becoming expressions of a kind of Romantic lost self, projections of self-misery to the extent that he might slip into a sobbing Romantic narcissism and lose the "selving" identity most expressive of his I-ness—his priestly vocation to selve Christ fully and absolutely in his life.

Such a crisis contended with the establishment in his understanding of the hermeneutic consciousness of history and tradition, what hermeneutic historians like Gerald Bruns calls the Classicist stage (196), that stage where interpretations of things in the past are handed down as a tradition to be appropriated as an aggregate of meanings, their variety cataloged, to be penetrated for their relative substance, and their structures as a set of paradigms of normative and binding meanings for interpretative acts assimilating the future. For Hopkins the Classicist hermeneutic stage was most crucially set in the Christian Patristic tradition and the institution of Roman Catholic Church.

The Romantic evolution of hermeneutic development, in which the self through the use of powerful feelings is imaginatively projected into some other selved thing or person to the point of suspending one's own identity and seemingly becoming the self of the Other from the inside, can be the beginning of a "selving" suicide. Gerald Bruns describes the debilities of this hermeneutic stage as a deconstruction of the self: "What I must give up is precisely my self-possession, my consciousness; I must evacuate my inwardness, leave my body, turn myself into I know not what, become a body for another to inhabit, or a mind for another's will to control" (167). The danger of such powerful imaginative self-projections are obvious. The real self looses control so that utterances now become such an depersonalizing objectification of the self that the self is dislocated, even intruded upon in a kind of ruthless invasion of privacy that can be come self-dispossessing. Hopkins exercised control over such Romantic projections in his "instress-inscape" hermeneutics through affirming the necessity of the volitional foundation of such self-projections as expressed in his carefully balanced circuit of perception, response, and projective utterance that reaches a kind emptying of the self for God's grace to fill, a kenosis that reconstructs the "selving I" to achieve a new, higher level of self-fulfillment. This "selving" situation is the hermeneutic of Faith, selving interpretation as the retrieval of the self through the giving of self in the flux of time and eternity, in effect, the forging of a new identity in the consciousness.

In these last poems, we find as well a second potential stage of hermeneutic development in Hopkins, one that can be seen to exhibit some Modernist aspects. Twentieth century modernists perceive meaning as masked by an allegorized recollective history, which keeps humans in a kind of hermeneutic bondage by analyzing and interpreting the past as the future gone by. Modernism of this sort is the hermeneutics of "suspicion" which attempts to unmask this historical institutionalization of meaning; a hermeneutic tradition, it is asserted, that aims to repress the chaos of history through a false hermeneutic of Reason and Faith, an inane trust in the hermeneutic integrity of recollection and retrieval— the tradition of ideas and ideals, institutions and language— that allege to express reality in time as it really is. Thus the "suspicion" of Modernist hermeneutics carries with it a deep anxiety that no meaning is normative and therefore no meaning is binding, "the horror of the Other . . . a repressed fear that time moves, after all, in the other direction, towards strangeness and difference, and that what lies ahead will be as full of primitive rage and incoherence, a rocky horror picture show, Chaos and Old Night, which is what the Modernist sees when he looks into the past" (Bruns 196-197).

The "terrible sonnets" are powerful anticipatory expressions of the "suspicion" hermeneutics of Modernism, which is why they have received the greatest attention by modern readers. These poems express the fright and horror in the consciousness when time and history cannot be understood as a narrative of ultimate cosmic intelligibility. When the contemplating consciousness is plunged into this hermeneutic chaos, the object of all contemplation tends towards the tormented subjective self, as Hopkins last poems show. Taken seriously, felt deeply, such self-denying "instresses" of the self's hermeneutic emasculation produces a poetry of searing I-destroying self-scapes, full of agony and sorrow, the only escape from which, according to Hopkins, is to regain the energizing assent to "a principle, Christ's gift ("The Wreck," Stanza 4), if a "selving" of hopefullness is to recommence. In the meantime, there is anxious contention: "birds build—but not I build; no, but strain, / Time's eunuch, and not breed one work that wakes. / Mine, O thou lord of life, send my roots rain" (177 / 501-503).

The "terrible sonnets" have been read as pre-Modernist anxiety about time and meaning. They have been read by many modern critics (Harris, Robinson) as the hermeneutic nightmare of the collapse of Hopkins' capacities to make his "instress / inscape" hermeneutic produce affirming "selving" utterance. However the frightful "selving" horror expressed in these poems is no mere playing with hermeneutical categories; the foundation of Hopkins' self-positing was his affirmation of the historicality of the Incarnation, the hermeneutic basis of his Faith. Nowhere did he express this trust than in his great "Wreck" ode. In Stanzas 5, 6 and 7 he wrote that the "stress" of the Incarnation "rides time like riding a river / (And here the faithful waver, the faithless fable and miss. / It dates from day / Of his going in Galilee." Christ is the "inscape" of God revealed in time, whose "stress" must be taken in by the human consciousness and reuttered ("mouthed to flesh-burst") if existence and time are to have universal, hence personal meaning: "His mystery must be "instressed, stressed." Only when our response to all hermeneutical situations begins with this incarnational assent can we construe the languages of history, culture, and institutions into the fullness of proximate and ultimate understanding, "selving" meaning: " For I greet him the days I meet him, and bless when I understand."

The last poem, "To R. B." (179), is a master statement of Hopkins "instress / inscape" hermeneutics of Faith. In the first four lines, the poet tells us about the "fine delight" of taking in an "inscape,"— "instressing." He tells us that meaning first comes as an intense, "hot" encounter with an "inscape's stress" upon the consciousness, "like the blowpipe flame." The dynamic of such an "inscape-taking" emphasizes pressure, vitality, and flashing potentiality, "Spur, live and lancing." The fourth line tells us that such experiences are sudden illuminations which, if not seized, flash out, "quenched faster than it came."

The next four lines move to the "stressed" consciousness, now pregnant with its appropriated "inscape." This passage is about the building of meaning and utterance in the consciousness. Hopkins used the time period of the gestation of a child as his figure for the way the "inscapes" are "worded" in the consciousness. The process is really mysterious though it is clear that "utterance" involves a kind of translation of the "inscaping" of the characteristics of language, an inchoate "immortal song," the production of which takes time, often much more time than the making of a child, yet similarly as the mother's body makes, "carries" the child, so does the poet (utter-bearer) actively carry ("wears, bears, cares, combs") its own child, word, as an expression of his "inscaping" selfness. Read as a hermeneutic process, Hopkins' verbs for natural pregnancy are figurative suggestions for the delicate activity in the consciousness of the embryonic growing in the stages of the wording "inscape." There is "wearing," the predisposition of bringing into existence, "bears," keeps and holds up for completion, "cares," actively sustains the ongoing process, and "combs," sorts out the parts into appropriate word-shapes as structured meaning as well as the design and sound as the expressive pattern at word-birth, utterance.

The next four lines focus upon the "maternity" of language birth. The consciousness is big with the "instressed" energy of the original "inscape," a kind of hermeneutic gene package which directs the gestation of meaning ("aim now known") into verbalized consciousness (("hand at work now never wrong"). The last line opens up the poet's maternal yearning for the seductiveness of such semantic siring ("Sweet fire the sire of muse"), the impregnating of the creative consciousness that will bring about the birthed child of meaning ("The roll, the rise, the carol, the creation"). This is the hermeneutic "bliss" that was missing in him, missing because for some reason that graced inseminating mediation between Nature and self has become dormant. God, "him that present and past, / Heaven and earth are word of, worded by." was not making the kind of "news" in his consciousness that moved him to speak back in exalting, affirmative responses. The world had come to seem un-Worded and in that blotting, the self becomes confused about its prime life's work—"selving" Christ as the lead story of Creation. This de-Christed state is true self-confusion in the face of which one is, as we have seen, frequently cast down into deep self-questioning. Hopkins last poems can be seen as the poetic "inscapes" of experiencing what culturally we know as Modernism, the hermeneutics of "suspicion," the anxiety that history is untranslatable and hence is an idiot tale. Beyond this hermeneutic stage is what some have called Postmodernism where the self becomes unraveled into broken systems of language, institutions that have become museums of dead meanings, and culture an unending quarrel of conflicted meanings. Hopkins never let this total blackening of the consciousness happen. He never lost his conviction that the universe is God's story and he was a character in it: his hermeneutics of Faith did become at risk, partly at least, because of his own "selving" prideful faults, though he never lost his place and closed the book. His last poems dramatize the hermeneutic horror that radical Romantic self-disposal leads to as do they depict that "selving" battle that must be won to hold fast to the ability to read the world as "God's news."

We have seen, in this hermeneutical overview, that Hopkins' writings span three central Western hermeneutical systems—Classical , Christian, and Modern. In and through each of these he strove to construct the "selving" hermeneutic consciousness of Faith. The rest of this book is a study of the deeper facets of his building of the hermeneutic consciousness of Christian hope with an eye towards its echoing in a Modernist Christian, philosophic frame—the Christian hermeneutic in the philosophy of Paul Ricoeur. While the focus will steadily be Hopkins' forging of his poetic hermeneutic Faith consciousness as expressed in his prose and poetry, I will attempt to sort out his specific hermeneutical predispositions as they relate to modern consciousness philosophy by showing how Hopkins' hermeneutics finds impressive echoes in the contemporary analysis of the Christian religious consciousness. Like Hopkins, Ricoeur attempts to ameliorate the Modernist / Postmoderniost conflict of interpretations by establishing a new hermeneutic of Faith based upon the meaning unfolding (narrated) "in front of the text," the semantics of hope decipherable in the futurity of time, the "passion for the possible," revealed in the story of Jesus. The echoes between the "selving" hermeneutics of Hopkins and Ricoeur are notable, even remarkable, a correspondence offering a fresh way to read Hopkins' spiritual writings and his religious poetry.

Chapter 1

Hopkins' General "Selving" Hermeneutics

Introduction

The situation of the human self making meaning is basically a hermeneutical predicament. The conscious self is confronted with a nest of questions about what goes on in the understanding of anything including its own selfness. Basically what Hopkins meant by "selving" is the unique processing of self-meaning that is the driving energy of every individual thing in existence. "Selving," then, in its most general sense, is the elemental activity in everything acting out its individuality meaningfully. To the "selving" human consciousness, every individual thing is a "text' to be "read" for its meaning as part of its own "selving" reflection.

On the deepest level of human consciousness, the direction of "selving"is towards an illumination of the subjectivity of the self. But the meanings that the hermeneutics of selving uncover are a complex of exterior and interior awarenesses. All "selving" involves questions of self-meaning which arise from all that is not the self, an Other, an Other that cannot be fully appropriated. Fully realized "selving" in the sense of total self-comprehension is not achievable. Therefore, the hermeneutics of "selving" the self always raises the question of the limits of self-understanding which meaning uncovers, a hermeneutic circle of comprehension that is always contingently partial.

While education is essentially a reprehension of historical interpretations of the way things are, the actualizing dynamics of the "selving" self soon awakens to the realization that the pedagogical frameworks of institutionalized "realty" interpretations do not finally reconcile the conflicts which are the historical part of hermeneutical tradition. "Selving," then, is a kind of living through this confliction of interpretations. Hermeneutics is an interpretative accounting of this experience. Each self, understood as the "text" of the "selving" consciousness, must wade through and in some sense suffer a host of conflicting interpretations in constructing a coherent hermeneutic of its subjectivity.

It is this hermeneutical "selving" account revealed in the writings of G. M. Hopkins that is the main subject of this book. Being a poet writing in the nineteen century, the essential character of Hopkins' "selving" hermeneutic stressed the role of the imagination as the prime texting faculty in understanding his experience of things. Of course, he inherited through his education the tradition of institutionally structured meanings. This was especially true in the area of his greatest interest, the religious meanings of things. But his "selving" being essentially poetic, his encounter with Christian Scriptures quickly went beyond the allegories of interpretative rationalization that make up traditional exegesis. In the hermeneutical spirit of Augustine, he viewed the meanings of the things of this world through a "cleansed eye" (Bruns 142) which brought him to a "selving" in which he felt his self had entered into the very ontological center of things, wherein he dared to imagine his self open to radical transformations. The hermeneutics of such a religious "selving" is the account of how meaning is disclosed through living spiritual experiences which recapitulate what the Scriptural texts declare as "the Kingdom of God." Hopkins' poetic acts of consciousness are redescribed "selving" appropriations of "seeing" himself in new religious modes of selfness.

Understanding the hermeneutics of Hopkins' poetic "selving" requires an examination of his views of language—phenomenological, poetic, and sacral— as a redescriptive "selving" processing of the experience of things as they are in all of their continuities and discontinuities. This analysis of his hermeneutics will result in a study of how his poetic imagination constructed an interpretative account of the conflicts, shocks or "wrecks" which divided his selfness and the universe, interiorly and exteriorly. Through such a descriptive analysis of personality and language formation, we will better understand how the religious consciousness is intrinsic to comprehending the hermeneutics of his "selving,"

To aid my analysis of Hopkins "selving" hermeneutic, I will use the hermeneutical theories of Paul Ricoeur to bring to bear the insights of a fully developed Christian hermeneutic philosophy on Hopkins' largely intuitive "selving" process. Hopkins did not construct a worked out, muchless a modern, systemic hermeneutic of the poetic religious imagination. What he did achieve was an amazing hermeneutical understanding of "selving" as a state of enacted religious consciousness, an understanding he little more than sketched out, but one which he powerfully realized in his poetry. By looking at Hopkins' writings, especially his poetry, through the prism of Ricoeur's consciousness philosophy, we can see how impressively prodigious was his understanding of the hermeneutics of "selving" from the point of view of modern consciousness hermeneutics.

The Self- Text: Interpretations of Interpretations

What twentieth-century readers have found especially engaging in the writings of G. M. Hopkins are the many ways in which he textualized his selfness in engaging his world, his surroundings, and his interpretative heterogeneity. His avid and appreciative readers have found in his self-scaping words a power, a meaning, and a music that together represent a kind of fundamental unity of achieved subjectivity that conveys a self-understanding strikingly realized.

Moreover, his wording of himself wording life, Nature, history, culture, God—his engagement with everything that made up his world of reality— is a vast process of interpretation in order to try to fit "truth" to "selfness." The nature of the "selving" hermeneutic conflict is confronted in his rich little essay on Parmenides (*Journals* 129-130) wherein he stated that the prominence of Being and the representations of thought—Parmenides' *"things are* or *there is truth"* —must be in some way be the same. Yet just how hermeneutic process mediates being and truth is an interpretative "selving" mystery. Hopkins affirmed that the basic human desire is to know absolutely, and that the questions about the true status of the objects of our knowing are mediated by interpretations, "utterance," in Hopkins' way of putting it: "The truth in thought is Being, stress, and each word is one way of acknowledging Being and each sentence by its copula *is* (or its equivalent) the utterance and assertion of it" (*Journals* 129). By writing, "Each word is *one* way of acknowledging Being," he implies that what fascinates the consciousness is the difference of every interpretation.

Hopkins explained in the same essay that the very essence of the interpretative act, the relating of the "is" to "it is or there is," involves a bridge, what he called "a stem of stress between us and things to bear us out and carry the mind over" (*Journals* 127). He held that words must be used to produce connections, universal and particular, between the ideas in the mind and the objects we encounter, to represent intelligible relationships between objects and ideas, and to fulfill our desire to come to "selving" understanding of our selfness in our world. Yet the plenitude of being and historical contexting of the traditions of interpretations produce words on interpretive words, interpretations of interpretations, so there is always a conflict of interpretations both subjective and objective.

Every truly creative expresser of the world of selfness, set in the world- frame of total experience, attempts to heal or assuage this conflict. Thus when we encounter a mind of Hopkins' caliber, what holds us is his interpretative word- bridge built between the thinker and things thoughtfully expressed. Such a bridge is a whorl of words that in their bridging order achieve a deep structured unity "between us and things," a mediation which draws us closer to the world and ourselves. Words also represent the heterogeneity of ourselves to others, and an articulation of our needs and desires, doubts and certainties, joys and sorrows. Taking my cue from Paul Ricoeur, I call this level of expressive selfness, this unification brought about by the self-reflective, expressive consciousness, "the achieved self."

Part of the enigma of hermeneutics of the "achieved self" is the self's projection into the things it experiences. Textually, this means reading in some sense becomes a way of entering the persona of the author. And while there is in part a kind of transference of the self in this hermeneutic process, there is also some blurring of subjectivity. This is to say that through a kind of "selving" projection, we uncover other potential selves in our identity. This hermeneutic involves a kind of play of masking and unmasking of "selving roles." Here the self reanimates the other selves it encounters as a process of making meaning. If the projective movement of energy is powerful, it often awakens a multi-self in which self-identity can threaten the coinherence of the "selving" consciousness itself.

This disclosure of meaning differs from that of Classical hermeneutic tradition where the self is, in a sense, reinscribed by experiencing the things (texts) of this world. This intersubjective hermeneutic movement of energy penetrates from without and, if powerful, will play a part in transforming the self. As we have seen, the movement of energy from text as medium inhabiting and reinterpreting the reader is historically part of the Christian tradition of Scriptural hermeneutics while the movement of projective energy emanating from reader to text is a shift emphasized by the Romantic Movement (Bruns 159-178). It is important to keep in mind that Hopkins' "selving" is complicated by both of these hermeneutic focuses, not surprisingly given his strong attachments to traditional Christianity and the Romantic literary culture of his time.

In general terms then, for Hopkins the "cleansed eye" senses a world of individual things scaled within an ordered cosmos. The consciousness, itself a shifting and adjusting apprehensive power, is thus confronted with the task of "reading" the "texts" of being as experiences of particularized selves, taken as a whole, expressions of an organically dynamic universe, though encountered in the reality of their separations, differences, conflicts, and crises. Hopkins "selving" hermeneutic, therefore, must contend with shocks, inside and out, to the consciousness in an effort to appropriate subjective and objective meaning from the things of the world. To make the world behave hermeneutically, Hopkins depended upon the poetic imagination to connect him with reality, to bridge the shocks in "dappled things" so that he could achieve a "selving" logos, which Gerald Bruns aptly describes as a "logic of discovery" (230). As I have outlined in the Prologue, the hermeneutic apparatus Hopkins used to describe his poetic logos is his well known twin onto-hermeneutic concepts of "instress" and "inscape." Hopkins rested his entire hermeneutic of "selving" the world though the apprehensions of the reflective consciousness's "instressing inscape" of the differentiated things of the world and poetically redescribing their separating but paralleled differences in an original "texting," disclosing order, meaning, and beauty in the universe.

The centrality of self-texting in Hopkins' poetic hermeneutic cannot be stressed too much. As already noted, for him being and thought are the same, and hence thought, thing, and word are inseparable. It follows that utterance is the meaning of the thing thought. Implicit in this wording is the notion of the polysemic metaphor, which is the expressive mode of the thing thought. In the making of metaphor, the consciousness becomes poetic, which is to say, the consciousness creates a verbal figurative form of the union of thought and thing. The resulting figurative utterance is an instancing of the formalized union of thought and thing as "meaning," a multiplex meaning that is as pervasive in the word as in the thing. The figure, as the verbalized incarnation of the thing, is the happening of meaning, a transfer from ontological individuality to its formal verbal equivalents— image, thought, sound, and movement fused into a symbolic form, for Hopkins the purest incarnation of being. When constructing meaning, specifically in a poetic formality, the consciousness is able to reproduce in language the ontological dynamic of thought/ things thereby uncovering their larger, more universal harmonic meanings. Poetic consciousness, then, is the power to make unique utterances of thought / things as symbolic forms possessing their own parabolic analogues of all parallel forms thereby infusing a high-rise of meanings— linguistic, natural, notional, sacral, and affective. The Hopkins poetic consciousness possesses intrinsic hermeneutic powers to make symbolic forms which in their repetitive pairing instantiates the canon of existence as an order of parallels, natural, human, and divine orders of meaning. For Hopkins the making of such metaphors through shaping powers of the poetic consciousness is the quintessential "selving" act of reflective consciousness in construing the meaning of the things of the world.

In the ensuing discussions of Hopkins' writings, particularly his poetry, I hope to produce and examine the phenomenological, hermeneutic, and religious interpretations which open up the "stem of stress" which bore Hopkins self out and carried him back to himself in "selving" disclosures. This book, as is any book of practical criticism, will be an interpretation of interpretations. Every reader's interpretative acts are grounded in other interpretations of texts—the author's, so far as they can be known, as well as one's own paradigmatic methodology of construing texts; however, since the reading of Hopkins in this study involves consciously applying a philosophic framework of a contemporary system of linguistic hermeneutics developed by Paul Ricoeur, some initial description of the melding of Hopkins and Ricoeur's hermeneutic paradigm at work in this book is called for.

"Selving" in Hopkins and Ricoeur

The imposing hermeneutic theory of Paul Ricoeur, whose systematic thinking about how consciousness and language work to synthesize perceptive and reflective experience into what we call understanding, offers a rich critical application to literature, poetry in particular, especially religious poetry, the hermeneutical linguistic locus of Ricoeur's philosophical thinking. What follows can be no more than an outline of the Ricoeurrian hermeneutical frame within which I will attempt to examine the hermeneutical implications of Hopkins' writings. The philosophical notions foundational to the epistemological frame, as well as the hermeneutical patterns functioning in reading texts within the interpretative circle of the frame, are derived from Ricoeur himself and / or his commentators. In applying Ricoeur to Hopkins, I will take cognizance of other interpretative sources, but always with the intent of reading Hopkins within the Ricoeurrian paradigm.

At base for Ricoeur, the issue of processing the self to "selving" understanding is essentially a linguistic process. Through language we go out of the self and return to the self changed. That change we call meaning. This change begins in the mystery of infant consciousness and continues as long we can utter. Thus the pure "I-ness" of the self-identity breaks into what we call existence. With the birth of utterance, the pure "I" is posited as this "I here speaking," the presupposition of every utterance. This transposition of the "I" from pure self-consciousness to the existential "I" is perhaps the first and most fundamental interpretative problem encountered in human self-expression because the pure "I" is always elusively hidden from the existential or linguistic "I"; therefore, every utterance is a kind of emptying of the absolute "I' into experience wherein it is posited into a linguistic self-reflection. Another way of understanding this positing of the self is that in entering experience through utterance, the absolute "I" acknowledges the priority of being to meaningful utterance, and in that acknowledgement, affirms being as the corrective to all self-expression, and thus experiences a kind of kenosis or self-alienation in the grasping of being. Hopkins anticipated, as we have seen, this contemporary notion of the first phase of the self going out of itself to being through language. As he put it, "the word is the stem of stress that carries us over to Being" (*Journals* 127), or in another expression, "the mind is foredrawn to Being."

Ricoeur expresses a similar dynamism between consciousness, language and existence. For him metaphor is the key action of texting in which the imaginative consciousness redescribes the futurity of being; meaning is thus the future intimated as new possibility. Figurative redescription goes beyond "being-as" to "seeing -as." Imaginative figuration is not just a replication of things. Nor is it mainly some kind of internal analysis of structural forms, nor is it an effort to decipher original intentionality. Rather it is an expansion through figurative utterance to match the creative dynamism that is the ever-productive creativity of being. Metaphor catches being in act, that is its becoming, which is the "ontological function of metaphorical discourse, in which every dormant potentiality of existence appears as blossoming forth, every latent capacity for action is actualized" *(Rule of Metaphor* 43). Both Hopkins and Ricoeur assert that things symbolized in the poetic consciousness as an event of language is an intrusion into being for purposes of disclosing new regions of reality. Ricoeur notes that the polysemy of language and being correspond: "the reference of metaphorical utterance brings being as actuality and potentiality into play" *(Rule of Metaphor* 307; Vanhoozer 70-73). This is the same incarnating process we have seen in Hopkins' emphasis that "Being and thought are the same" and that wording is an acknowledgment of this coinherence.

There are difficulties in moving from oral to textual phenomenological discourse according to Ricoeur On the way to creating the reflective language of the symbolizing consciousness, the self encounters increasing degrees of self-distancing, a growing disunity in the secure positing of selfness in the appropriating process. The mind's metaphors become opaque which disorders the "selving" consciousness. For example, moving from informal verbal utterance to formalized textual language projects the "I" posited into the written text under the formalities of a linguistic order, a structuring well beyond the originary acts of interior wording. The act of formally texting the "I" is experienced as a state of further estrangement beyond spoken utterance because the symbolized appropriations of things and thoughts by the "I" expressed within the formal text becomes an authorial "I." Yet the circle of distanced "I's" can be closed, for the text, as transformed oral utterance, offers the possibility for the self to return to itself in self-comprehension, that is, the "I" recognizes itself objectified in the very concreteness of text as a meaningful possibility "for me to be" (Klemm 14). This recognition represents an hermeneutic unity based upon a selving recomprehension, a kind of returning of selfness to the self-positing "I."

Hopkins' view of "selving" infers, as we shall see in some detail, the condition of hermeneutical conflict in human personality and the "selving" impetus towards unity of thought, word, and thing in the expressive "I"-consciousness: he wrote, "All thought is of course in a sense an effort at unity" *(Journals* 83). He drew a careful distinction between the desire for unity as an ideal in art and morality. Art represents the continually varied self-positings of the "I," and thus is subject to the creative-expressive processing of unity as a foredrawing to being, the reality principle in all art. The ideal of morality is that attraction wherein the "I" chooses at a more lofty level of desire to achieve the purest self-appropriation, as perfect a self-realization of some ultimate ideal as is within human powers. As Hopkins put it, "Why do we desire unity? The first answer would be that the ideal, the one, is our only means of recognizing successfully our being to ourselves, it unifies us, while vice destroys the sense of being by dissipating thought . . . [and] wickedness breaks up the unity of principle" (*Journals* 83). In hermeneutic terms, Hopkins' desire to close the circle of self-interpretation is at base an ethic of self-unification in the phenomenology of selfness, but it is more. Self-unification reaches beyond the conflicts of self-interpretation to a new, transformed selfness, to what Hopkins called that "chastity of mind" that he attributed to Christ *(Letters to Bridges* 174) which Ricoeur has described as the "the passion for the possible." Herein enters the whole realm of the contemplative consciousness functioning at the level of cosmic horizons more commonly known as the meditative tradition in Christian spirituality and religious poetry.

For Ricoeur, the call within selfness to self-reflective acts of linguistic interpretation that reveal a relationship to being, is the theme of his philosophical anthropology. His commentators have summed up this theme in the question: "What does it mean to be human?" (Klemm 45). In opening up this theme, Ricoeur starts by depicting the model structure of human phenomenology as having three levels: the theoretical, the practical, and the affective consciousness. Each of these levels in their discontinuity operate as dysfunctional elements in the integration of understanding and sensibility within the self giving rise to what Ricoeur calls the "pathetìque of misery" (Klemm 52). This misery constitutes what Ricoeur calls "fallible man" who is ontologically a contradictory mixture "because his act of existing is the very act of bringing about mediation between all the modalities all the levels of reality within him and outside him" *(Fallible Man* 3-6), a mediation that is very difficult, because all the levels are in some way discontinuous. Thus any study of the discourse of self-reflection will be a study of the "pathetìque of misery."

As a philosophical anthropologist, the intent of Ricoeur's thought is to discern some notion of a transcendental method of pure reflection and to consider its limits. He concludes that pure reflection can describe noetically what he calls "human mediation," but the description is abstract and does not disclose the disruption that is endemic at the concrete level of individual consciousness: "Pure reflection is unable to make the transition from fallibility to fault, from the possibility of evil to its actuality in concrete existence" (Klemm 54-61). Pure reflection being so limited, a new starting point for deciphering faulted selfhood must be found. For Ricoeur this new beginning must be based on a linguistic hermeneutic through which selfness can be posited as meaningful, however bound up with the condition of fault. The poetics of human utterance is the key to human meaning for Ricoeur. It is in the surplusage of expressed figurative meaning beyond mere perception through which the self is more clearly deciphered. This is so because the "I" consciousness perceives *perspectively,* and words these slanted perceptions in language that always has a surplusage of emergent self-meaning. Later we shall see that this surplus of self-meaning opens up the hermeneutic role of metaphor and narrative in human experience and sets the stage for a religious horizon in the self-reflecting consciousness.

Ricoeur offers an elaborate analysis of the conditions that emerge in the self in passing from the "I think" to "I will" (Klemm 53-76). The center of Ricoeur's analyses of practical selving *(Fallible Man* 70-219) is the meaning of freedom in personhood, which in any self-reflective act involves, in general, a mediation between the infinite (perceiving, signifying, seeing, and saying) and the finite (knowing, feeling, and doing) aspects of the self. Ricoeur describes the functions of the practical "selving" through an analysis of affective perspectives in limiting the will, perspectives rooted in a desire for obtaining some practical end. Affectivity in the self is heavily modified by a deeply felt attachment to one's difference from others, the role of habit in doing, and the elusiveness of personal motivations. According to Ricoeur, human beings are fallible because of a disproportionate relation of finitude to infinitude, a disproportion that sets up the whole movement of human existence, a movement to reconcile the general self's originating affirmation at an infinite level (I aim to be bountifully happy). But the fallible "I-ness" confounds this desire for specific happiness by its multiple perceptual perspectives and by the split between thinking and choosing (thus allowing the possibility of failing through inner conflict, including the deliberate corruption of the self-mediating process).

Out of this anthropological analysis arises the hermeneutic task according to Ricoeur. Klemm sums up Ricoeur's view of hermeneutics: "Reflective philosophy is self-grounding but blind to that ground. For self-reflection to proceed, it must recognize with Dilthey that the self is lost, fallen and alienated in the works, ideas, images, institutions that objectify it. Consciousness of the self is not a given but a task of appropriating what is lost and self-alienated in language. Reflective philosophy must reconstitute itself as hermeneutics in order to recover the meaning of the "I" of the "I am" in its act of existing by deciphering the meaning of that self as it has become sedimented in the linguistic tradition" (60).

How the "I" of the self hermeneutically bridges the dark holes in "selving" its "I am" is what it means to be human. Hopkins stated the complexity of this "selving" mystery memorably in one of his lesser known prose passages. Writing about the volitional mode of the self's "I" expressing its "selving"-identity in constructing its personality, he wrote : "so far as it is a definite self . . . it is identified with pitch, moral pitch, determination of right and wrong"; on the finite level, "this pitch, if it might be expressed, if it were good English, *the doing* be, *the doing* choose . . . And such 'doing-be,' and the thread or chain of such pitches or 'doing-be' 's,' prior to nature's being overlaid, is self, personality . . . when the self, the person comes into being with the accession of nature . . . As besides the actual world there is an infinity of possible worlds, differing in all degrees . . . like so many 'cleaves' or exposed faces of some pomegranate . . . cut all directions across; so there is an infinity of possible strains of action and choice for each possible self in these worlds . . . of which we see at best only one cleave. Rather we see the world as one cleave and the life of each person as one vein or strain of colour in it" (*Sermons* 150-51). Hopkins, like Ricoeur, understood that "selving" the human self involves partly, but critically, a hermeneutic of volition.

Let us now look in more detail at how Hopkins understood the hermeneutical pattern of human "selving," achieving an identifying "I"-self that can lead from the diaspora of the chaotic self to the possibility of an integrated consciousness, free at last and hopefully beatific. Juxtaposing Ricoeur with Hopkins will reveal how amazingly precocious he was in his understanding of the dynamics of consciousness philosophy. Such a paralleling will require, at times, frequent reiteration of the basal "selving" paradigms of each thinker in order to examine fresh facets of the hermeneutic implications of each account of the self and personality. In returning to the foundational concepts each time, the reader, it is hoped, will gradually build up a contextual understanding of each hermeneutical system, separately and comparatively.

Chapter 2

"Selving" the "I Am" in Hopkins

The Monodramatic "I"

There are two pervasive aims which thoughtful people seek in today's world. The first is to authenticate the role and meaning of the self that each of us is. The second is to be rational about how we explain our ourselves and our world. The goal of both aims is to "selve" oneself in understanding human nature. Let us see how Hopkins tried to accomplish these aims and goals of the achieved self, the "I am" of the "I" as a harmonized state of consciousness.

Hopkins started, as I believe most modern phenomenological thinkers do, with the concrete experience of the "I" subject and the process of self-perception of the world within ourselves (*Sermons* 122). The subject-self and the perceiving "I" conscious-self, according to Hopkins, are unique modes of an ontic energy Hopkins called "instress" (fusing Aristotle and Newton, and Coleridge and Newman, and arguably anticipating modern particle physicists and the genetic biologists). "Instress" is that "energy of being" which passes through universal creation shaping each thing in its distinctive form which he called "inscape," making all being in the world individually singular and intelligible. Perception, then, is a conduction of such energies. Nothing in Hopkins' canon demonstrates this notion more than his diaries, which are filled with all kinds of displays of energies drawn from a broad range of Nature, notebooks which could well be jottings of a Faraday, von Helmholtz, or Peter Guthrie Tait— the energy scientists of his day (Zaniello 35-58).

Hopkins held that everything in the world is singular. What did he mean by this? It is the characteristic of energy that "chance left free to act falls into an order as well as purpose" (*Journals* 230). Order and purpose are attributes of the "inscape" of energy that produce thingness, that abrupt uniqueness each being possesses expressed as its design-principle and pattern formation. The particles of energy coalesce into larger collections or centers of energy whose formation Hopkins called "scaping." Since the patterning of energy into distinct being is a result of an inner dynamic of energy, the design principle of a thing is called its "inscape." Close observation of the "inscape" of a thing will reveal its own texture, its surface scape , and its design formation in its most minute detailing as produced and sustained by its "instress," that is, its skeletal lines of force, its network of energies. (Such a notion, incidentally, is a remarkable anticipation of the scientific descriptions of the behavior of particles by modern particle physicists) (Polkinghorne 43-62.) All things, according to Hopkins, share difference in their sharing the energy of being. Taken together, all things are discovered to be part of a structured whole, each separate thing fitting into a larger purpose. Thus the energy of being, not only produces individualizing micro-form, but it also structures the whole plethora of being into a macro-universe.

Hopkins' concept of the energy of being which is the carrier of the intelligibility of the "inscapes" of things he called "instress." This energy, of course, an energy like no other in natural existence, permeates all the textures and structures of all being, a unique communicative energy that interacts most powerfully with the intellective / affective system of the person: the human consciousness. "Instress" is the medium that makes the "inscapes" of everything understandable to a conscious observer. Within the consciousness is the "I" of the self, that elemental driving energy of "I-ness" which is readily distinguishable from the contents of the consciousness as "me." It is the "I" of the consciousness which unifies the self as a knower of self and the world. It is this "self- knowing" that is the crux of positing self-identity. In Hopkins hermeneutic words, the monodramatic "I" must "stress, instress" its own "inscape."

Paul Ricoeur's account of the self-consciousness echoes and responds to Hopkins' discussion of "selving" consciousness. The positing of self, Ricoeur notes, is the first truth of the modern tradition of philosophy, for twentieth century consciousness philosophers, the most important event in contemporary personalist culture— the act of individual personhood. Ricoeur wrote, "For this tradition (which we are considering as a whole before distinguishing its principal representatives), the positing of the self is a truth which posits itself" (*Conflict* 326). But for Ricoeur, how is the existence of the self affirmed? Only by consciousness, he argues, enacting itself through self-reflective acts, is the self posited: "Incapable of being either verified or deduced, it is simultaneously the positing of a being and an act, a form of existence and an operation of thought: I am, I think; to exist for myself is to think; I exist insofar as I think. Since this truth can neither be verified as a fact or deduced as a conclusion, it must be posited in reflection; its own self-positing is a reflection" (*Conflict* 326-327). And what is reflection? It is a deciphering of self in and through its "I" selfness, that is, the self reflects on its self-representations, acts, and works which objectify its "I-ness." This is the prime task of consciousness "selving," finding what Ricoeur calls the "*ego* of the *ego cogito* in the mirror of its objects."

Such self-positing is richly exemplified in Hopkins famous narrative description of his "I-ness." In writing his now famous affirmation of the existence of his selfness ("I find myself both as a man and as myself"), Hopkins started outside the whole tradition of his priestly philosophical education by choosing to reflect on the psychic "world within," thereby preferring to make sense of the Christian belief in Creation in introspective terms of his own selfness, that is, the interior evidence of selfness; thus the character of evidence he used is subjectively individualized and more powerful than "outside" evidence: the "world within . . . takes on the mind more hold." In starting this way, he was applying his own intellectual framework to the theology of John Duns Scotus and *The Spiritual Exercises of St. Ignatius*, of course, but he was doing more than an academic exercise. He was taking seriously the notion that "selving" the "I" of the self is central hermeneutic task of human selfness, as Ricoeur asserted a century later.

Using the "selving" reflections which posit the self, Hopkins, not only attempted to posit the "inscape" of his own selfness, but also the intelligibility of the"inscapes" of all being energy, and most of all, he attempted to posit the "inscape" of God as the Creator. In other words, in positing the self-reflections of his own "I-ness," he was lead through his self-understanding to insights about the origin and nature of the cosmos. I cannot stress too much the extraordinary leap in understanding that Hopkins' initiating act of "selving" philosophic reflection constitutes. His insights, and their phenomenological implications, make him our contemporary because he started his speculations, not out of inferences from the external order of things, but rather where all consciousness philosophers have begun in trying to make sense of the self and the world, the hermeneutic process of positing the "I" of the self.

Let us look at his famous "selving" statement in this context. I take up those passages (*Sermons* 122-123) which specifically depict his selfness. First and foremost, Hopkins wrote about the self, his selfness, from the perspective of his own self-reflections, his own turning inward upon the "I-ness" in him. He wrote, "I find myself both as a man and as myself something most determined and distinctive than anything else I see." And again, " I find myself with my pleasures and pains, my powers and my experiences . . . more important to myself than anything else I see." He kept on delving: "when I consider my self-being, my consciousness and feeling of myself, that taste of myself, of I and me above and in all things, which is more distinctive than the taste of ale or alum . . . Nothing else in nature comes near this unspeakable stress of pitch [energized individuality]." And again later, "Searching nature I taste *self* but at one tankard, that of my own being. The development, refinement, condensation of nothing shews any sign of being able to match this to me or give me another taste of it, a taste even resembling it." Finally, "And even those things with which I in some sort identify myself, as my country or my family, and those things I own and call mine, as my clothes and so on, all presuppose the stricter sense of self and *me* and *mine* and are from that derivative."

Could any passages more exemplify what Ricoeur called "positing the self in self-reflection"? Hopkins here established through his self-reflections, not only what the act of reflection is, but how reflection works as an effort to comprehend selfness, namely, that self-consciousness is produced through the mediation of images, acts, works, things, which are the contents of the "I's" acts of reflection in the consciousness. What Ricoeur has pointed out, Hopkins was doing in his texted self-reflection: he identified his selfness as singularly unique, absolutely differentiated from everything else; he found his selfness to permeate all that his being is, all he owns, all he chooses to do; finally, he pointed to the location of his "I-ness" in its mirroring representations in the contents of his consciousness—pleasures, pains, powers, experiences, deserts, guilt, shame, sense of beauty, dangers, hopes, fate. So it is fair to say that Hopkins understood the self and the nature of consciousness much as it is considered in modern consciousness phenomenology. Moreover, this positing of the self is for him the first truth of his general philosophic inquiry into the origin and nature of all existence, as it is the starting point for many modern philosophers of consciousness phenomenology.

What then is the meaning of human existence according to Hopkins and Ricoeur? It is the "selving" energy of "I" self to be and become its achieved self through its self-reflections mirrored in its acts. In other words, "selving" through the reflective consciousness is the job the "I" takes on to try to locate and expressively affirm its truest selfness in order to achieve its destiny—full and final self-realization.

Another striking parallel between modern phenomenological thinking and Hopkins' notions about the character of the self is what Ricoeur calls the "concept of appropriation." He explains "that the original situation from which reflection proceeds is 'forgetfulness'; I am lost, 'astray' among the objects of the world, separated from the center of my own existence, just as I am separated from others and the enemy of all. Whatever may be the secret of this separation, this diaspora, it signifies that I do not originally possess that which I am. The truth which Fichte called 'the thetic judgment' is situated in the emptiness of an absence of myself" (*Conflict* 328-329). Thus it follows, according to this line of thinking, that the task of appropriation for each self is to consolidate personal experience with an affirmative "selving" of the "I am" in the consciousness. This validation is the fundamental desire and effort of every human being; the "I's" alienation must be transformed into "selving-action"— self-approval, freedom, and hope—in constructing the "I" of the self. But this task is daunting, overwhelmingly daunting, given the isolation and opaqueness of the "I" in the complex of the consciousness.

Hopkins recorded this same sense of self- isolation, loneliness, and separation in his description of the reflexive self. However, Hopkins did more than attribute this ego isolation to an "absence" of fulfilling identity in the self. While he did stress a sense of dispossessing isolation, Hopkins explained this separating emptiness differently. He wrote: "The development, refinement, condensation of nothing shews any sign of being able to match this to me or give me another taste of it, a taste even resembling it. One may dwell on this further. We say that any two things however unlike are in something like. This is one exception: when I compare myself, my being-myself, with anything else whatever, all things alike, all in the same degree, rebuff me with blank unlikeness; so my knowledge of it, which is so intense, is from itself alone." Thus, central to his understanding of "selving" emptiness is that he found the uniqueness of his own distinctiveness which shares only difference with everything else, an incommunicable, hence profoundly separating, difference: "Nothing else in nature comes near this unspeakable stress of pitch, distinctiveness, and selving, this selfbeing of my own. Nothing explains it or resembles it, except so far as this, that other men to themselves have the same feeling" (*Sermons* 123). The distinctiveness of the I-self produces a sense of radical separateness from "selving" fulfillingly its "I" identity in the consciousness.

Hopkins was probably influenced in developing his notion of the idiosyncratic self by John Duns Scotus, a medieval scholastic, though it seems certain that Scotus affirmed rather than determined Hopkins' sense of the unique self. Scholars early (Christopher Devlin, *Sermons* 338-351, W. H. Gardner in Roberts' *Hopkins' Critical Heritage* 337-344) and late (Ellsberg 87; C. Phillips, "The Mixed Emotions" 142) have noted how much emphasis Hopkins placed on a Scotus-like idea ("Hacceitas") of the individualized self, first existing in the mind of God before its creation as a mind and body. This particularized self is what distinguishes a person from every other self, what Hopkins called " the selfless self of self," hence the source in the finite self of the incommunicative, isolated individuality.

A critically important inference here is that if this particularized state of the self is what God intended, and Hopkins believed that it was, then J. Hillis Miller is wrong (*Disappearance* 270) to assume that such a "selving" state is unholy, even diabolical; for, as Walter Ong has noted, "The world within the self, the "I" or "me" . . . is holy in its very idiosyncratic isolation. The human self implies a creator God who is, in Hopkins' words, precisely a 'selfmaking' power'" (143). It is out of this existential "selving" resemblance between God and the individual that the self is opened to community and love. But such achievement requires help from outside the self to subdue into "selving" harmony the insistent "I" in the self.

The Hermeneutics of the "I-selving" Consciousness

We have seen that both poet and philosopher assert that human I-ness involves an abiding sense of self-absence; as well, each of us is left to make sense of ourselves in a world of "selving" alienation. Self-positing, then, as the task of "selving" reflection tries to overcome these "selving" barriers by the actualizing recreation of our "I-ness" (appropriated from our self- acts) in order to achieve a fulfilling identity in the plenitude of all being through which the "I's" "selving" possibilities are realized. Each of us, then, is left to interpret ourselves to ourselves in the experiential texts of our activities in a difficult, differentiated world.

There are two considerations here in "selving" the "I am": How does consciousness organize perception so as to reconstruct the I-self, and if so, what are the means of doing so? Are there prime mediating signs in our "selving"-texts, and is there a basal pattern in interpreting them?

If it is true as Ricoeur holds, that human beings can know themselves only through their reflective acts, these acts must be essentially hermeneutic in character, that is, these acts of reflection must have the clarity and depth of self-interpretative implication so as to become authentic revelations of the distinctiveness and singularity of the I-self. Further, it follows that arriving at authentic self-consciousness is an interpretation. What does the self interpret? The "I" enacting its selfness. This is to say that the I-self finds objectifications of its "I-ness" in the culture of its conscious acts, acts which are symbols that mediate the recomprehension of the "I" in the self. The "I," then, can be uncovered indirectly and dialectically through symbolic representation and interpretation. This hermeneutic emphasis focuses upon language as the key to the phenomenology of human "selving."

Positing the self, then, means "reading" the symbols of "I-ness" in the acts of self-reflection. Saying this is to assert that reflection is open to interpretation and moves toward hermeneutic acts. Ricoeur wrote: "Reflection here appeals to interpretation and seeks to transform itself into hermeneutics. Such is the ultimate root of our problem; it resides in this primitive connection between our activity of existence and the signs which we manifest in our works; reflection must become interpretation, for I can grasp the activity of existence only through those signs that are scattered through the world" (*Conflict* 326). It is through language that humankind expresses individualized self-understanding. In an elemental sense, individualized humankind is the sum of its language, for language provides a means to reappropriate the human self, to try to find the floating *ego* of the *ego cogito* amid the streams of energies called the world.

Hopkins basically answered the question of how selfness is restructured in the same way. Like Ricoeur, Hopkins thought that the world confronting the self for each of us is disparate. The energy of being that issues forth in the "inscape" of selfness produces a world of separates before which the human self stands in baffling isolation. The self is the fixed point from which is encountered the swirl of individual things fluxing all around: "The unchanging register of change / My all-accepting fixed eye," of an early poem (*Poems* 77). How can all of this disharmony and dispersion of the energy of being be organized into some perspectived reality in which the self will find self-mediating identity?

Like Ricoeur, Hopkins determined that the experience of the self experiencing the world of energized being can be brought into some kind of unity of pattern and self-identity through the mediation of the semantic, phonic, and symbolic nature of language. To assert this Hopkins had to demonstrate the philosophic credibility of language as somehow implicated in the reality of being. Like Ricoeur, he had to affirm a connection between the mind, words, and things.

Hopkins, however, came to his insight, not by considering the nature of self-reflection, but by pondering the great divide between the stress of energy and the non-stress of energy. In thinking about a text from Parmenides that "Being is and Not-being is not," Hopkins interpreted the text in his own "selving" terms: the chasm between Being and Non-being is the difference between things that are and things that are not. "Things are" is another way of saying there is truth—*it is* or *there is*." Based upon this reading, Hopkins then wrote his reflection upon this elemental insight: "But indeed I have often felt when I have been in this mood and felt the depth of an instress or how fast the inscape holds a thing that nothing is so pregnant and straight forward to the truth as simple *yes* and *is*." This insight leads to a crucial insight in the way that the self and the world are interconnected by the being energy Hopkins called "stress." Hopkins went on to say about the absence of the being energy that generates "yes and is": "There would be no bridge, no stem of stress between us and things to bear us out and carry the mind over: without stress we might not and could not say / Blood is red / but only / This blood is red / or The last blood I saw was red / nor even that, for in later language not only universals would not be true but the copula would break down even in particular judgments" (*Journals* 127). Hopkins has here stated that "selving" is a hermeneutical act by which the "I" self knows itself in and through its reflections of the world of being.

This insight lead him to posit the key truth about the energy of Being and the energy of the self: "To be and to know or Being and thought are the same. The truth in thought is Being, stress, and each word is one way of acknowledging Being and each sentence by its copula is (or its equivalent) the utterance and assertion of it" (*Journals* 129). This is to say that words are unique formalities, "inscapes" of the stress-energy of the self; unique in that that energy we call the mind possesses a means of knowing other being outside of itself, a binding action in which the world is internalized and then reconstructed into a new, reexpressed "inscape" of the self. To put this notion fully in Hopkins' own terminology, words, naming an individual thing, appropriate the "I's" selfness in the very "inscaping" energy of wording the "inscape" of stress-energy of the thing named. Words are a means by which the self grasps the world and, in grasping the world, grasps itself.

How this notion works in practice is plentifully revealed in Hopkins' diaries. His jottings are often a series of discrete wordings of individual things, jottings which are careful attempts to preserve the separateness of things including keeping a space between the observer and things observed. But the journals are not just a long series of isolated encounters with the distinct "inscapes" of individual things; rather, they are both perceptive discoveries (through wording) of the uniqueness of each thing as well as a "selving" amalgamation of the expresser of these individual things. Through the colors, textures, and patterns, things are organized into a world wherein there are perceived fields of patterned order, groupings, in which there is discerned a universal structuring of the stress of being-energies into a grand "inscape" of universal being which is called the universe. The universe, then, is discovered to be a great collection of distinctly patterned things, difference categorized into kinds, and kinds having shared likenesses which mimic sameness in variety and variety in sameness. This is the world field the self words in wording itself. Wording the self in the world is the prime work of humankind.

What I have described is the way Hopkins thought that the self reaches out and grapples the world to itself. Again the key is what he called, "the stem of stress between us and things to bear us out and carry the mind over," that is, the "selving" consciousness energy we summarize as "wording." Like Ricoeur, Hopkins located the vital action of self-reflection in language. The energy of the self, which is essential to positing the self, is the self-defining energy of language. For Hopkins and Ricoeur, language is a function of "selving-understanding." Language is the mode through which each of us carries on the task of constructing the "selving" consciousness, wherein lies I-self-objectification.

If language is that "stem of stress" by which the self grapples with all otherness, then, of course, all facets of language play a role in carrying the mind over and bringing the world back. Words participate mimetically in the nature of what they name, which is to say that "selving" language is essentially poetic in character. Thus, for example, rhyme becomes a key naming function of wording the world and wording of the self. In the energy of being Hopkins called "stress," all things, though individually unique, are like one another in some way. All things rhyme, hence all words, the "stem of stress" of being, echo and imitate the parallel structures of the self and the universe. The same can be said for other attributes of language— cadence, structural form, denotation, connotation, and recurrence in language. Each is an aspect of that unique "inscape" of being-energy called the word. And each has its own role in the "inscaping" the I-self in grasping the things of the world. Moreover, among these attributes of words, metaphor for Hopkins (symbolic metaphor for Ricoeur) is the central linguistic energy by which the word organizes the self and the universe through self-reflection

It is useful here to see the connection between Hopkins' general notion of "wording" and his definition of poetry. In his *Journal* (84-85) in a short essay titled, "Poetic Diction," he set down his idea of poetry from the vantage point of hermeneutic structure. He wrote:

> The structure of poetry is that of continuous parallelism . . . . Parallelism is of two kinds necessarily—where the opposition is clearly marked and where it is transitional . . . . Only the first kind, that of marked parallelism, is concerned with the structure of verse—in rhythm, the recurrence of a certain sequence of syllables, in metre, the recurrence of a certain sequence of rhythm, alliteration, in assonance, and in rhyme. Now the force of this recurrence is to beget a recurrence or parallelism answering to it in words or thought . . . the marked the parallelism in structure whether of elaboration or of emphasis begets more marked parallelism in the words and sense. And moreover parallelism in expression tends to beget or passes into parallelism in thought. This point reached we shall be able to see and account for the peculiarities of poetic diction. To the marked or abrupt kind of parallelism belong metaphor, simile, parable, and so on, where the effect is sought in likeness of things and antithesis, contrast, and so on, where it is sought in unlikeness.

What we see here is how Hopkins' notion of "selving" language— being, thought, word—engenders his idea of the "principle of parallelism" in the structure of poetic language. Poetry possesses extra expressional energy in that it utters striking and powerful juxtapositions of thought and diction thereby heightening its capacities for a more complex communication: "And it is commonly supposed that poetry has tasked the highest powers in man's mind: that is because, as it asked for greater emphasis of thought and on a greater scale, at which stage it threw out the minds unequal to further ascent." Here Hopkins has defined the character of poetic consciousness while suggesting that the expressive productions of such a consciousness "carry us over" to heights beyond the language of prose. Anticipating Ricoeur, Hopkins placed the poetic imagination at the power center of the upper ranges of the "selving" hermeneutic process. This is to say that "selving the I" in the consciousness is a poiesis, a making of self-identity.

Figurative language, then, is central to self-reflection, especially metaphoric language that fuses images with words in a compact surplus of meanings. The symbolic metaphor is at the heart of Ricoeur's hermeneutics. Consciousness is a hermeneutic construction of the "I" self "reading" experience through symbolic expression. Ricoeur writes, "I wager that I shall have a better understanding of mind and the bond between the being of mind and the being of all beings if I follow the indication of symbolic thought" (*Conflict* 355). In analyzing the interpretative modes of symbolism, the experience of the "selving" subject is the focal point. Ricoeur approaches the formative symbolism of anthropological self-consciousness through analyzing the primitive metaphors embedded in the consciousness of evil. He holds that these primal verbal symbols, "stain," for example, reveal the linguistic structures through which experience the autochthonous self arises.

Ricoeur suggests that hermeneutic of symbols has two levels of semantic indirectness, the relationship of experience to expression and the equivocal subjective character of linguistic figuration. Within these levels, he asserts, language mediates states of feeling so that "selving" fault, for example, takes on linguistic objectification: "This language of confession is the counterpart of the triple character of the experience it brings to light: blindness, equivocalness, scandalousness. The experience . . . is a blind experience, still embedded in the matrix of emotion, fear, anguish. It is this emotional note that gives rise to objectification in discourse; the confession expresses, pushes to the outside, the emotion which without it would be shut up in itself as an expression of the soul" (*Symbolism of Evil* 7). The language of such discourse is indirect, then, because it is based upon imagery that is opened through symbolic metaphor to a multiplicity of affective meanings.

Moreover, according to Ricoeur, symbolic expression operates in the field of experience as emotions function in the field of experience. There is an empathic vital link between word and self. Ricoeur writes, "A characteristic of the symbol is never to be completely arbitrary. It is not empty; there is always a rudiment of a natural relation between the signifying and the signified " (Ihde 97). This notion leads to the basic point that symbolism is part of the very constitution of the consciousness of the self: "The consciousness of the self seems to constitute itself at the lowest level by means of symbolism " (*Symbolism of Evil 9*). The empathic self is a constituent of "selving" language. Only through symbolic language can the self parse experience of itself experiencing the world, for without symbols, all experience would, as Ricoeur notes, "remain mute, obscure, and shut up in its implicit contradictions."

These notions about language and symbols round out Ricoeur's concept of reflection as "selving"-expression. In sum, then, the phenomenology of the "selving" the "I" is reflective, a process wherein the self moves towards the objective world through hermeneutic linguistic patterns of the I-objectifying consciousness. Ricoeur writes: "When we speak of word as a positive, vital reality, we are suggesting an underlying connection between word and the active core of our existence. Word has the power to change our understanding of ourselves. Word reaches us on the level of the symbolic structures of our existence, the dynamic schemes that express the way in which we understand our situation and the way in which we project ourselves into this situation" (*Conflict* 454). Finally, an examination of historical symbols that span the development of human consciousness reveals that there have been extensions of symbols into "selving" myth systems, an elaboration and expansion of the linguistic possibilities of symbols. Clearly, for a linguistic phenomenologist like Ricoeur, language figuration, personal and cosmic, is central to the "selving" revelations of the "I" in the reflective consciousness.

Turning to Hopkins, we have found a similar focus upon selfness and figurative language. As we have seen earlier, for Hopkins, building on the insight of Parmenides, the self's act of reflection is one facet of the energy of being, the "inscapes" of Nature's myriad otherness and the interactive consciousness mediated through the "stem of stress," that is, language. The stress of these energies of being are the forces which unify the world, a unity that posits universal relationships, particular judgments, and the existence of individual "I" selfs. Focusing upon that energy of being that is the word, Hopkins extensively investigated the powers and strengths with which words can integrate the self and other selves through expressing certain in-depth realities about both. For Hopkins, language as utterance of universal being is the great sounding of the buckling together of all the energies of being into a unified voiced chord—the song of the universe.

To couple the vast assembly of difference that makes up the "inscapes" of individualized energies of the world involves word energies which have incredible elasticity of sound and extensivity of meaning. The matching of the "inscapes" of stress is all the more intricate when words yoke the "inscapes" outside of the consciousness with the inside "I-scape" of the beholding-expressing, "selving" consciousness, what he called a "canon of feeling," a validation of one's feeling that Denis Donoghue defines as Modernism—"converting apparent external images and events into inwardness, personal energy." No wonder Hopkins noted that the poise required to produce a true "inscape" of the "inscapes" of anything is always a rare moment. Even more rare is authentic poetic "inscaping," a dazzling interplay of the energies of "inscaping" of things, self, and words. Let us dwell on this a bit more.

What is the extraordinary character of the energy that results in the "inscaping" power of words? It is the centripetal / centrifugal powers of symbolic figuration. At the first level it seems that metaphoric words are primarily kinesthetic ways of catching distinctive features of an "inscape" in Nature. However, implicit in the linguistic figuration of the action of metaphor is the symbolization of a relationship between the "inscape" of the sayer, the "inscape" of the things worded, and the "inscapes" of things compared. This is to say, metaphors open up a new consciousness reality, a world of relationships which, though essentially different in their "inscapes of energies," are in some way experienced as meaningfully related, ordered, or connected. Thus for Hopkins, metaphor is a central way of "seeing" the particularity of things and a way of "seeing" the paralleled overlaps with other particularities of things in their totality, the world order of being-ness. In other words, if anything is comparable to anything else, then everything has something in common. This insight applies to the comparer and all the things he compares. Hopkins' notebooks, not unsurprisingly, are in large part lists of metaphors, lists in which he is trying out the figuration of the "inscapes" he has taken in. His notebooks contain the most lavish collection of figurative words extant in any poetic canon. (See his incredible list of cloud metaphors, for example, *Journals* 27, 36, 67, 138,139,142, 153, 165, 206, 207, 240, 260).

Another way to understand Hopkins' "selving" through symbolic metaphor is the distinction between vision and visuality. Vision is the perception of things as they are, evidence of the senses whose mental images capture things as observable evidence for purposes of the objective accounting of the other. Visuality, however, is a product of the metaphoric "selving"consciousness which confronts evidential images with connective, far ranging parallels, whose associative powers produce in the consciousness a kind of hypervision, a visuality, "seeing" the distinct thing as part of a larger order, and hence possessing a higher register of meaning, thereby introducing a subjective or "selving" significance to common sense experience. In a fundamental way, the difference between vision and visuality is the crux of the modern imagination—the ascent or descent of the self.

For Hopkins and Ricoeur, then, the link between reflecting consciousness and the "selving" experience is language, especially that metaphysical potential of language which configurates language, Nature, and consciousness. Every selved thing is an "inscape" of the energy of being; human selfhood is so as well. The symbolizing powers of language, themselves "inscapes" of the stress of being, are the ways the human self, through the hermeneutic enactments of its reflective consciousness, reappropriates its "I-ness" in and through the experiences of all otherness. The verbal symbol that is the product of reflective judgment keys the "inscape" of energy that is the "other" of the universe as it keys the "inscape" of energy that is the "I" self. Hopkins wrote: "To be and to know or Being and thought are the same" (*Journals* 129): Ricoeur writes, "The unity of being and logos makes it possible for man to belong to being insofar as he is a speaking being" (*Conflict* 462). The echo between the poet and philosopher is clear in their accounts of the hermeneutic creation of the "I am" of the self.

Chapter 3

The Poetics of Volition in Hopkins

The Adamic Consciousness

We have seen thus far that the poet and the philosopher both understand being, consciousness, and language in similar ways. Both account for the energy of human self-being by starting "inside," that is, through acts of reflection. These reflective judgments are the means to posit the self, to initiate the tasks of consciousness, which are to discover the particularity of everything, the commonality of everything, and, in making these discoveries, to locate the "I-inscape" of the discoverer. Both assert that the vital creative energy which links being and consciousness is the stress or energy of words, for all are modes of the one and the same being-energy.

We now turn to the structural character of the consciousness through which the self seeks to be objectified. Here too there are interesting similarities between the poet and philosopher.

We begin by noting that both Hopkins and Ricoeur consider the consciousness to be essentially poetic. In designating the consciousness poetic, both poet and philosopher mean that the medium through which the consciousness enacts reflection is the figurative image which imaginatively coalesces the energies of consciousness into the analogies of symbol. This is to say, that the thetic (poetic) positing of self is contained in the intentionality of the symbol. The energy of the "selving" poetic is the very birthplace of language which, through its expressivity, yokes experience to the consciousness in the rich analogues of symbols.

Both Hopkins and Ricoeur start with the Pre-Socratic notion that the Being in things is the being in the self and the being in words—all the same universal being. Hopkins meant by "being" that "stressing-energy" in the consciousness with which the self infers that the perceptions produced in its awareness represent real things external to itself, the same energy with which the "I" infers its creating "I am" (*Sermons* 128, 284). Ricoeur emphasizes this "selving" energy as logos, "Being brought to language," hence "A being who interrogates Being" (*Conflict* 464). For both, the poetic word is the base and field of the hermeneutics of selfness. Now we must see how "selving" linguistics initiate the tasks of consciousness.

For Hopkins the prime symbolic characterization emerging from within the consciousness is the "I-ness" abiding in the self. Figuration is the mode of insight in self-symbolization, hence the revealing source of selfness. The symbolization of the self, in its acts of self-reflection, reveals the singular distinctiveness of the self. Hopkins, pondering this awareness, was led to considerations which caused him to dismiss chance as the source of selfness and self-causation of the beginning of all selfness. There must be, then, a universal Self outside of the inmost self, a Selfness that has its own selfness, a more distinctive being than one's own: "For if this [distinctive being] is what I find myself to have above all other things I see, except only my peers in nature, other men, this self, in its taste to me so distinctive, how much more this greater being" (*Sermons* 126).

But it is not only the existence of universal Selfness— God —that the distinctive "I-ness" symbolized in the self reveals. The existential link between the selves which are "more distinctive, more selved, than all things else" (*Sermons* 125) of the world and the Universal Self, "the most exquisite determining, self-making, power," is that "instress" of energy he called Being. The commonality of Being is crucial to asserting a relationship between the Self who contains in Himself all the matrices of all possible and actual selfness in the super-distinctiveness of His own Selfness and the self's reflective consciousness objectifying its distinctive "I-ness." If in some way there is a common being- nature between universal and particular selfness, then God is present to all things in some manner. But the deific presence is mediated by a difference of scale, as Hopkins noted, since "a being so intimately present as God is to other things would be identified with them were it not for God's infinity or were it not for God's infinity he could not be so intimately present to things" (*Sermons* 128).

At this stage of reflection, the deity is present to all distinct things and yet hugely distant. This separation, then, is an absence in the "I am" of all Selfness. Hopkins is saying In the discovery of myself I have found, in the being of my selfness, the image of the most highly distinctive Self of all. However, the commonness of the "inscape" of energy which is encountered affirms the presence of difference, not identification. The positing of selfness, then, involves the discovery of an elemental ontological limitation—the finitude of human selfness. It is precisely here, at this stage of Hopkins' self-reflections, that Ricoeur begins his philosophic inquiry into the interpretation of self-consciousness.

As already noted, Ricoeur, starting with a perusal of those symbols which lie in the myths of Western culture, finds the character of the predominating cosmic symbols to be that of evil and guilt: fallibility, then, is a basic structure of human existence. All of these symbols, reductively combined, as an interpretation of the reflection of the self, express forgetfulness, being lost, "being separated from the center of my own existence" (*Conflict* 328-329). Looking at mythic symbols in the form of narrations, which are beyond the categories of the specifics of history and geography yet indigenous to all, Ricoeur studies experiential expressions of finitude at three levels of fault symbolized as evil: evil as defilement, as sin, and as guilt. There is a progression in the phenomenology of selfness in this pattern of symbolized experience towards self-interiorization, a movement from evil as a primitive realism to a state of ethical idealism. Ultimately, then, the human experience of evil is a state of subjectivity in which the lower symbolic forms of evil are absorbed into higher forms of fault. Indeed, Ricoeur states that it is in the subjectivization of symbols that the symbols become open to the inquiries of phenomenological interpretation: "I would even venture to say that defilement becomes a pure symbol when it no longer suggests a real stain at all, but only signifies the servile will" (*Symbolism of Evil* 154-155).

Ricoeur finds, in reading the primordial history of mankind that is myth, that the human encounter with the sacred that constitutes religious consciousness, starts from the beginning of human experience: "Man first reads the sacred *on* the world, *on* some elements or aspect of the world . . . First of all, then it is the sun, the moon, the waters,—that is to say, cosmic realities—that are symbols. . . . For these realities to be a symbol is to gather at one point a mass of significations which, before giving rise to thought, give rise to speech" (*Symbolism of Evil* 10-11). The progress to speech is, of course, a progression to subjectivity, which is to say ethicity.

The main types of myth dramas in human experience in historical order, according to Ricoeur, are those of creation, tragedy, exile, and eschatology. In the first, the focus is on the interiority of evil; humankind discovers evil and continues it. In the tragic myths, a person is the victim of evil by which evil becomes diabolical. These myths portray human experiences of evil and good as ambiguously innocent, a complication of the creation myth, for the human race now becomes involved in a kind of disproportioned creation as forms of violence. Prometheus stole powers from the gods in his effort to gift humankind. The myth drama of the exiled soul introduced a new variant in symbolization of evil. Humankind experiences itself as divided in its essential being. Somehow in the process of being human, the soul, divine in its origin, becomes exiled in the experience of evil, an event as Ricoeur depicts the myth, "that inaugurates the humanity of man and makes man the place of forgetting, the place where the primordial difference between soul and body is abolished. Divine as to his soul, earthly as to his body, man is the forgetting of the difference. " (*Symbolism of Evil* 280). This phase of myth drama sets the stage for the eschatological, for the narration moves forward to a "fall"into the earthly followed by a path of recovery, education through punishment being its significance.

This brings us to the myth drama where Ricoeur and Hopkins meet— the Adamic eschatological myth. According to Ricoeur, this myth drama introduced a new intentionality in myth, marking the full progression of the interiorization of the experience of evil, from evil as an external reality to evil as a complex interior lapse of individual choice. The myths which locate evil in a state of being Ricoeur calls "speculative," while the evil that begins with man and locates the experience of evil in an human act of will, he calls" reflective." In the Adamic myth drama, evil comes to be through human choice a radical and absurd event, an event that initiated evil in all humankind throughout human history. The radical new intentionality of this myth is the introduction of ethical vision into the arena of evil experience. As a result, evil now is examined as the condition of human powers and human responsibilities.

Moreover, in the context of what Ricoeur calls the dialectic of mythic drama, the gradual objectification of the evil experience through symbolization reveals that good is dramatically separated from evil: in the beginning the biblical God is infinitely holy and innocent, and biblical man is finitely good and innocent; creation begins as essentially good at both the divine and human levels. Evil enters the world through a calamitous ancestral deviation. However, Ricoeur points out, the primordial forms of evil in the speculative myths still find symbolization in the Adamic myth through the figure of the serpent who, in the initiation of evil in the act of will, represents an evil already present. Adam's fall, then, is an alienation from a destiny that might be called the goodness of finitude.

The presence of the serpent keeps alive in the anthropological myth of Adam the notion that choice implies a destiny, what can be called the fate of finitude. This fate is a kind of other limit to human possibility which restrains ascribing an ultimate possibility to the ultimizing of the ethical view of evil. Ricoeur comments about this dialectic of the early objective myths and the subjective Adamic myth: "Here . . . is a fault no longer in an ethic sense, in the sense of a transgression of the moral law, but in an existential sense: to become oneself is to fail to realize wholeness, which nevertheless remains . . . the dream . . which the Idea of happiness points to." *(Conflict* 312-313).

The notion of the exile of Adam and Eve as symbolically an "inner exile" also surfaces, to some extent, as the philosophical myth of the separation of body and soul. Gradually this symbolism entered into the Adamic myth as a kind of sin-body, soul-good dualism. Ricoeur notes that this orientation of the body-soul myth became strong in the language of St. Paul, in whose account the fall of Adam is secondary to exile, thereby focussing more on the separation of the spirit and flesh and the amalgamation of selfness that is to occur in the resurrection of the body. This reading of Paul and the Adamic myth makes the myth less a descent into the humanity of man than an affirmation of man's innocence which "will become a fantastic innocence, accompanied by knowledge, bliss, and immortality, whether by nature or surperadded gift; at the same time, his fault instead of being a case of 'going astray' will become truly a 'fall,' an existential downgrading, a descent from the height of a superior and actually superhuman status" *(Conflict* 334-335).

All of this discussion of Ricoeur's account of evil in the human experience is basically an account of the process of reflection by which the conscious self becomes a religious consciousness. The long human process of the making of symbolization of the experience of evil has resulted in a reflective state that is called the volitional consciousness, which experiences evil both as a discovery and an enactment. We have seen that Ricoeur as linguistic phenomenologist focuses upon the interiorization of experience and the making of symbols by which the consciousness becomes religious. Hopkins, as we shall see, begins with evil as well, but focuses more upon the intentionality of choice going beyond duty. His model is Christ's service of love that transcends the servile will.

Turning to Hopkins, we find that his affirmation of the consciousness as religious begins with the discovery of ontological evil. The human person is uniquely his / her finite selfness; God, in His summing of all selfness, is infinitely His Selfness. If the extraordinary pitch of self-energy posits some extrinsic power as the causal energy of the selfness of all things, why does this Super-Self seem so existentially separated from its creations? This sense of distance, and even abandonment, is, perhaps, the most striking feature of the religious character of the human consciousness. It is not too much to say that all religion revolves around the paradox of the actualizing presence of God in the consciousness and his mysterious non-participative absence. The sense of God's absence is the most acute experience of isolation and thus loneliness of the "I" in the human consciousness. The theme of God hidden is a staple of all religious experience and hence much religious writing. It is no less so in Hopkins both in his early writing as well as in his most mature compositions. The early "Nondum" is a good example (*Poems* 78):

> God, though to Thee our psalm we raise
> No answering voice comes from the skies;
>
> *****
>
> We see the glories of the earth
> But not the hand that wrought them all;
>
> *****
>
> We guess, we clothe Thee, unseen King,
> With attributes we deem are meet;
> Each in his own imagining
> Sets up a shadow in Thy seat;
> Yet know not how our gifts to bring,
> Where seek thee with unsandalled feet.

In this, and a whole series of early poems, Hopkins described the sense of isolation he felt in his religious consciousness. Isolation suggests abandonment, and abandonment suggests something incomplete, undesirable; maybe evil (see "Myself unholy, from myself unholy," *Poems*

61), in the self is the reason that God is absent from his creations. How, then, can the reflective self overcome this sense that the author of his and all other being is unavailable, unattainable? The general, categorical answer, as we know, was Hopkins' essential Christianity and his eventual conversion from the Anglican to the Catholic Church from which traditions he deepened his spiritual union with God-Christ's communicative Presence in the Holy Eucharist. But such an answer does not adequately explain the gradual working out in Hopkins of a deep and abiding interior awareness of God continually present in his consciousness—the making of his unique religious consciousness in Christ. As is frequently the case, the coming of faith precedes any illumination of pattern of its coming. Thus, in Hopkins' case we must look to both his pre- and post-conversion "selving" meditations to see his self-reflections on the gradual changes in his religious awareness. This we will do when we read the narrative of his spiritual consciousness that his poetry is.

Hopkins' awareness of the isolation of the self—and all the selves in the world—became symbolized in his consciousness in the form of the Adamic myth. Like Ricoeur, Hopkins' religious reflection upon his feelings of isolation coalesced with his feelings of evil in his own experience. Something must have happened which brought evil into the world and into his own selfness. Like Ricoeur's account of the symbolization of evil, Hopkins interiorized the Adamic myth as the narration of symbolized experience which best objectifies the religio-ethical dilemma of the disproportion between the intentions of freedom and the experience of finitude in the reflecting consciousness. If the "objective myths" of creation and tragedy are the best expressions of exterior evil, then the most salient symbolization of evil in the reflective interior self is the myth of Adam. In a series of written explications, Hopkins sorted out the meanings of this myth touching on such subjects as personality, grace, and free will (*Sermons* 146-159) as well as such topics as creation, redemption and "the great sacrifice' of Christ (*Sermons* 196-209). We should remember that his prime mentors in his reflections were John Duns Scotus and Ignatius of Loyola, about whose roles in Hopkins' intellections of his religious consciousness much has been written, and thus I say little in this chapter about their influences. His own direct treatment of these topics, however, will be touched upon.

Hopkins discerned four significant meanings in the Adamic myth. First, the myth narrates a state of radical innocence in our human ancestry. That is, the moral anthropology of human beings originated in goodness, a goodness that was related to the Creator's "inscaping" of his "selving" energy that we know as Creation. Second, the Creator raised the "inscape" of energy we know as human selfness to the level of reflective consciousness, thereby constituting in this class of "inscapes" a unique capacity to choose freely in the employment of its energy potentials. Thirdly, because of the unique character of the human self, the Creator made a covenant in which the parents of the human race agreed to maintain a stipulated relationship which in effect affirmed the holiness and innocence of God and the goodness and integrity of humankind. This covenant was an acknowledgement of the difference in the character of the "inscape" of energy that is God, that is infinite divinity, and that of the "inscape" of energy of humankind, that is, finite humanness. Fourth, evil (non-being as a kind of pre-existent death) was present even before human experience of evil, and thus there was a moral condition of human experience that might have been avoided, hence the stipulation in the covenant regarding the tree of the Knowledge of Good and Evil.

Hopkins discussed his understanding of the Adamic myth using his concept terms of "instress," the selving energy of being and "inscape," the manifesting shape of the selved energy. One poetic figure he used to symbolize the narrative of the Adamic myth was that of a great choral ode (*Sermons* 200-201). God, the supreme composer-creator of the "instress"of energy that is the song of Creation, "inscaped" both the music and the singers. In this massed choir of glorious "inscaped" energy, there were four components. The first was the lead singer / conductor whose part contained all the hymning of all the other parts, the perfect expression of the Creator— the composer as the conductor himself in virtue of his Son / Christ. The second component was the massed angelic choir. Hopkins speculated much about angels in his religious writings. He saw them as spirits created, like Adam and Eve, with the perfection of sanctifying grace (being beyond death), grouped in nine choirs to honor and serve their Creator according to the song — the covenant against evil and death— of praise composed by their maker, perhaps the soprano and tenor voices. The third choir was made up of the voices of the human race whose part—covenant— called for obedience and service by singing the middle and lower registers of voices in the song of Creation.

Hopkins discerned a ground bass counterpoint in the person of Lucifer who began to sing his own song, a hymn praising himself, perhaps in discovering that God had given the chief role and solo to Christ, His Son, who, according to Hopkins, existed in eternity as the highest angelic figure, Christ being God's first intention in creating. Thus Christ willingly became a creature—singer— who was glad to adore the Father-Creator-Composer, and sing His song, a perfect "selving" of God's selfness.

Hopkins explained the musical rebellion this way. Speaking of Lucifer's rebellion [who according to Isaiah (xiv, 12), was named for the beauty that was once his and in Job (xxxviii) was the precentor in the hymn of praise, sung at the dawn of creation "when the stars sang together, and all the sons of God shouted for joy"], Hopkins explained: "For being required to adore God and enter into a covenant of justice with him, he did so indeed, but, as a chorister who learns by use in the church itself the strength and beauty of his own voice, he became aware in his very note of adoration of the riches of his nature; then when from the first note he should have gone on with the sacrificial service, prolonging the first note instead and ravished by his own sweetness and dazzled, the prophet says, by his beauty, he was involved in spiritual sloth . . . and spiritual luxury and vainglory; to heighten this, he summoned a train of spirits to be his choir and contemptuously breaking with the service of the eucharistic sacrifice, which was to have a victim of an earthly nature and of flesh, raised a hymn in honour of their own nature, spiritual purely and ascending, he must have persuaded them, to the divine; and with this sin of pride aspiring to godhead their crime was consummated" (*Sermons* 179-180).

Now exiled for his actions, and renamed Satan, Lucifer lies in the tract of all existence to be able to approach and attack everything innocent and virtuous. As Hopkins put it, "God gave things a forward and perpetual motion; the Devil, that is, thrower of things off the track, upsetter, mischiefmaker, clashing with one another brought in the law of decay and consumption in inanimate nature, death in the vegetable and animal world, moral death and original sin in the world of man (*Sermons* 198-99). Hopkins, in analyzing the symbol of the snake or serpent as the Devil, thought that the depiction was most apt, for the serpent, a form of dragon, is a material configuration of several vertebrate characteristics, the combinations of which Hopkins found fitting as a "type of the Devil to express the universality of his powers, both the gifts he has by nature and the attributes and sway he grasps, and the horror which the whole inspires. . . . The dragon then symbolizes one who aiming at every perfection ends by being a monster, a 'fright'" (*Sermons* 199).

"Selving" the Fallible Self

Just as Ricoeur suggests that religious consciousness arises and is shaped through reflection upon evil in the form of primordial symbols, so Hopkins explained the making of religious consciousness by interpreting the biblical symbols of the Adamic mythos to elucidate the anterior evil human kind encounters, and also like Ricoeur, Hopkins read the temptation myth in the Garden of Eden as moving evil from a category of being to an ethical event in the history of Creation. Both interpret the symbols narrating the act of disobedience by Adam and Eve in the Garden as a radicalization of the character of evil. The Adamic myth partially transformed evil from a category of being to an interior condition of the will alone—partly through its expressions of its structural fault and partly due to its narrative of self-induced betrayal.

However, Hopkins, the poet of Christian theology, and Ricoeur, the hermeneutic phenomenologist, offer different explanations of what both consider the enigma of evil to be in the human condition. Ricoeur explains the enigma as a dialectic of myths in which the old speculative myths, locating evil in the status of being as chaos, focus upon evil as an existential precedent overcoming man, thereby becoming a limit to the Adamic myth, which locates evil in the will alone. Thus the will does seduce itself, but only to a limit. Herein lies, of course, the genesis of the tragic myth form. In Ricoeur's reading, fate is a hidden root of choice. Hopkins, on the other hand, interpreted the Adamic myth as prophetic theology, and therefore accounts for existential evil and the fallen will entirely within the symbols of the rebellion of the angels who establish evil as a category of non-being in their efforts to reject the goodness of the finite world, and humankind becomes destined to a good though finite fulfillment. These rebellious creatures in the figure of Satan, the serpent in the Bible, then, are powerful moral forces which betray the destiny of created humanity by inducing a willingess to choose to contend with their Maker. The consequences, according to this reading, are an historical calamity forever altering humanity. Hopkins, in a trenchant passage, depicted the divided personhood of humanity: "Each of these *persons* {italics his} wants to be the world to himself; he hates his brother whom he sees and therefore the God whom he does not see and the not seeing, the blindness, is part of the hatred" (*Sermons* 172).

The difference in emphasis, then, between Ricoeur and Hopkins is that Hopkins thematizes evil as an act of will having eschatological implications, whereas Ricoeur, wishing to keep the phenomenological contexts of the symbolic opacity of evil intact, understands the avowal of evil as human because in and through the human will, evil enters the world, but a part of this avowal is non-human because of the anteriority of evil in existence: " Because fate belongs to freedom as the non-chosen portion of all our choices, it must be experienced as fault" (*Conflict* 312-314).

This exterior existential fault has a counter-fault in the structure of the human personality according to Ricoeur. To him, the human volitional condition is a play between the infinite as a human possibility and the finite as a limit to human reality. This is to say that mankind is fallible, subject to the possibility of evil. This phenomenological fragility, belying an idealized transcendental synthesis of the human powers of the self, is located in the knowing, willing, and feeling components of human personality. Ricoeur identifies the human phenomenon of fallibility as the condition of perspective in knowing, choosing, feeling, what he calls the "perspectival limitation of perception" (*Fallible Man* 32) that is the condition of every act of reflection by the consciousness.

In hermeneutic terms fault is involved in the basic intentionality of humankind, Hopkins' "instress" to signify self; language plays the intermediary between the intention to transcend to infinitude and the means by which the expressive word signifies the finite point of view. Thus fault may be expressed as the failure of the intention to signify human transcendence. So the word is paralleled with the will in that it possesses an infinite field of possible human expressions or signal motivations articulating the general aim of true personal happiness. But this intention is limited by character, which narrows the fields of possible choice or expression, for choosing and feeling are finite actualizations of personhood. Full personhood, then, an abiding unfulfilled intention, is the task of consciousness which, given the limits on knowing and willing, remains unachieved and thus unfulfilled.

Additionally, a central factor of this structural fault in human consciousness is affectivity, a kind of obverse bodily side of the objectifying selving consciousness. Desiring, unlike knowing which exteriorizes and objectifies (thus separating subject and object), is counterpoised by an affective locus in the self which attempts to relate, unite, and bond the subjective / objective hermeneutic of "selving" in a dual complex of knowing. The model for integrated personhood is the union of choice and desire. In Ricoeur's words, "The investigation of authentic human affectivity, therefore, must be guided by the progress of objectivity. If feeling reveals my adherence to and my adherence in aspects of the world that I no longer set over and against myself as object, it is necessary to show the new aspects of objectivity which are interiorized in the feelings of having" (*Fallible Man* 171).

Affectivity, as an essential component of human existence, then, reveals self-existence as a transcending feature of self in its attachment to the Other through its attempts to integrate self and Other, efforts to internalize the Other in a kind of felt possession—mine, part of me. The polarity of knowing and feeling, then, is another expression of potential structural fault in the human personality, as Ricoeur notes: "By interiorizing all of the connections of the self to the world, feeling gives rise to a new cleavage of the self from the self. . . . It seems, then, that conflict is a function of man's most primordial constitution; the object is synthesis; the self is conflict. The human duality outruns itself intentionally in the synthesis of the object and interiorizes itself affectively in the conflict of subjectivity" (*Fallible Man* 201). We now have the key to Ricoeur's account of the ethicalization of evil as structural fragility: fallibility is a felt conflict within the self.

Hopkins discussed the poetic dialectics of the will as freedom and hope in one of his most protracted essays, "On Personality, Grace, and Free Will" in his *Sermons and Devotional Writings* (146-159). Students of Hopkins familiar with this essay will have already recognized, in my broad sketch of Ricoeur's rich discourse on the structural phenomenology of the self, the clear parallels to Hopkins' understanding of the self— finite and fallen.

Hopkins, like Ricoeur, pointed to the interiorization of the experience of evil. However the context of Hopkins' reflections is theological rather philosophical. If the "instress" of energy in the "world's inscapes"— selfness—in all Creation is the same being energy as that of the Creator, then self-expression is irrevocably an intentionality which is shared between God and creature, an Adamic intendance that is subject to fault in positing the "selving I" through the fallible, expressive reflections of the consciousness. Hopkins attempted to penetrate the formation of the self to understand evil as a structural fault in human personhood.

"Selving" Volition

As noted earlier, Hopkins construed the self along the lines of Scholastic philosophy mentored by John Duns Scotus. We need not sketch here a detailed diagram of notions with which Hopkins traced out the faculties of the mind. Rather to see the echo between the modern philosopher and the nineteenth century theologian-poet, we need only focus on the structural design of the consciousness. The human heart, to use Hopkins' collective word for the whole self, is a complex congeries of energies, one pattern called memory, another understanding, and another will. It is the human will, the energy of choosing, on which Hopkins centered his key notion of "selving," the making of personality.

Human will-energy is a divided energy. One part is the dominant determinative energy, a power that is most like God, "an absolute which stands to the absolute of God as the infinitesimal to the infinite" *(Sermons* 153). Hopkins called this authenticaing, voluntary the *arbitrium* in the structure of the self the "bare self"; the other part he designated its nature, that is, the affective energy through which the determinative will *(arbitrium)* functions. This general energy of volition, a tiny replica of the whole Personality or Selfness of God, is that energy which constitutes the finite personality or self of humanhood— individual human personality. Freedom, then, is the interaction of these two volitional energies that creates the personality of the "I am."

Limitation in the structure of the human self lies in these two aspects of human volitional powers according to Hopkins. Three of these mental energies—memory (which includes the imagination in the Scholastic concept), understanding, and affectivity are attracted to and interactive with the "inscapes" of energies of the finite world and thus are not, to be accurate, expressive of the individuality of the self. Though they are part of the deliberating process of human determination, and in this capacity play a role in free choice, they are, strictly speaking, in themselves able to choose only that to which they are interactively attracted. On the other hand, that energy which is the distinctivising power of the individual self, the elective will, is able to discriminate between the "inscapes" of energies encountered and to choose freely to affirm, that is, reexpress those energies in the "instress of inscape" of its own "I am." Moreover, according to Hopkins, only the elective power of the volitional soul can seek to transcend the "inscape" of energies of the finite world and attempt to interact with any possible energies described as infinite "inscape" energies—God. This split between the energies of the self constituted for Hopkins the structural fault in the phenomenology of the self. (I do not address here the issue of whether Hopkins has exaggerated the Scholastic understanding of the powers of soul by his postulating the structural fault in human volitional powers; I, and others, have addressed this question elsewhere [See Downes, *The Ignatian Personality of G. M. Hopkins* Postscript 11].

So for Hopkins, like Ricoeur, the positing of the human self is snagged with an internal fallibility. Both thinkers discern in the self a split between the energies of knowing, feeling, and choosing, so that hermeneutic ambiguity lies within the configuration of the "selving" energies we call the self. It follows, then, that the definitive "I" reflected in selfness lies hidden in the opaque images and symbols which the consciousness reflects upon in order to discover those representations of self which identify its "I-ness" with expressive accuracy. Of course, for Hopkins as theologian, this fault in the array of human volitional powers is construed differently than for Ricoeur, the philosopher. For Hopkins, this fallibility in the self makes for a spiritually destructive interaction of energies so that the self is betrayed into corruptive representations of the self in the very process of corrupting the "inscapes" of energies of other selves that make up world, what we call in human nature "sin" and evil in Nature. This chasm in the phenomenal structure of self is what Hopkins meant by the Fall— each human self "so selfbent, so bound, so tied to his turn" (*Poems* 156).

We now are able to see that the genesis of religious consciousness in both thinkers lies in their notion of the general phenomenology of the self and particularly in the "selving" hermeneutics positing the self's "I am." For Hopkins, distinct finite selfness posits distinct infinite Selfness. From this insight arises religious consciousness, that is, the possession of a radical awareness that all the energies in existence are God's utterances of Himself, and thus all the energies He put into existence are dependent upon and subservient to his Selfness. The multifarious being-energies of Creation are symbols of his powerful creativity and of his generous goodness. Hopkins clearly put deific Selfness in a hermeneutic context of what he supposed the "selving" consciousness of God to be when he wrote: "God's utterance of himself in himself is God the Word, outside himself is the world." God's wording, then, is the wording of all Creation, especially human consciousness: "The world then is word, expression, news of God.Therefore its end, its purpose, its purport, its meaning, is God and its life or work to name and praise him."

This theologico-hermeneutic insight gives rise to two considerations regarding the task of human consciousness in uttering human selfness. First, in Hopkins' words, "the world, man, should after its own manner give God being in return for the being he has given it or should give him back that being he has given." This is to say , in Ricoeur's terms, that the "I-ness" that constitutes the unique self has an obligative dimension in its task of energizing the reflective consciousness that overrides the dictation of the *ego* in the *ego cogito*; there is the task of *disaffirming* the ego as the principal task of consciousness. Secondly, to use Hopkins' words again, "This is done by the great sacrifice. To contribute then to that sacrifice is the end for which man was made" (*Sermons* 129). Under the heading of the "great sacrifice," Hopkins developed the whole of his theology of the religious meaning of God, the Creator, Christ, the Word, His triple Incarnation (one in angelic time, the second in human time, and the third in Eucharistic time). The Kerygma of Christian faith, then, becomes the key to understanding the formative actions of religious consciousness, a "passion for the possible," as Ricoeur called the Christian religious consciousness, mediated by poetics of the religious imagination—symbols, parables, and the mythic Gospel narratives.

"Selving" the Christed Assent

It is in understanding Christian Kerygma that the echoes between the poet-theologian and the hermeneutic philosopher become a dialogue. We have seen how both Hopkins and Ricoeur understand the self-descriptive reflections of the consciousness, how each encounters the experiences of evil both as an external force and an inner ethical dilemma, how each depicts and accounts for the structural faults in the "selving" of the human consciousness. Now we come to the nexus between faith and consciousness.

According to Ricoeur, that nexus lies in the kerygmatic core of ethics. Here is his way of answering Hopkins' logic of the Christological interpretation of the event of salvation. Starting with ethicalized consciousness, Ricoeur writes:

> I would unite the notion of value with the dialectic between a principle of unlimitation, linked to the desire to be, and a principle of limitation, linked to works, institutions, and structures of economic, political, and cultural life. I would not project value into the heavens, where it becomes an idol. If value is an event, if it is announced and attested to only in the element of witness, then value is the *event,* if it is a *commencement or beginning*, if it is a *historical mystery* which is announced and attested to only in the element of *witness,* [author's italics] then value is the event of a kerygma which relocates man— man and his law, man and his ethics—in a history of salvation, that is, in a history where everything can be lost and where everything can be saved or, rather, in a history where everything is already lost on the basis of an event which endlessly occurs, the Fall, and in a history where everything is already saved on the basis of an event endlessly remembered and signified, the death of the Just One. It is this

contextualization of man and his human ethic in relation to the evangelical summons that constitutes the kerygmatic moment of ethics (*Conflict* 343).

Ricoeur goes on to define that "Kerygmatic moment" as "What can I hope for?"— the fundamental question in the face of radical evil. He attempts to posit a religious consciousness as promise. The object of religious reflection is the archetypal representation of "the good"; Ricoeur writes, here "is where the Christology which the theologian takes as his space of intelligibility is related to the will in the philosophy of religion. The central question of the philosophy of religion is this: how is the will affected in its most intimate desire by the representations of this model, this archetype of a humanity agreeable to God, which the believer calls the Son of God?" (*Conflict* 345). The agent which the Kerygmatic moment reveals is Christ, who, to the philosopher, is a surcharged, radiant image of fulfillment: in Ricoeur's words, "for the philosopher, Christ is the schema of hope. He comes from a mythicopoetic imagination, which concerns the completion of desire to be" (*Conflict* 346). The "desire to be," which is the primal driving energy of the human consciousness, then, is a dialectic of volitional powers which on the one side confronts self-accusation, and on the other promotes self-consolation. The theme which emerges from this dialectic unites these two powerful symbolic "selving" agencies in the image of fatherhood as love, the love that is the Kerygma of Christ. Herein enters Hopkins' theology of grace.

We now come full circle with the introduction of the notion of Christian grace as the perpetuity of the Christological "Kerygmatic moment," the reflection elevating the "selving" consciousness to a new level of symbolized hope and fulfillment. Let us first look back over the dialectical curving before we close the circle.

We have traced how both Hopkins and Ricoeur start their reflections with selfness, and then assert that the task of self-consciousness is the positing of the unique "I-ness" of the self. The central implication of selfness for philosopher Ricoeur is the mode by which the self carries on its task of achieving consciousness—the hermeneutics of symbolism. For the religious poet Hopkins, the main implication of selfness is the "selving" fatherhood of the universe—the process of the creative personhood of God. In both philosopher and poet, the experience in the self of evil as suffering and alienation, accusation and guilt, are interpreted as an external deforming energy and as an internal disordering energy entering into selfness—volitional evil. Thus both see a fallibility in the self as a structural fault which has made the will servile. Both look to interpret the magnitude of "selving" fallibility in the narration of the myths whose symbolism posits evil in the typology of a super-narcissism resulting in a self-exiling captivity, whose antitypology is the achieved self in the figure of Christ. This is to say that the positing of selfness involves the creation of religious consciousness wherein "I-ness" is transvalued from hopelessness to hope. Every self is lost and found in the mystery of the "selving" religious consciousness. Such, both thinkers find, is the basic "selving" predicament of every human being.

Now the circle of echoes becomes integrated. Both Hopkins and Ricoeur address evil and guilt by looking to that representation in the consciousness which, in Ricoeur's words, "expresses in an objective language the sense that man has of his dependence on that which stands at the limit and at the origin of the world" (*Conflict* 391). This sense, which both thinkers share, necessarily leads them to sacral language, the sacred in the Bible, especially the New Testament. For both, the task of consciousness is to find the "selving newness" of the Gospels in the time-scoped here and now for achieving the true positing potential of the "I am " of the self, the personality of full "selving" plentiude. which Ricoeur stated this as "the correspondence between the Christ-event and the inner man" *(Conflict* 385), and of which Hopkins wrote, "the just man . . . / Acts in God's eye what he is— / Christ," that is, every person is a Christ-event (*Poems* 115).

Both writers find their basic textual symbolism for an exegesis of full human selfness in St. Paul. For Ricoeur it is Romans 5:12-20, where St. Paul interprets the Adamic myth as the logic of grace, in Paul's words, " If the reign of death was established by the one man through the sin of him alone, how much more shall the reign of life be established in those who receive with profusion the grace and gift of justice by the one man Jesus Christ." Ricoeur comments: "The logic of punishment is a logic of surplus and excess. It is nothing else than the folly of the Cross" (*Conflict* 375), and "It is only when we have crossed the border, into grace, that we can look back on what we have been exempted from" (*Conflict* 374).

The impact on the self of achieving this "graced" level of religious consciousness Ricoeur interprets through the myth of Job. The story of Job seems to be about suffering, the issue being accusation, but Ricoeur asserts that the key symbolism in Job is faith: "Job in fact receives no explanation of the meaning of his suffering. His faith is simply removed from every moral vision of the world. In return, the only thing shown to him is the grandeur of the whole, without the finite viewpoint of his own desire receiving a meaning directly from it. A path is thus opened: that of a nonnarcissistic reconciliation. I renounce my viewpoint: I love the whole as it *is* *[italics the author's]*" (*Conflict* 351).

The kergymatic meaning for Hopkins of the Christ-event is located as well in St. Paul, in Phillippians 2: 5-11. Here is Hopkins' reading: "For the divine nature was his from the first; yet he did not think to snatch at equality with God, but made himself nothing, assuming the nature of a slave. Bearing the human likeness, revealed in human shape, he humbled himself, and in obedience accepted even death—death on a cross." Hopkins commented, "It is this holding back that was his right, nay his possession from past eternity in his other nature, his own being and self, which seems to me the root of all his holiness and the imitation of this the root of all moral goodness" (*Sermons* 108). Christ, then, is the exemplar in the consciousness who provides the recuperating selving energy, the gift of grace. Once across this spiritual border, the mystery of self-sacrifice is entered into where the consciousness can begin to experience freedom from the accusation and guilt of evil, where consolation begins, and hope becomes possible.

Crossing this "selving" border requires difficult spiritual surgery as St. Paul noted: "If true knowledge is to be found in Jesus, you will have learned in his school that you must be quit, now, of the old self whose way of life you remember, the self that wasted its aim in false dreams. There must be a renewal in the inner life of your minds; you must be clothed in the new self, which is created in God's image, justified and sanctified through the truth" (Eph 4: 22-24), and again "You must be quit of the old self and the habit that went with it; you must be clothed in the new self" (Col 3: 9-10).

Hopkins elaborated these insights in his discussions of the elevations of grace that the consciousness may experience, the difficulty the "I" has in renouncing its narcissism, and the radiance felt in acknowledging the intimations of transcendence in conjoining the energies of selfness with the energies of Christ in a self-transforming self-sacrifice— a new song of selfness. Hopkins never stated more passionately the possibility of the transformation of the self possible in the achievement of Christian consciousness as a triumph over evil and death than in his famous Resurrection poem, "That Nature is a Heraclitean Fire" (*Poems* 174):

> Flesh fade, and mortal trash
> Fall to the residuary worm; world's wildfire, leave but ash:
> In a flash, at a trumpet crash,
> I am all at once what Christ is, since he was what I am, and
> This Jack, joke, poor potsherd, patch, matchwood, immortal diamond,
> Is immortal diamond.

We now can hear, in the echo and response between Hopkins' religious and poetic contemplations on the sacred and Ricoeur's philosophic hermeneutic reflections on the true positing of selfness, a dialectical harmony whose theme is at the very conflictive center of twentieth-century Modernism: Is there any basis for hope? We know all too well the powerful answers to the possibility of hope that many leading modernist thinkers have decreed, in Sartre's terse summary of them— "no exit!" Yet the perennial question of hope resides in the human heart. In the "selving" dialectic of Hopkins' Christological tradition and in Ricoeur's phenomenological hermeneutics of selfness, we are presented with a refashioned sense of the hermeneutic response to the possibility of human hope of which the Incarnation and Resurrection of Christ are, for them, the key disclosing "selving" figurative signs. For both Hopkins and Ricoeur, this Christed sign, a sign beckoning the I-self to be reappropriated anew, offers the positing "I" a new "selving," full of passion for a transcending hope and freedom. However, both make clear such "selving" work must achieved by a "graced" felicific choosing by and within every self to accomplish its full passion for possibility.

Chapter 4

The Poetics of the Sacramental Word: Hope and Freedom

The Poetics of Ricoeur's Religious Imagination

The focus of this Chapter is on Hopkins' understanding of the nature of the poetics of the "selving" consciousness. However, at the outset it will be useful to lay out the general parameters of Ricoeur's hermeneutics of the religious imagination as a contemporary counterpoise to Hopkins in order to readily see the currency of his ideas about "selving" and the poetic religious consciousness.

We remember that for Ricoeur, the meaning of the "I" of "I am" must be rescued from self-alienation through recovering the meaning of the self in the disclosures of language. This healing through self-positing emphasizes expression as an self-objectifying knowing mode; expression also utters the thought and experiences of the utterer as the subjectifying mode of consciousness "selving." This dual operative "selving" pattern in the self parallels the structure of language, words that are concepts and words that are symbols. Concept words express an objectifying intentionality bearing attributes of univocal, logical expression, while symbol words bear a subjectifying intentionality possessing the attributes of plurivocal, figurative expression. For Ricoeur it is in metaphoric language that new self-revealing meaningfulness is uttered by which the "I" reconfigures its "I am."

Both kinds of expression proclaim meaning as sense and reference, the linguistic duality of expression being that conceptual language is a single-meaning wording while symbol words carry multiple meanings. While Ricoeur concentrates on symbolic language, it is important to note that, for him, the language manifold is a unified operation which produces the dual levels of concept and symbol, depending upon the hermeneutic intentionality of the "selving" consciousness (Klemm 62-66).

Another of Ricoeur's views of language must be noted. Human expressivity arises as cosmic utterance (myth) "spoken" to the self from without. Out of the symbolic structuring of the elements of the world arises a "selving" meaning, a primal meaning that typically involves interpreting deep feelings of the subjectivity of evil. Of the avowing confession of evil in the self, Ricoeur wrote: "It is this emotional note that gives rise to the objectification in discourse; the confession expresses, pushes to the outside, the emotion without which it would be shut up in itself, as an impression in the soul. Language is the light of emotions" (*Symbol of Evil,* 7). Moreover, the symbols of this emerging language as cosmic symbol and psychic expressivity are inextricably linked: "Cosmos and Psyche are the two poles of the same 'expressivity'; I express myself in expressing the world; I explore my own sacrality in deciphering that of the world" (*Symbol of Evil* 12).

It only remains to be added that the self processes new self-meaning in passing from the primary cosmic symbol of expressivity through interpretative stages: from the unity of symbolic cosmic myth and subjective consciousness through the disunity of evil and exile, where the consciousness reflects the subjectivity of alienation and discontinuity, to the restorative hermeneutic of the sacralizing symbol, wherein the intentionality of the self achieves a new self-meaning by way of a progressive "selving" actualization. Cosmic myth symbols and the "selving" subjectivization of moral evil are the expressive means, powered by the metaphoric configurations of the sympathetic imagination, by which the self achieves a new consciousness: "This "I" is no longer the existential self that is in direct relation to the symbol, but is the "I" that synthesizes direct self-world relations" (Klemm 73).

The "I" of the self can achieve a new "I am." The occurrence of this new dialectic discourse of "selving" expressivity, for Ricoeur, reaches its fullest manifestation when it moves from orality to textuality: "Writing is the full manifestation of discourse" (*Interpretation Theory* 25-26). David Klemm comments on this declaration: "The reason why for Ricoeur text is the full manifestation of discourse is that with the inscription of meaning and its isolation from event, language displays the full scope of its creative and renewing capabilities" (Klemm 81).

In Ricoeur's hermeneutics, then, living speech opens the horizon of "selving" dialogue, but the event of discourse changes when the speaking is made in written form. Meaning and event in discourse becomes separated so that the dialectic now becomes explicit (*Interpretaton Theory* 25-26). The full manifestation of "selving" discourse that is writing now must deciphered by the reader. The text now becomes the coded clue to be actualized into a new meaning event. As text structure, the reader encounters composition (a system of wholes and parts), genres (the dynamics of production),and style (the assertion of individuality in the unique forging of the text) ("The Hermeneutical Function" 36-37). Authoring and reading are the two sides of the "selving" event.

In the duality of notion and symbol that is the medium of written expression, especially so in the language of religious discourse, the plurivocity of symbols, the basic units of figurative expression, points to a sacred universe. The linguistic process of symbolic action emerges in three different horizons of meaning: the cosmic set, which temporalizes the sacred universe and uncovers natural and human disorder; the pyschic set, which interrelates the expressed (the world) with the expresser (the reflective decipherer) so that all self-expressions are in some way expressions of the world, and all explorations of the world are in some way expressions of the self (Klemm 66-69).

The third horizon of meaning, the most central to our interest here in encountering sacral texts, is the imaginative, which is the subjective, creative response to the primary symbols of the cosmos and the psyche. Through the imagination, the self attempts to restore a radical unity with the universe, a transformation that involves appropriating the mythic narratives of the primary symbols, Nature and the fallible "I" the individualized self attempts to transcend the disclosed rift in the order of being caused by evil, now perceived as a self-infection and an alienation from the Creator's intended order, by accepting personal responsibility to restore the lost wholeness of Being. Here the hermeneutics of text involves a process of self-conscious alteration whereby the self becomes involved in a reconciliation through a newly textualized consciousness that finds a self-transcending mode in which to find a new bonding relationship between self and the Master Intelligence of the universe. This new event of meaning, for Ricoeur, and for Hopkins, is exemplified in the texting Word of the Incarnation—"the Christ event." Such "selving" refiguration amounts to a hermeneutical description of the religious imagination.

The zone of the hermeneutics of imaginative texts, out of which the religious imagination springs, is, in general, a product of the hermeneutic horizons of poetic diction by which direct redescription becomes a part of the allusions of fictive metaphoric and symbolic expression: "Fiction removes us from the perceived world in order to open up new possiblities for being-in-the-world accessible to the imagination in that the imagination constructs the fictional text-world as a place in which a new mode of being is manifest" (Klemm 86). According to Ricoeur, then, imaginative consciousness, as an hermeneutic process, is the "world of the text" in which we go beyond connecting ourselves with some being-object (ontological meaning) to an undreamed of connection of relational meanings between "I-ness" and the world, "a new mode of being," which brings disclosures of a new "I," that is, a new state of "selving" of the consciousness. Reading secular poetry and fiction, thus, can pass from "playful " new modes of being-in-the-world to transforming self-reflections of truly actualizing new modes of self-formation. We see that the religious imagination is phenomenologically rooted in the creative, productive appropriations of the world of the text we generally call imaginative consciousness; however, the religious imagination moves beyond playful projections of self and the world, from meaning as fanciful projection to meaning as a new aspect of reality sometimes emerging out of what often seems, at the referential level, absurd, nonsensical. From this hermeneutical theory of the dynamics of the religious imagination arises Ricoeur's approach to the sacred texts of the Bible.

The unique character of the religious imagination according to Ricoeur is its power to bring us to a new apprehension of reality. It is the hermeneutical act by which we become more fully human through a process of recontexting the "selving" word. As creatures of the "word" we encounter the semantic innovations of metaphorical symbols that disclose a newly emerging set of meaningful "selving" relationsips on a wholly different plane of reality perspectives that reveal the possibility of an uplifted psycho-spiritual kinship within self and between the self and cosmos: "What is at stake in a metaphorical statement is making a 'kinship' appear where ordinary vision perceives no mutual appropriateness at all" ("Biblical Hermeneutics" 78-79). Metaphor, keyed into symbol as cosmic meaning, is the bridge by which cosmos and self "testify to the primordial rootedness of Discourse in Life"; metaphor projects onto a trans-semantic plane of symbolic meaning "creating a new mode of being" (*Interpretation Theory* 59, 88). The world of the text, then, becomes a projection of a new world—referentially and imaginatively—to which the reader is open to enter into a process of altering self-understanding.

This general notion of the self going out of itself in encountering transfiguring symbols and returning to itself in the appropriation of these symbols on a new plane of self-recovery is at the heart of Ricoeur's hermeneutics of religious texts. A confession of "selving" faith, then, arises out of a discourse mode embodying symbolic forms to which an open, sensitive reader may respond, a response empowered by the poetic imagination. For Ricoeur, a classic religious text is a biblical text, and, while there are several genres in the Old Testament Bible (narrative, prophecy, wisdom, laws, hymns), all are linguistic forms of a generic naming of God. God is disclosed in the opacities of these text forms, for the Bible as a whole is a polysemy of the transfiguring names of God.

In the New Testament, parables, proverbs, and eschatological sayings are different linguistic modes through which the open- hearted, sensitive reader can achieve a new self-meaning. Such religious texts are in kind poetic texts, that is, the literal referents move from the literal plane to the figurative in and through which a real experience is redescribed in new ways, for religious texts go beyond the merely poetic in that the possible new modes of being extend into a new horizon, that of the infinite as the background of the finite. This is to say that God becomes the referent, and as such becomes the new meaning by which the self comes to a new self-meaning (*Philosophy and Religious Language* 83).

This altering, "selving" hermeneutic process is engendered by sacral texts which express confronting limits (covenants in the Old Testament and "the Kingdom of God" in the New Testament) which test the widsom of common experience in all of its conventional assumptions and attitudes. The narratives, through their metaphoric actions, qualify the redescriptions of real experience so radically, that the heuristics offered by the parabolic symbols become surcharged with a surplus of meaning. Hidden in the metaphorical action is the provocative possibility for the sensitive reader of acquiring a new self-meaning. Faith is an assent to accept this difficult challenge of overturning the finite "selving" limits of temporal existence (*Philosophy and Religious Language* 83). It must be stressed that such self-transformations do not happen automatically by just encountering religious texts; appropriating the religous meaning of "Love your enemies, do good to those who hate you" (Luke 6:27), for example, confronts the reader with a limit that only an understanding of a wholly different level of referential meanings—cosmic and self—must come into awareness before the reader can begin to achieve a new perspective about what seems an unreachable way of life. And even a firm assent at any given time will need to be tested against the limits of experience again and again. Thus Jesus asked Peter, "Do you love me?" And Peter answered with a fervent assent, an affirmation that asserted that Peter would attempt to live in the world at a new limit-breaking level of "selving "existence. But as we know, the trial of faith goes on in the story of Peter, involving more promises, kept and unkept.

With this recapitulaton of Ricoeur's hermeneutical theory of the transforming powers of the religious imagination, we come to his understanding of the central issue of Christian religious texts, Jesus as "the Christ Event" in the Gospels. In its hermeneutic perspective, the Incarnation is a symbol of the perennial human predicament, the constant struggle between the clock of the universe, the psychic time in the self, and time's suspension in the contemplative religious consciousness. The energy that travels this complex web is called hope, which for Ricoeur, and for all Christians, is that latent force of desiring aspiration buried in the heart that is the hidden meaning of every personal self-history—life towards eternity. Self- history is nothing more or less than this secret story of the self. From the vantage point of human consciousness, the medium in and through which such meaning becomes known is a narrative wherein the self structures the timed sequences of personal experience into intimations of eternity. Just as the Incarnation is the story of God personally entering time, faith is the story of the self entering into eternity. In this context, it is clear why Ricoeur is interested in the heuristics of the historicity of Jesus' way of living in time.

Lived action in time is every person's life-plot, the basic structure of narrative, by which each of us refigures the meanings of our lives. "Selving" transformation can happen because certain narratives do more than tell the chronology of human experience; some narratives remake human experience. These we call religious narratives. And in their hermeneutical remaking, a work of the religious imagination, we not only retrace our own temporal story, but we can also be enabled to refigure our lived time into spiritual time, a new plane of self-meaning in a transformed time frame, yet within the transitory patterns of cosmic time.

Of course, any phenomenological account of such a transformation involves what comes out of our encounter with the fates of cosmic time. For existentialists in general, as we know, what comes out is sudden or prolonged suicide; another variety of existentialist response might be named "the pathetic Romantics" who choose to try to make the tales of their consciousnesses esthetic. There are other varieties of humanism that have been put forth in facing cosmic time. All are what Martin

Heidigger has identified as **essential** existentialism, "being-towards-death, wiith one **existiell** response, the stoical mask of mortal despair (Vanhoozer 195). It is precisely here that Ricoeur sees fictive narrative offering a different "existiell" response. Narrative, free of linear patterns of time and the sequences of historical tracings, can freely explore the limits of time. Such exploration constitutes human freedom, a capacity that is at once the core of any hopeful humanism and a potential to revise the meaning of the world as something more than a mysterious accident. It is at at this outer cosmic limit the symbol of Creation is able to be uncovered as the gift of transcendent existence.

The hermeneutics of the Creation symbol offers the potential for a new way to refigure cosmic time and human meaning. This primal symbol subsists in biblical time in the form of narrative. The parables of the New Testament, for example, are stories in ordinary lived time, but their plots are so constructed that they force a confrontation between natural event in linear time and the possibility of a new vision of the meaning of biblical time, what Ricoeur calls, "the 'miraculous' dimension of time" (*Bibical Hermeneutics* 102). Ricoeur uses the parable of "hidden treasure" as an instance of what he means: "The kingdom of heaven is like treasure hidden in a field, which a man found and covered up, then in his joy he goes and sells all that he has and buys that field" (Matt. 13:44). "Finding" connotes gifting rather than laboring or fighting-tales of ordinary time, a gifting that opens up a different way of understanding living in time. Such an "Event," unforeseen, undeserved, and unexpected, can, if responded to with openness and commitment to its meaning, reverse the consciousness of individual being-in-time (selling), and with perseverence, be the basis of a profound personal change, a decision (buying) to try to live in sight of the new vision of the self in cosmic time— spiritual time, eternity, the "Kingdom of God " (Vanhoozer 197). What Ricoeur is saying about biblical tales, like the parable of the "hidden treasure," is that they are opportunities for "events" in which the reader can be opened up to the discovery that Jesus' life was like the parable He told, which is what the Kingdom of God is like. Ricoeur says of this pattern: "This succession is full of sense: the Kingdom of God is compared to a chain of these three acts: letting the Event blossom, looking in another direction, and doing with all one's strength in accordance with the new vision" (*Philosophy of Paul Ricoeur* 241).

Ricoeur understands "Event" as the transforming happening by which Being and possibility come to the "selving"consciousness through the powers of poetic speech. Treasure gifted in the parable becomes treasure gifted in the self. Moreover, such "gifting" is not of the reader's making; rather the gifts are lodged in the figurative meanings of the narrative texts as out-riding new meanings flooding the text's amplitude. This rich surplus of possible meanings is especially evident in the parables Jesus told, and hence the parables are powerful in their poetic capacity to reorient the reader: "The poetic power of the Parable is the power of the Event . . . it is in the heart of the imagination that we let the event happen . . . To listen to the Parables, it seems to me, is to let one's imagination be opened to the new possibilities disclosed by the extravagance of these short dramas" (Vanhoozer 198). Such is the character of the biblical imagination, a potential conferrer of a profoundly transformational gift of self re-vision, what Ricoeur calls "Event," and theologians call grace—the new temporality of God blazing into the head.

Taken together, then, the stories in the Bible, while in different literary forms, are an elaborate single story about the Event of the Kingdom of God. Each single story narratively interacts with every other story in some way to form a complex system of spiritualizing symbols in which the meaning of God's Kingdom is textualized. Ricoeur calls this linguistic phenomenon "Intertextuality" (*Philosophy of Paul Ricoeur* 242). The charge to each of us is, as hearers and readers, to recontextualize the Bible into our own lives (*Conflict* 384-385). Thus all Jesus' parables are the tracings of his preaching the Kingdom of God during his own life time, and the Gospels are stories about Jesus living His life at the kerygmatic level of spiritual consciousness. Together, Jesus' own story and his story-telling, as symbolic, poetic figurations of the what the Kingdom of God means, represent a rich, deep, extended metaphor combining narrative as story in ordinary time and heuristic in supernatural time. The work of the reader is to grasp the hermeneutics of intertextual meaning in the world of biblical texts whose poetic powers can engage the imaginative powers so that "Christ Event" of new Being will become the reader's own individualized speech.

Of course, Jesus' own story is the major plot of the New Testament narratives. What is different about his story, and all the other stories in the Bible, is that his story, taken as a whole, is more than a complex symbol illuminating what the Kingdom of God means; his story is actually about the eventuality of the coming of the Kingdom of God. His own historicity is the meaning of the end of cosmic time, a meaning that cannot be calendared. The Event of the Kingdom of God sponsored by the Gospel text for each individual is immanent in the very ordinary events of lived time. The stories of the Bible, singly and intertextually, call for reponsive choice to the "Christ Event" in the text. In ordinary time, we are called to do "something" about our insights into the eternal provoked in and by the the Gospel stories; that "something" is opened up in the narrative symbolism of Jesus' own life, but particularly his Passion. The Passion story is the ultimate instance of the temporal "limit" experience in human time. The story of Jesus' temporal life is essentially about what Ricoeur has called the "passion for the possible." For Jesus' story is about how one lives in ordinary time with the consciousness of supernatural time, that is, understanding in the spirit of faith every little or big happening in one's life, keeping the promise of hope and the affirmation of love, because of the gifts of Creation coming from the goodness of the Creator.

As narratives, then, the Gospels are fictive paradigms expressing the event of hope that goes beyond cosmic time limits to the eternal because the eternal (Jesus) entered human time to show the way. The Gospels are also tales about eternity, for their poetic configurations open a kind of outline of the eternal beyond the time barrier, a vision, as we say, of the hereafter, a transcending consciousness. The Gospels, as well, are a sounding of the name of God, taking us beyond the Old Testament Jahweh, the name of God "out there," to the Christ, the God "in here." Of course, narrative, prophecy, wisdom, hymns, and proverbs all name God, all tell of God's involvement with humanity, but Jesus' story adds a most significant dimension, namely, the naming of God as rejection, loss, failure, sacrifice—death in ordinary time that is to be transfigured into meaning pointing to supernatural time—the Resurrection and Ascension. The new name of God in the story of Jesus is grace, the paradox of God as a creative power actively immanent in the very processes of the world, working in and through the very frames of cosmic time according to the sequence of ordinary time, but at some level, revealing the Event that offers a hopeful vision that we call faith, a hope that "sees" through and beyond to a new time-transcendent freedom.

It must be said emphatically again that such a transformation in consciousness is not something that occurs automatically in encountering the horizon of sacred texts. A reinterpreted life becomes a transformed life only in and through the kerygma of the text as Word, that is, the text possesses a communicative power to alter consciousness, a kind of creative, expressive passion that Christians call the "living Word" that is the necessary condition to afford the possibility of transformation—the grace of the Spirit. This circumstance of self revision, of course, is a story, as it must be, in the Christian narrative, the story of the sending of

the Paralcete to the Apostles. Jesus' Ascension and the sending of the
Spirit is at the heart of this story (for example, in Luke 24 and in Acts 1;
also John 14:16-17; 16: 7-11) of Jesus' fearful followers in the upper
room when Christ appeared to them and told them how the testimony of
His passion would continue in ordinary time. At issue in these texts is
the revelation of how the Jesus of history became the Christ of faith.
There is opened up the connection between Jesus "going" and the Holy
Spirit "coming down." In the story, these parallel actions tell of how
Jesus is reconstituted in ordinary time through the Spirit of faith as the
Christ abiding in the Holy Eucharist in the Church, an enduring
community bridging cosmic time and supernatural time: "Death may
have come through Adam, but something greater than death came through
the second Adam, Jesus Christ. Whereas the first man Adam became a
living soul, the second Adam has become life-giving spirit (Cor. 15:45).
In other words, Jesus is the Christ because through his Passion,
Resurrection and Ascension he is able to send the spirit, the power of the
Christian possibility" (Vanhoozer 255).

But the power of passion for the Christian possibility, personal
liberation, as Ricoeur reads the Gospel texts, demands on our part an
imaginative encounter with the revelatory narratives so that we are opened
up to the entry of a new consciousness (*Essays in Biblical Interpretation*
111-139). The Word / word has the power to transform us, to bring us to
a new self-understanding, but we must reach what I would call the
contemplative stage of reflection, that is, a level of consciousness in which
our rising up to an open-ended possibility of surrendering our old ego-
fixated selfness is answered by what only can be described as a coming
down of a new vista of the surrender of self-meaning. This experience is
ineffable, surely; it is experienced as both an entering of an outer force
from an upper level of a new self-reality yet seems, strangely, to be a
kind of a rediscovered inner power, manifested dimly in the self, but
quickly forgotten, even lost, but somehow mysteriously resurrected into
a soul-changing, new selving-possibility. Such are the powers, according
to Ricoeur, of encountering the texts of the Bible with the exercise of
one's imaginative powers appropriating the Gospel narrative metaphors
with their conferring illuminative graces.

This contemplative state can be called an assent to a new reality of
selfness, a kind of verification of a new self-existence that reinterprets
our lives. This reinterpretation can be understood phenomenologically
as the essence of freedom, for this new "faith"consciousness is an entrance
to a new life, hence the possibility to become a new self on a higher level

of consciousness (Bultmann I, 331). However, this Christian possiblity comes about, it must be emphasized again, in the preachings of Jesus, that is, in the texts of the New Testament; again and again they tell of how ordinary experience can awaken us to a revisioning of the world in ordinary time as Creation, and in appropriating this new perspective, we see that Creation consciousness is conducive to our human freedom. Ricoeur is quite emphatic about this understanding of the Gospel narratives: "I believe that the fundamental theme of Revelation is this awakening and this call, into the heart of existence, of the imagination of the possible. The possibilities are opened before man which fundamentally constitute what is revealed. The revealed as such is an opening to existence, a possibility of existence" (*Philosophy of Paul Ricoeur* 237). It might be added that such an approach to reading the Gospels transcends textual arguments about the historical accuracy of the accounts of Jesus which so absorbs biblical scholars, for the mediative powers of the texts adequately express the universal significance of the eschatological story of Jesus' life, a source of transforming powers in human lives that is the evidential progress of the Christian community, a history full of abundant testimony.

From the reader's vantage, the process of encountering and interpreting texts involves a free, democratic movement from text to the world of the text. This transition releases the literary powers of the text which open up, touch, and change the reader. Such is the unfolding of the text in and through the reader's intellective-imaginative powers. In Ricoeur's religious hermeneutic, the new being that is faith is a plumbing of the metaphorical world of the text to the level of refigured self-consciousness. The word, then, becomes the Word in a kind of co-creative process, the figurative powers latent in the narrative text interacting with the creative imagination of the reader. What I have called "contemplation" Ricoeur calls "awakening" (*Philosophy of Paul Ricoeu*r 231). "This wake-up call" occurs in the normal time-frame of ordinary experience, but does not lift beyond cosmic time in any absolute way. At some upper level beyond time-consciousness, the awakening spirit figured in the text allows us to "see" new self-being, new horizon reality, even though at a lower level the world follows its cosmic patterns and human nature in general remains encompassed in the cosmos. This is to say that from the beginning, Creation has within its existence the presence of the Incarnation, which became visible in Jesus and remains "visible" in the Christ-Wording through the Holy Spirit.

But the "seeing" to believe must come through the reader's in-taking of the Gospel text. The gift of Faith is latently present in the figurations of the text (Ricoeur would say the "superabundance" of "folly of the Cross" and "the wisdom of the Resurrection" at the heart of the biblical texts, (*Conflict* 409-410), but it is in and through thetext that the reader must achieve in some way the new contemplative consciousness. In his hermeneutics, Ricoeur stresses less the ethical responses to the texts, getting right with God, than the redemptive, refiguring powers of the reader's self response. His emphasis is eschatological. What, then, according to Ricoeur, is the reader's work in appropriating religious texts? The achieved self, in his view, is less a work in the sense of something done; self-changing assent is not so much a doing, a taking, or a making; rather it is a kind of self-surrendering, a giving of a new selflessness to the usually I-centered ego that renders the self open to new perspectives of reality and self-reinterpretations. For Ricoeur, it is in the revealing world of the text which possesses universal powers of disclosure to refound our human meaning (*Interpretation Theory* 94-95).

The Christian understanding of self and the world, then, what is called faith, is an empowering freedom that is awakened in and through the contemplative imagination unfolding the sense and reference in the world of the sacred text. Reading in the fullest meaning of the word is part of a redemptive action insofar as such an act alters our mode of being-in-the-world. Such reading is not limited to religious texts exclusively, for such powers of change reside in secular texts as well. But for Ricoeur, clearly it is religious texts, especially the bibical texts, that are surcharged with the figurative powers to transform our existence, because such texts bring us so forthrightly to "the limit experiences" which press us to be reinterpreted: "Faith is the attitude of one who accepts being interpreted at the same time he interprets the world of the text . . . the response to the proposition of a new being which opens up new possiblities of existence for me. Hope, unconditional trust, would be empty if it did not rely on a constantly renewed interpretation of sign-events reported by writings, such as the Exodus in the OT and the Resurrection in the NT. These are the events of deliverance which open and disclose the utmost possibilities of my own freedom and thus become for me the Word of God" (*Philosophy of Religion* 84).

But what gives sanction to such a deliverance in the Word of God? Even if cosmic symbols can be interpretatively connected to the cosmos, how do they interact with metaphors which hermeneutically float freely beyond the actual world? In other words, are texts enough, even religious texts? Ricoeur's answer is the authentication of texts through "testimony." Testimony is the actualizing assent that someone has been changed through the world of the text. Symbol and metaphor become grounded in the lived reality of changed self-being: "Only testimony that is singular in each instance confers sanction of reality on ideas, ideals, and ways of being that the symbol depicts to us and which we uncover as our ownmost possibilities" (*Essays on Biblical Interpretation* 109). In testimonial assent to our new self-being, we acknowledge an absolute and eternal meaning to human experience and cosmic history. This is to say that the meaning of human existence and of all being is founded in an ultimate transcendency. This is the flower of religion of which testimony is the seed.

"Testimony" is a wording, a narrative of historical perceptions that are discovered in the foundation of actual events. Hence authenticity of testimony is always a kind of test or trial, always subject to falsity, but true testimony notably has the mark of existential verification. Testimony is not only a discussion of empirical evidence, which can never be adequately found to verify the transcendent consciousness; rather, confirming authenticity of testimony is actually undergoing the consequences of achieving a new self-reality, whatever the personal cost. From this perspective, even the narrative witnesses of such authenticity do not necessarily achieve "selving" testimony in their own lives. In the temporal order, the ultimate test of testimony is suffering until death to achieve a new spiritual self.

For Ricoeur, the Passion of Jesus is the mysterious temporal paradigmatic witness test for all truly radical spiritual testimony. The Passion story is about giving meaning to the ideas and ideals of the "Kingdom of God" in the absoluteness of lived temporal reality. This paradigm gives to the word, "testimony," an astonishing ultimate connotation when one contemplates the Passion story of Jesus as the testament of the Christed Son of God. Hopkins described the essence of this mystery to Robert Bridges: "Therefore we speak of the events of Christ's life as the mystery of the Nativity, the mystery of the Crucifixion and so on of a host; the mystery being always the same, that the child in the manger is God, the culprit on the gallows God, and so on. Otherwise birth and death are not mysteries, nor is it any great mystery that a just man should be crucified, but that God should fascinates—with the interest of awe, of pity, of shame, of every harrowing feeling" (188). The engendering power of truly entering such a "text-world," as Hopkins here exhibits, lies in discovering the authentic spiritualizing meaning in the text and humbly accepting the full significance of the self-meaning that has been found.

What "selving" vision, then, did the life and death of Jesus inaugurate? First of all, there was transmitted a holistic vision of who and what He was in the "testimony" of his words and acts. Second, while Jesus' life is a true story of dreadful failure and ignominious death, such narrated events constitute testimonial symbolization disclosed in their "text-world" contents. The apocalyptic testimony powerfully proclaimed in the poetics of these biblical texts is the rich metaphor of the Resurrection, called by Ricoeur "that great poem of existence" (Vanhoozer 263). The narrated historical event in the text is straightforward and clear as to its literal telling. However, its eschatological meaning, in passing through the contemplative hermeneutic process, becomes the sponsor of a "selving" opening, a life-affirming, envisioning consciousness of hope as an achievement of the possiblity of salvific love. The hermeneutics of the biblical story of the life and death of Jesus, especially his Resurrection and Ascension, bear "witness" to the possibility of a destined personal transcendence. Out of the unique particularities of these narrative texts arise the poetic proclamations of apocalyptic hope, which can reinterpret the deep reader's personal, "selving" meaning in radically altering its temporal and spiritual planes of existence.

A transformed self-understanding which is evoked out of the poetics of the sacred word is what Ricoeur means by the "passion for the possible." Out of the real historical event (story) emerges the spiritual idealism (the text as theology) which is translated (hermeneutics) into personal, human, "selving" meaning—a newly redeeming self-meaning that encompasses an ultimate destiny. The matter of this regenerating act is the sacral word, and the formality is the contemplative, religious imagination. Together they constitute what may be called an " eighth" sacrament by which grace is conferred. Such grace operates to unlock the consciousness to appropriate the narrative logic of the biblical stories: "Creation is a gift so full of love that God sent His own "Being" into Creation to communicate the fact of and the meaning of this love, the climactic testimony of which is the epoch-making event of the Resurrection which grace (Ascension) further revealed omnipresent in Creation, the constantly descending Holy Spirit that is kergymatically 'the Giver of Life'" (Vanhoozer 262-265).

Such spiritualized passion opens up, beyond the conflicts of "selving" interpretations, the possibility of human meaning as perennial hope and freedom at last. It must be emphasized again that while it is the grace of the imagination which opens up the sacramental powers of the word / Word, Ricoeur makes clear that "seeing" new self-possibilities will not refigure the self. True achievement of a new self involves the confluence of the contemplative imagination and the poetics of the will to choose and change to a new level of personal meaning. We must follow the "Oh, I see" in the head (possibility) with "Yes, I will" in the heart (passion). For Ricoeur, such transformation can happen in discovering the gift of Creation as a personal grace extended to us all; in Creation's free gifting lies the hope which overcomes the pollution of cosmic despair and achieves a mysterious love, a love which realizes capacities to acknowledge our world as a gift, an insight to our humble place in it, and a capacity to cherish it ourselves, and all its Christed inhabitants. According to Ricoeur, in sum, the sacral texts prepare the way as John's Gospel declares: "When all things began, the Word already was"; "the Word became flesh"; "This is the testimony . . . ."

Hopkins' "Selving" Hermeneutics

Now that we have examined Ricoeur's hermeneutic philosophy as it applies to encountering religious "selving" texts, we are ready to explore Hopkins' thinking about the "world of the word," and, later, how his own creation of religious poetry might be understood in Ricoeurrian contexts.

Again, the keys to Hopkins' understanding of the general linguistic process are the onto-hermeneutical concepts denoted by his coinages, "Inscape' and "Instress." To further discuss them in their hermeneutical implications, we must first begin with two short essays on language, Parmenides, and the hermeneutic consciousness titled,"Notes on the History of Greek philosophy" (*Journals* 125-130) which focus on the processing of meaning.

The "Parmenides" essay posed a central problem to Hopkins' understanding of the hermeneutic process. Parmenides was interested in the unifying universal of thought, but he was not interested in how we know particular things: "For the phenomenal world (and the distinction between men or subjects and the things without them is unimportant in Parmenides)." Hopkins was interested in both, which he acknowledged in his essay on the Parmenidean unity of knowing utterance: "The way men judge in particular is determined for each by his own inscape, which depends on the mingling of two elements . . . ." (*Jounrals* 129). Perhaps Hopkins construed "elements" literally in the Heraclitean context of fire and earth, but my point here is that Hopkins' own evolving understanding of basic hermeneutics focused upon finding a "mingling" in utterance (self and word) of the individuality of "inscape" and hermeneutic unity at the horizon of all being. Again, the "mingler" is the reflective consciousness which must find, in the parallels of the dense diversity of persons and things, self-meaning parallels in the self-wording expressivity of the selving "I." "Selving" arises out of particularity, self-being and its "wording."

In rather an astonishingly simple way, Hopkins anticipated contemporary thinking about the nature of language when he opened his essay on words with the sentence: "All words mean either things or relations of things: you may also say then substances or attributes or again wholes or parts" (*Journals* 125). He began with the fundamental proposition of modern phenomenology, namely, that spoken or written words construe meaning through diverse relationships. Hopkins did not elaborate the areas of verbal correspondence beyond existential interrelationships, though his statement logically extends from "wholes or parts" to the parallelistic complexity of the relations of things and the ways that words relate in sentences (poems, for example), including the correspondences between oral and written structures, grammar, and logical patterns.

What he goes to immediately in his essay is the heart of the matter in the hermeneutics of language, the ambivalent nature of words as expressers either of the subjective or objective poles of utterance. In the second brief paragraph of his essay he wrote: "To every word naming a thing and not a relation belongs a passion or prepossession or enthusiasm which it has the power of suggesting or producing but not always and in everyone." Words that name ("instress") things as a particular form ("inscape") are also forms ("inscapes") of the expresser. Hopkins here pointed out that there is a subjective aspect of words, what he called their "prepossession or enthusiasm which has the power of suggesting or producing" a subjective meaning which functions as an affective analogue to the objective aspect of words. Hopkins goes on in his essay to assert that the words of language operate as definitions, and that every definition is multileveled: "every word may be considered as the contraction or coinciding-point of its definitions." He then described generally what each verbal linguistic contraction consists of, that is, "its prepossession of feeling," its abstractive definition which also includes its utterance, whatever the form, and its application or "extension" to the concrete things it names. However complex the associative levels of the word, Hopkins emphasized that the essential hermeneutical nature of the word is its "inscaping" of the "I" of the expressser: "For the word is the expression, *uttering* (italics his) of the idea of the mind." He went on to note that this "idea" takes the form of the "image (of sight or sound or *scapes* [italics his] of the other senses), which is in fact physical and a refined energy accenting the nerves, a word to oneself, an inchoate word, and secondly the conception."

We see here that Hopkins basically understood language as do many modern hermeneutic philosophers. Language as discourse possesses a subjective-objective polarity, where discourse is actualized as a personal event and through which discourse becomes meaning (Klemm 77). Moreover, it is clear that for Hopkins utterance of words is a complex play of associations comprising the utterer's subjective intention and the objective referentiality of the utterance. Thus Hopkins sides with Ricoeur regarding the nature of linguistic theory of discourse. Both preserve a notion of language as possessing an objective reality-based referenciality and self-based subjective intentionality. Moreover, Hopkins understood what modern philosphers like Bernard Lonergan, Paul Ricoeur, and a host of others have analysed, that langauge constructions are experiential sources of potential meaning that must be made into actualized meaning by the the intelligent experiencing of language itself ("Knowing and Language in the Thought of Bernard Lonergan" *in Language, Truth, and Meaning* 67).

Also for Hopkins as for Ricoeur, the creativity of expressivity is a continuing process of human "selving." This is to say that the subjective pole as symbol and the objective pole as concept are irreducible elements of human utterance. Both symbol and concept are distinct significations of meaningfulness as to the utterance of the "I" and the referential character of the uttered word. Ricoeur and Hopkins understand language as possessing this basic duality, each conveying meaning essential to the creation of the "I am" of the "I."

What in things produces the ontological utterance of themselves as themselves, and what in the consciousness creates insights into the parallels between external things and the internal wordings of the self?

That is, what are the hermeneutic energies of the consciousness? Hopkins coined his famous term, "instress," to name those energies in things and the mind that achieve the paralleled correspondences we call meaning hermeneutically and being ontologically. However, "instress" is interactive in its meaning with the meaning of "inscape," his other famous coinage; hence, some sorting out must be done in the context of their associative, phenomenological applications.

"Inscape" denotes something is its unique self, and as an existent, asserts its selfness in the very peculiarity of its manifested differentiated being. Every being-thing, then, is a field of ontic energy out of which emanates its simple (unified) shaped being-ness,the reality of which can be worded as *"things are* or *there is truth.* Grammatically it = *it is* or *there is . . .* how fast the inscape holds a thing that nothing is so pregnant and straight forward to the truth as simple *yes* and *is" (Journals* 127). (A further refinement to "inscape" is Hopkins' word for the absolute distinctiveness of each individual thing, which he called "pitch," an analogy to a single tone in a musical scale, here ontologically a specifc degree of self-development in the "scale of Being"). To the senses, the energy of "inscape" in all natural things appears rough or smooth, and a myriad of textures in between, all of which take on unique patterns down to the most delicate fineness of surface and coloring. Behind and within this outward appearance in every thing is a network of girding strands of energized materials upholding it as a thing unified in its wholeness. These highly energized fields of inner and outer structure, which each thing in Nature is as a "shape," is what Hopkins meant by "inscape" (Miller *Disappearance* 287-294). His diaries are full of carefully delineated descriptions and drawings of the "inscapes" of things.

While the "inscape" of a thing is its exterior manifestation of its interior being-energy, the images of things in the consciousness as "inscapes" suggest that though they are richly multiple and varied, they are not randomly organized. To Hopkins it seemed that things and their images are scaled in patterns in an order of correspondence. Hopkins constantly noted in words and sketches inhis *Journals* the paralleled patterns of everything. Thus the principle of parallelism is a key factor in the making of meaning.

Ricoeur makes a similar hermeneutic declaration about the nature of discourse as constituting a subject-object relational referentiality answering to the structure of the selving "I," out of which parallel arises a dialectic between event and meaning as well as between sense and reference (Klemm 76-77).

What orgainizes the energy of "inscape"? The energy which creatively organizes the structure of a thing ("inscape") must be the same energy moving throughout the entire universe. The force of energy which expresses itself as 'inscape" in every thing and which arranges the ebb and flow of all things in the universe, Hopkins called, "instress." He made quite clear in his writings that these two terms are hermeneutically and ontologically co-functional: "But indeed I have often felt when I have been in this mood and felt the depth of an instress or how fast the inscape holds a thing . . . " (*Journals* 127). These terms may be taken as the verbal equivalents of the dual "selving" energies of the utterer and language: "inscape is structured "instress"; "instress" is as well the "selving" energy of the receptive consciousness which connects (makes meaning of) self and the world of things. Such is the nature of "selving" discourse.

Thus in identifying these energy fields of being in his Parmenides essay, that is, "all things are upheld by instress and are meaningless without it," Hopkins pointed to the hermeneutic factors involved in scapes and stress. He also noted that the entire interpretive process runs through a canon of "selving" structural problematics. Meaning to any degree of fullness happens irregularly, which is to say that the "instress of inscapes" cannot easily be "seen." In his experience, "inscapes" often seemed to be a question of "catching" them (*Journals* 231); and he judged that most people never do (*Journals* 221). For him "instress of inscapes" happened only when he was alone (*Journals* 182, 228). He felt that the mind had to be especially fresh and clear to take in, "instress inscapes," and even so, the season of the year alters opportunity (*Journals* 205).

The ideal inner state for effectively taking in the "instress of inscapes" into the consciousness he called "a canon feeling" (*Journals* 135-136), by which he meant the "instress" of the consciousness mediates the "instress" of the incoming "inscape" in a pattern of meaningfulness which realizes a true correspondence between the feelings of the perceiver and the "instress of the inscape" of the perceived. Both retain their distinctiveness while corresponding to the selfness of each other. Hopkins' "canon of feeling" has a counterpart in Ricoeur's understanding of the affectivity of language. Parallel to Hopkins, feeling for Ricoeur is an important part of the subjective intentionality of knowing through which rapport is developed between things and persons. Along with this connectiveness, there is engendered on the part of the self an affective interior response to forge a bond so that the experience "touches" the self deeply. About such openness to Being, Ricoeur wrote that feeling "is the manifestation of a relation to the world which constantly restores our complicity with it, our inherence and belonging in it, something more profound than all polarity or duality" (*Fallible Man* 129). Additionally, like Hopkins' momentary sense of the "canon of feeling" that is open to a fully realized "instress of an inscape" of a thing, so Ricoeur emphasizes the fragility of feeling because affectivity is the mediator (courage) between the finite feelings of natural life and desires of a longing spiritual aspiration for some kind of cosmic bonding—perhaps the most fragile condition in the subjectivity of the conflicted self (Klemm 56-59). The problematic conditions of "instressing" that Hopkins noted are at the very heart of the "selving" conflict of human feeling in the fallible self.

Because these moments of meaningful self-integration are rare and transitory human experiences, texting them is important; otherwise, the self would never fully encounter the "inscapes" of the world. This is what Hopkins meant by the powerful acknowledgment of a "pregnant and straightforward . . . simple yes and is. . . There would be no bridge, stem of stress between us and things to bear out and carry the mind over: without stress we might not and could not say . . ." (*Journals* 127). The centrality of meaningful, "selving" referential utterance is powerfully emphasized in Hopkins' understanding of the "selving" hermeneutic process as a "saying" wordedness that is the essence of the event of language becoming meaning. Utterance for Hopkins is at the heart of all "selving"; moreover, utterance encompasses all forms of language modes. Thus his attitude is fully compatible with that of Ricoeur who holds that oral discourse is transformed in its hermeneutic elements when spoken discourse becomes written. Ricoeur asserts that writing is a fuller manifestation of living speech, a view that is answerable with the Hopkinsian notion of the "inscaping" word that fully "instresses" the self who in turn utters ("stresses") the "inscape" of the "selving" experience. For both Hopkins and Ricoeur, "texting" experience with the intentionality of expressing a perspectived disclosure is the positing of the distinctness of the "I" of the self, an act that constitutues a reflective reworking of the powers of the consciousness of the self.

The hermeneutic implications of "instress and inscape" are complex. They are verbal signs for the ways the images of things become clarified as meaning in the reflective consciousness; to this end, "selving" sensibilities / word correspondences are sorted out in the intersubjective dynamism of the self. "Instressing" is, as well, a paralleling process in the consciousness wherein correspondences between the shapes of things ("inscaped instress") and the self are translated ("instressed") into some form ("inscape") of utterance. There are three dimensions of instress in selving utterance. They are the subjective component, the "prepossession of feeling," which is a creative expressive power, an ideational component (abstractive definition), and actual utterance, vocal or textualized.

Hopkins understood the energy he called "instress" as taking two patterns. One he dubbed "transitional," when "one thought or sensation follows another, which is to reason," and the other pattern he named "contemplation" in which the consciousness dwells deeply on one "instressed " scape. While both are active energies in "instressing any inscape" in the consciousness, contemplative energy (*Journals* 125-126) is significantly increased in the "selving" stress of the arts both as to creativity and response. This latter mind energy is an abiding kind of mental energy by which the consciousness dwells upon the internal words that the transitional mind energies produce in its apprehensions of the outside world. Such an interior ruminating energy is especially "exacted," as Hopkins put it, in experienceing literary art, the visual arts, and music. Contemplative energies bring us to a more penetrating realization of the diversity of apprehended things, what Hopkins called, the "instresses of inscapes," so that we become more aware of the character of the fusion of their deversified parts into unified whole entities. Hopkins described this state as one "in which the mind is absorbed (as far as that may be), taken up by, dwells upon, enjoys a single thought." Hopkins here suggested the role of symbolization in the consciousness, a special transmutation of the the appropriating reflective process by which the consciousness comes to a clarifying grasp of the density of a perception, the complexity of the "selving" response, all expressively mediated through the cynosure of a unfying, imaginative ikon. Here lies the power of the arts and religion, for both depend upon contemplative mind energies to activate their special expressive, symbolic powers.

Central to the basic "instressing" energy in the self is the processing of the parallelism in the world order of things. Parallelism involves the consciousness in the hermeneutics of diversifying and unifying. The deeper the expressive form of utterance, that is, the greater degree to which the diverse paralleled components are organized, the more expressive the form both as to the "inscapes instressed" and to the "selving-stress" uttering these "inscapes." The parallelism principle is especailly applicable to works of art: "The further . . . the organization is carried out, the deeper the form penetrates, the prepossession flushes the matter, the more effort will be required in apprehension, the more power of comparision, the more capacity for receiving that synthesis of (either

successive or spatially distinct) impressions which gives us the unity
with the propossession conveyed by it" (*Journals* 126). Here Hopkins
defines the function of parallelism as a key hermeneutic activity of
"instress and inscape" in its richest applications.

Metaphoric language is implicit in Hopkins' linguistic hermeneutics.
Poetic consciousness is Hopkins and Ricoeur's most important
hermeneutic connection. Key to the figural notion of poetic consciousness
is the duality of language. Ricoeur's hermeneutic is directed towards
analysing the image / figure / symbol / text component in language as an
insight to the operations of the "selving" intentionality. To him the
reconstruction of human meaning is essentially the appropriation of
metaphorical language as "selving," interpretive utterance. The same
apparoach is true for Hopkins. For him, language, while bearing
grammatical, historical, and logical associations, conveys at its most
radical expressive level the authentic "I" in the self: " For the word is the
expression, *uttering* of the idea in the mind. That idea itself has two
terms, the image (of sight or sound or *scapes* of the other senses [italics
his]). which is in fact physical and a refined energy accenting the nerves,
a word to oneself, an incholate word, and secondly a conception"
(*Journals* 125). From the perspective of the uttering self, "Being and
thought are one" in the hermeneutics of the "selving" ("instressing
inscapes"). Ricoeur emphasized that positing the self is a poetic act.

Again it must be emphasized that Hopkins' perspectives of
hermeneutics arise from his epistemological notion of parallelism in
things and thoughts. In his assertion in his Parmenides essay that "Being
and thought are one," we must concentrate, from a hermeneutical point
of view, on the rest of his declaration: "and each word is one way of
acknowledging Being and each sentence by its copula is (or its equivalent)
the utterance and assertion of it" (*Journals* 129). The hermeneutic
question immediately arises: Given Hopkins' view that all things exist
as a manifold variety of individuals, how is it that the self "instresses"
reality as a diversity and words utter a unity in this variety? Hopkins'
answer was, as we have noted, that unity (words, utterance) comes about
through the "selving" energies of the "I's" appropriated parallelisms—
"instressing inscapes" to the level of a unifying worded self-scaping
utterance.

Parallelism is, then, the central hermeneutic medium of "instressing
an inscape" of anything, the process whereby the being-energy of the
consciousness interacts with the being-energy of things in the deciphering
of their existentially parallel, manifesting shapes. Moreover, the

sensibility that produces an image / idea of a thing perceived also produces a parallel feeling in the affective subjective consciousness; both are paralleled in the "coinciding-point" of the defining word. Hermeneutics for Hopkins is a processing by the self of existential parallels. The term names the self's capacities to "grasp" the distinct parts of beings holistically, that is, to appropriate the diversity of every thing as sensation, image, "prepossession of feeling [affectivity]," and idea, each and all reconfigured as an internal word. Out of such complex paralleling of the apprehensive / reflective powers of the consciousness arises its linguistic powers to reexpress the bridge, "stem of stress," between the mind and being.

What we see, then, in Hopkins' two short notes on Parmenides and language, is a working out of the hermeneutic consciousness similar to Ricoeur's account. Linguistic hermeneutics for both is a "selving" reflective mode in and through which perceptual images become meanings / words to find meaningful interrelationships at an univocal level, (notional framework), at a figural level by which words become symbols (mythic frameword), and by interlocutor words expressing a plurivocal meaningfulness (secondary metaphoric meanings). Moreover, we also see the ontological principles on which Hopkins thought the hermeneutic consciousness operates. The cosmos is an ontic order of difference and similarity (scaled "pitches of inscapes"); the "selving" consciousness "knows" ("instresses") the cosmos as being answering being ("prepossession," concept, and contemplation); and words (the hermeneutical principle of "instressing") are the communication network between being and all being, the bridge "between us and things," immediate and horizonal, universal reality.

The hermeneutical consciousness is complex, for the mind, in encountering the transphysical horizons of things, must keep making whole-part comparisons to work out the unity of the whole. This contemplative state, in affirming this particular being, also asserts being at a global horizon of consciousness, and in so doing names multileveled correspondences in the consciousness, subjective and objective, as the hermeneutic foundation of "instressing" things—images, "pre-possessions," concepts, and words. We will come back to the figurative stress element in this hermeneutic experience in discussing what Ricoeur calls "limit" experiences in Hopkins' uses of metaphoric language.

This brings us again to elaborate further on Hopkins' notion of "instress" as a "selving" mind energy correspondent to the being-energy residing in all being. Basically, "instress" is the unique empowering energy for the making of human meaning in and through our reflective consciousness. Moreover, "instress" as an unfying energy in the "selving" consciousness is the essence of what Hopkins called contemplation. Contemplation, we remember (*Journals* 125-126), is an abiding kind of mind energy which is a reflective force in the consciousness for dwelling upon the internal words that the "instresses of inscapes" of things produce. Such an interior dwelling energy is especially "exacted" in experiencing literary art, visual arts, musical art. Contemplation brings us to a more penetrating realization of the imaginatively reexpressed "instress of inscapes," a dwelling on their paralleled formal unity, so that their diversified parts become clarified into a synthesized unity as a whole being wholly expressed.

In achieving this contemplative sense of artistic unity within diversified experience, the consciousness mediates the constituent elements of the paralleled parts / wholeness of the experience redescribed (in visual art, for example, the parallels between a picture's esthetic expressive forms and its counterpart to real entities); moreover, this contemplative energy also mediates the paralleled parts / wholeness of our subjective "instressing / inscaping" creative consciousness, whose intentionality is to grasp esthetic experience in self- "inscaping" words. In managing this dual complex of reflective unified-diversity, we engage our affective consciousness, which, we remember, Hopkins called our "prepossession," the creative "enthusiasm" produced in the subjective complex of the worded experience. This is the poetic energy in us which "has the power of suggesting or producing" (*Journals* 125), that is, empowers us to reexpress, as our own "instressing" self-scape, the "instress of the inscapes" we have taken in (objective intentionality) as well as our "selving" relationship to such experienced objects (subjective intentionality). The direction of these insights is to assert the possibility of a hermeneutic composite or unity of opposing verbal polarities in the utterances of positing the self. The contemplative energy of the consciousness penetrates this deep symbolic form (images and words) of artistic creation.

Hopkins worked out, in his short essay on language, the dynamics of these two mind energies as the word-play discourse between and within direct apprehensions of things, and their interactions in the reexpressed productions of the creative arts. Again, the drive in the force of these energies is towards grasping the unifying framework of their expressive structures. Both the intellectual and the artistic expressive forms demand contemplative mind energies, but it is the work of art that forces the consciousness to range more widely in that art forms add, more fully, the subjective pole of hermeneutic intention: "Works of art of course like words utter the idea and in representing real things convey the prepossession [the affectivity of the subjective self] with more or less success." In applying his notion of contemplative mind energy to his own medium, Hopkins is saying that the contemplative energy is the hermeneutic foundation of the poetic word as the "inscaped, inscaping" word: "The further anything, as a work of art, the organization is carried out, the deeper the form penetrates . . . the more effort will be required in apprehension . . . the more capacity for receiving that synthesis of . . . impressions which gives us the unity with the prepossession conveyed by it" (*Journals* 126).

The diverse particularity of "inscape," the "passion" of the subjective word "intressing" the world and the self, the paralleling expressive form of art as unifying image / word, as an uttered synthesis, can be penetrated by the dwelling-on energy of the contemplative consciousness. Hopkins' priortizing of the poetic expressive energy in the self as an unique "selving" expressivity is an account of the hermeneutic process which finds a counterpart in Ricoeur's hermeneutic notion of the positing of the self, especially in its focus on the drama of poetic parallels working throughout the reflective consciousness. This drama Ricoeur called "tension," the heart of human linguisticality, that is central to the figurating language which posits the self.

For Hopkins, as for Ricoeur, the highest hermeneutical levels of the consciousness are poetic. Hopkins' notions of poetry and poetic language as "selving" suggest connections with Ricoeur's notions of the metaphoric process of the human making of the "I am" of the self.

We have seen that being for Hopkins meant the utterance of individuating difference—all things speak themselves. What this notion emphasizes is that, in the most general sense, all being is a form of language. Hopkins forced this point very heavily. As we know, he even coined a term to denote when a thing authentically utters itself. He called it "pitch," by which he meant the direct expressivity of the individualing "I," "being more high pitched, selved, and distinctive than anything in the world" (*Sermons* 122). About "pitch" as expressivity, Hopkins wrote, *"pitch* is ultimatelysimple positiveness, that by which being differs from and is more than nothing and not-being, and it is with precision expressed by the English *do* (the simple auxiliary), which when we employ or emphasize, as 'he said it, he did say it', we do not mean that the fact is more a fact but we the more state it. . . . So that this pitch might be expressed, if it were good English, the *doing* be, the *doing* choose, the *doing* so-and-so in that sense [italics his]. Where there is no question of will it would become mere fact; where there is will it is free action, moral action. And such 'doing-be', and the thread or chain of such pitches or 'doing-be's, prior to nature's being overlaid is self, the person, [which] comes into being with the accession of nature" (*Sermons* 151). We see coming together here three central notions that form the basis of Hopkins' hermeneutic self. The first is "pitch" as distinctive individuality; the second, "pitch" as the perspective utterance of the unique self; and third, "pitch" as the verbalizing of the imagining self, that is, the understanding of "pitch" under the register of language as a form of choosing, saying, doing—the active verb as self-actualization, the volitional word of personality, the uttering "selving" word.

We remember also that Hopkins thought of words as correlates to things, that the business of words is to "instress the inscapes" of things (objective intentionality) and inevitably as "selving" expression, words "inscape" the expressor (subjective intentionality). This intimate participation ("instressing") of language in being, "selving," and wording, we also remember, is a reflective echoing of the patterns of diversity in real existence. Thus we have seen that the principle of parallelism is a dynamic of "selving," knowing, and expressing. We also must remember that for Hopkins such meanings, while comparative, are nonetheless true understandings of real existence. For language itself is a part of Nature, part of the "works" of God, and hence has its own reality-laws, patterns, "inscapes." Hopkins collected words in his diaries like butterflies (Milroy 52-53).

Hopkins' famous terms, "instressing inscapes" are, then, hermeneutically speaking, a figure-making process by which we take the world into the intersubjectivity of the consciousness and utter meanings as our own self-uttering meaning of the everything not us, what Ricoeur calls the "world of the word" that is essential to the "selving" reflections in the positing of the "I am" of the self.

Hopkins' "Selving" Poetics

Few poets have had Hopkins' knowledge of the linguistic base of poetry. This is most powerfully seen, of course, in the vital varieties of his use of language in his poetry. But the depth of his understanding can also be discerned in his definitions of poetry wherein he brings together the linguistic, hermeneutic, and ontic strands of expressivity. All his definitions are rooted in the hermeneutic process of utterance: "Poetry is speech." Living speech, emphatically. Not poetic diction, not the language of prose which generally possesses an objective intentionality of logicality, but the language, he insisted, that was the speech of active consciousness uttering its living self (Milroy 100).

While language takes many forms, it must be emphasized that for Hopkins all language is to some degree poetic, that is, all language works through some comparative figuration in representing real things. Moreover, language, we have seen, works at many levels in echoing the similarities patterning the specific differences of things. Poetic language organizes itself in the broadest and deepest expressions of the range of being. The "instressing" of poetic language can capture the pattern of "inscaped" particulars of the world and elevate them towards the horizon of a cosmic order of being. It is language in poetic forms that possesses the fullest powers of creative expressivity. Only poetic language can reach the level of full human expressivity because the language of poetry possesses a "selving" richness to utter the complex of the reflective consciousness uttering itself in wording real things. Poetry is the exquisite speech making power in the consciousness which, we remember from Hopkins' essay on words, expresses the subjective state of the expresser, has its own"inscape," yet names real things in world. The self and the world of being are unified in the multifoliate poetic word.

Let us look at the specific linguistic / hermeneutic aspects of Hopkins' definition of poetic utterance: "Poetry is in fact speech only employed to carry the inscape of speech for inscape's sake—and therefore the inscape must be dwelt upon" (*Journals* 289). First, Hopkins noted that poetic words in general have their own special linguistic-hermeneutical functionality; poetic speech, as an "inscaping" utterance of language, has unique verbalizing energies ("instress") which forge unique structural manifestations such as audiality (phonology), word order (grammar), and sensibility (the affective subjectivity). A second linguistic aspect is what Hopkins called "heightening": "the poetic language of an age should be current language heightened " (*Letters to Bridges* 89). By "heightening" he meant employing language devices such as rhymes, syntax, and speech vocabulary which build poetics upon ordinary speech formations. There are also special hermeneutic implications. The dwelling powers of contemplation must be employed to reach an imaginative appropriation ("instress") which inwardly shapes the expressive form (unity) of a poem as the poet's "selving" utterance: "selves—goes its self; *myself* it speaks and spells."

But these normal poetic language facilitations are not enough. In order to express the "inscape" of the poetic word for its own sake, often the poet must repeat the "inscaping scape" of poetic speech, "repetition, *oftening, over-and-overing, aftering* [his italics] of the inscape must take place in order to detach it to the mind and in this light poetry is speech what afters and oftens its inscape, speech couched in a repeating figure" (*Journals* 289). To accomplish this echoing of the "inscape," a second level of linguistic tools must be used such as alliteration, compounding, word-blending, and various other syntactic changes. These "heightening" aspects are formally analysed by Milroy and Plotkin (114-229; 71-145). Hopkins himself prepared some lecture notes on creating "heightening" devices which have never been adequately studied as yet, perhaps, because these exhibit an imposing grasp of the expressive potentials of language reaching into the technical capacities of specialist language theorists and certainly beyond the expertiz of many practicing poets during and since his time. See *Journals* 267-288.

The ontic aspects of language according to Hopkins we have already reviewed. but we should keep them in mind in discussing Hopkins' notion of poetic speech. Let me briefly reiterate his general ideas. Words and Nature are interfused, thus words are a way of taking in the things of the world. Indeed wording is the way we are able to grasp the "stem" of reality, that is, seize an understanding of particular things in some frame of expressed meaningful relationships. And while all words are in some way figurative in their ontic-semantic relations (the parallelism principle), only poetic words catch ("instress") the full flush of the expresser expressing—sounding— the very patterned "noises" of beings themselves ("inscapes").

There is one other aspect of Hopkins' poetical hermeneutic approach to "selving" through language which again must be emphasized. This is the character of the thetic "I." Like Ricoeur, Hopkins held that the selving "I" is a going, doing, but especially, a speaking "I"; positing the self is the "pitch" of the "I" uttering, declaring the distinctiveness of the self. Active "selving" is active "verbing" from a linguistic perspective. Words utter the "I" generally, but only poetic words capture the fullness of the "I's" expressive, subjective intentionality. Thus it is through poetic language we attempt to achieve an original view of ourselves in our experiencing of the world. Both Hopkins and Ricoeur agree in this understanding of the hermeneutics of the self as do they agree that accomplishing this kind of meaning is a kind of moral action by which the "I" self changes its self-understanding. Both agree that, linguistically as well as psycho-linguistically, the bridging "selving" mode is the result of the metaphorical function of language. Metaphor opens up the self to a new consciousness of possibility of "selving" reality through which interpretations we can choose to be in the world at a different consciousness horizon of living relationships. Metaphoric language opens up the "I" to a way of being so that it can choose to reconstruct a new self meaning in its "selving."

The notions of hermeneutic parallelism, the achieving of the "pitch" of the "I,' the role of "heightening" in uttering the "inscape"of self and things, and the volitional nature of the revealing poetic word in Hopkins are clearly echoed in Ricoeur. We can see such echoes in the following much abbreviated account of a commentator's exposition of Ricoeur's theory of the hermeneutics of poetic language:

> Ricoeur claims that the metaphor exposes the very heart of linguistic process. For Ricoeur, metaphor is a matter of semantic innovation by which new information about reality is discovered as newly created linguistic disclosures. The term *metaphoric process* names the activity occurring within historical language by which the concepts and insights that illuminate and evoke concrete experience are brought into light. In the process of writing as a mode of understanding, metaphor functions as a key for Ricoeur's overall philosophical intention, which is to sustain the query: "What does it mean to be human?" Humankind are word creatures. According to Ricoeur, metaphor is a verbalizing phenomenon of disclosive semantic innovation. Metaphor teases the mind into thinking something new by virtue of seeing a resemblance previously unnoticed and unthought: "What is at stake in a metaphorical statement is making a "kinship appear where ordinary vision perceives no mutual appropriatness at all" (Klemm 96).

When the poet says that "Nature is a temple where living columns . . . . , " a tension is set up between two interpretations: one is a literal interpretation "whose sense emerges through nonsense . . ." and the other, an imaginative interpretation where "nonsense" envisions new meaning. The new meaning that emerges through this tension is sensed as peculiar because it catches an aspect of reality not brought to light in ordinary use of language. There is the realization that in metaphor language has organized reality in a different way; metaphor has "made manifest a way of being of things which is brought to language thanks to semantic innovaton." More precisely, in metaphorical language, the literal level of meaning abolishes itself in a self-destruction and because of this self-destruction of sense, the literal reference founders, metaphorical meaning emerges with an interpretive "twist" on the literal meaning.

The metaphorical "twist" extends the meaning so as to make sense out of nonsense. One technique for producing the "twist" by which figurative meaning emerges is the poetic technique of tying literal sense to the sound of words in the context of rhythmic cadences, resemblance and opposition between syllables or words, and metric equivalence. New relations of meaning can then "be introduced by the recurrence of phonic form. This proceeds through an interplay . . . that seems to possess an "iconic solidity." The further step is that sense-sound relation can include relations to other sensorial dimensions of meaning through synaesthetics (Klemm 96-98).

In this short commentary on Ricoeur's discourse on the metaphoric hermeneutics of the "world of the text," I submit, there are apparent multiple echoes to Hopkins' notions of the character of poetic utterance as well as a hermeneutic analysis of what he called the poetic energy of positing the "I" consciousness through the figurative word. In the poetics of both men, the hermeneutic dynamic of parallelism, working through the metaphoric process, is a text "heightening" element. Literal meaning is set against figurative meaning producing the "twist" of metaphrical parallelism out of which emerges the heightened meaning of new "selving" insight. Parallelsim for Hopkins is the character of the ontic scale of being; Ricoeur emphasizes the linguistics of parallelism as a semantic innovation. For both the parallelism of being and language are the sources of the poetics of the metaphorical world—the wording poetic imagination.

"Instress and inscape" have another Ricoeurrian hermeneutic aspect, that of the "limit experience." We recall that Ricoeur meant by this phrase that kind of metaphoric statement which so qualifies the heuristic figure redescribing the experiential world, that there enters into the metaphoric reflection an extreme point of transfigurative meaning carrying over to multiple horizons of possible meanings. This is what religious language is all about according to Ricoeur.

We see the same hermeneutic "reach" in Hopkins' notion of the contemplative mind energy which, when successively employed, draws the consciousness towards awarenesses of the possible ultimate unities of the "inscapes" of universal being imaginatively correspondent to the heightened unity of "inscaped" language of the poetic form. In both Hopkins and Ricoeur's hermeneutic, there is what might be called a cosmic disclosure available through the reflections of the poetic consciousness, and for both, such disclosures are linked with feelings of assent, what Ricoeur called "total commitment" and Hopkins called the "passion of prepossession." Indeed, it is not too much to say that "instress and inscape" in Hopkins are equivalent to "symbol making" and "self reconfiguration" in Ricoeur as "contemplation" and a "canon of feeling" are equivalents to Ricoeur's "event of appropriation," which, we remember, is that stage in which the reader catches himself reflected in the language figures of the text so that he affirms his own authentic being in and through the world of the text. These parallel hermeneutic principles are "selving" dynamics through which the self is revealed as being part of and thus having a destiny in a unified cosmic order.

Finally, both Ricoeur and Hopkins affirmed the possibilities of "seeing" the self relocated through the imagination in new realities in existence, and in this poetic vision the possibility to reconfigure self-meaning so as to be opened to the world at a different level of lived consciousness. The text-world of Christianity offers, both writers affirm, the richest sacral field for encountering the transforming figurative word which produces "Faith," the "passion for the possible." For Hopkins, it must be remembered, the "Book of Nature" is also a key part of this Christed text-world wherein to read transfiguring word-scapes. Nature's Book for Hopkins is more than the literal "texts" of Nature; Nature's texts are sacral "wordings" of Creation, the "words" of God uttering his divinity. Hopkins called Creation God's "news."

In general, then, poetic assertion is "selving," a hermeneutical process in the consciousness through which self-utterance is made. The utterance may be the word as a clarifying of conception (including its extensions to "concrete things coming under it," called objective knowledge, or utterance as image, "(of sight or sound scapes of the other senses)," but essentially a fusion of affective awareness as an expressive form of the self, "a word to oneself, an inchoate word." This subjective knowledge utterance is as much an acknowledgement of universal being as is its objective concept term counterpart. As has been noted, subjective intentionality employs a different consciousness energy from that of the transition energy of the objective intentionality, the energy of contemplation. This energy affectively fixates the consciousness on the parallelisms of worded images of sensation and thought in a kind of "trance" which affords a new horizon of global understanding.

Turning to the operations of Hopkins' own hermeneutic consciousness, his actualized poetic powers, we find an astonishing instance of textual "selving" through his use of metaphorical language, so central to Ricoeur's hermeneutic philosophy.

The problematic condition of matching the exterior "inscapes" of experience with interior "self-scapes" puts heavy emphasis on figurative language. Different mind energies, as Hopkins noted, are at work to come to different reflective insights. It is clear in Hopkins' remarks scattered throughout his writings, whatever the complexity of the relations of language and consciousness, that he held constantly to the principle he stated in his Parmenides essay: "To be and to know or Being and thought are the same. The truth in thought is Being, stress, and each word is one way of acknowledging Being and each sentence by its copula is (or its equivalent) the utterance and assertion of it" (*Sermons* 129). But to acknowledge being fully, language must go beyond a basic threshold to an upper level of expression, from concept to figure and symbol. In any case, truth (subjective or objective thought) is reality worded and asserted in its existential mode. In delineating the dual levels of language, Hopkins, like Ricoeur, kept clear the distinction between scientific and poetic language.

The key rhetorical principle in Hopkins' notion of poetic language lies in a statement he made in his short essay on "Poetry and Verse: " . . . poetry is speech which afters and oftens its inscape, speech couched in a repeating figure . . . poetry is . . . speech wholly or partially repeating some kind of figure which is over and above meaning, at least grammatical, historical, and logical meaning" (*Sermons* 289). In these remarks Hopkins declared what Ricoeur affirms, in his hermeneutic approach to language, that language is two-staged, that the second stage (figurative) generates meaning beyond the concrete mode of reality, that is, meaning at an upper horizon of being, at what Ricoeur called the metaphoric stage. At this heightened poetic level of language there emerges in the consciousness the canon of religious language.

Hopkins used figural language with amazing frequency and expressiveness. Few extant writers have exhibited such a constant flow of metaphors in all kinds of writing. This penchant for figuration came not only from stylistic purposes, a freshening of diction, but also, perhaps primarily, from Hopkins' interest in achieving a higher match between his "instressed" sense experiences and their reexpressions in words. Such wording consciousness has "the power of suggesting or producing" what Hopkins called an expressive form analogous to the soul, that is, poetic words "inscape" the self. As a poet he sought to use such words which uttered himself ever so exactly while uttering fully other beings.

Moreover, since his understanding of universal being as an order of patterns of contrasting similarities, deep perception involved seeing, afresh and aboriginally, hidden juxtapositions, revealing similarities, dramatic contrasts, at a totalized consciousness horizon of being. This is the verbalizing hermeneutic action of figuration which can make the transfer to the higher level of contemplative consciousness, and in so doing, can capture what Hopkins called the "prepossessive passion" and "enthusiasm" of wording being. This understanding of poetic consciousness is an accurate correlate to what Ricoeur meant by the "symbol-making consciousness."

As terms of creativity, "instressing inscapes" means to use the figurative language of poetry to selve the "I am" of the self. Hopkins filled his writings with an incredible number of "selving" metaphors, that is, "instressing inscapes" of language "inscaping" his unique sensibility. Any cursory look through his journals, for example, will reveal literally hundreds of metaphorical figures (for example, "Eyelids like leaves, petals, caps, tufted hats, handkerchiefs, sleeves, gloves" *Journals* 72), some merely named in what seems to have the possibility of an infinite series, some worded fully in dense detail, a veritable flood of figurative language. At work here is poetic reflective consciousness seeking through metaphor to come again and again to fresh nuances of reality, hidden beauties of the cosmos allied to the prepossessions of the expressing self. What emerges in such wordings of "selving" reflections is a kind of figurative paralleling at many psycholinguistic levels within the wording consciousness, a hermeneutic process effecting a correspondence that takes on a kind of echo and response, a rhyming sounding together captured in the "inscaping" of configuring language. This is what Hopkins meant by saying that poetry repeats its figures, "oftening, over-and overing, aftering"; the "inscaping" of the uttering sounding of poetic language itself answers to the "steming" parallels between beings and the expressive, poetic consciousness.

Ricoeur expresses awe at such rich expressive powers of such poeticizing: "What would the stirring spectacle of this perceived world, the matrix of our existence, be if the artist did not convey to us the joy of it . . . . By preserving color, sound, and the flavor of the word, the artist, without willing it explicitly, revives the most primitive truth of the world of our life which the scientist shrouds. By creating figures and myths, the artist interprets the world. . . . *Poetry is a criticism of life*" (*History and Truth* 174).

Finally, Hopkins' general approach to language is in accord with the development of modern linguistics. James Milroy has detailed Hopkins' expertize in the subject, noting that his knowledge of language was surprisingly up-to-do-date and forward-looking for his time. Specifically, Hopkins' grasp of the figurative nature of words is evident in his work as a philologist. Milroy underscored Hopkins' basic understanding of words in the linguistic assumptions underlying his work on etymology: "first, that series of words that are related in meaning can be shown to be derived from a limited set of monosyllabic roots; second, that the meanings of words within these series are associated in a broadly metaphorical way always going back to a root with a physical or 'sensible' meaning, no matter how abstract some of the derivative senses may be; third, that there is a connection between sound and sense, so that 'onomatopoetic' or 'echoic' theories about word-origins are found illuminating" (Milroy 53). The Ricoeurrian factor in Hopkins' view of polysemous language lies most heavily, of course, in his emphasis upon the notion that linguistic transactions generally, semantic change especially, hermeneutic transformations particularly, occur by way of the figurative engendering of meanings. Metaphor is the very "selfhood" of words.

Hopkins' Incarnational Consciousness

Another crossover between Hopkins and Ricoeur is their notion of the time-frame of consciousness. For Ricoeur, the human consciousness temporalizes its reflective acts as narrative: "The world unfolded by every narrative work is always temporal" (*Time and Narrative* I, 3). And, as we have seen, Hopkins considered the energies of consciousness as in a time-frame:"A word then has three terms belonging to it, or moments" (*Journals* 125), and his notion of "transition" words and "contemplation" words involve time patterns. Implicit in the making and the experiencing of narrative is a created redescription of the human actions (motivations), which is to say that the poetics of narrative moves towards ethics. Human meaning is shown to be bound up in what we do, and what we do, we do in time.

There are then two time-frames, "natural time," which we know as history, and "poetic time," which we know as fictional time. For both Ricoeur, the philosopher, and Hopkins, the poet, they are deeply interrelated as modes of narrative discourse. Both would subscribe to

Aristotle's analysis of the matter in his *Poetics*: "The distinction between history and poetry . . . consists really in this, that the one describes the thing that has been, and the other a kind of thing that might be. Hence poetry is something more philosophic and of graver import than history, since its statements are of the nature rather of universals, whereas those of history are singulars" (*Works* I, 7). Narrative (plot-making) is really making (poetics) human meaning of historical experience.

Hopkins construed the concept of time into more levels than history and narrative, though his delineatons fit bascially into the two frames of natural time and human time. Hopkins, in fact, postulated four versions of the narratives of time: Creation, Incarnation, whose time frame is universal (eternal, angelic, and natural time), cosmic history, and Pentecostal or Christed time. The core source matters of these time notions is, of course, Christian Scripture and theology, but Hopkins worked out his own narrative versions which became the subtextual time-frames and themes of his religious poetry. Again the principle of parallelism applies. The historical dimensions of time (past, present, future), he asserted, have working within them " a positive pitch and direction," that is, God's Creational plan passes through ordinary time whose plot is the incorporation of the universe into the Mystical Body of Christ (*Sermons* 196, 306).

Hopkins elaborated his story of Creation in a supernatural Trinitarian time frame (*Sermons* 108-115, Chapter Eight). God began making the universe in what he called the "internal and intrinsic procession of the Trinity." In his narrative, Hopkins, probably taking some cues from spiritual mentors commenting on the *Spiritual Exercises of St. Ignatius*, pictured the story of Creation as a kind of time-ordering of intentionality in the mind of God. At the heart of God's plan for Creation was His intention to express Himself in Creation as "Son." Assuming an ordered sequence of actions following God's first intention, Christ was present in the first instant of Creation time, called angelic time, a kind of instant of duration coterminous with the whole time-frame of natural time, or instants of duration coterminous to a single instant of natural time. The narrative of the Incarnation, for Hopkins, began as a progression out of Trinitarian time to angelic time. He supposed that Christ descended into this first outer ring of time, angelic time, which presupposed that the Incarnation was prior to the creation of the angels, a notion he likely took from another of his religious mentors, Duns Scotus. But Christ's presence as the chief and highest angel was unknown to the host of angels, and when he was discovered, the result was rejection out of envy, leading to the revolt of Lucifer and his troops, their fall, and their enmity to all that is good—the Fall from the Garden, the "in the beginning" of the human narrative in historical time.

The next, the middle episode of the narrative is, of course, the entrance of Christ into human time as Jesus, again hidden, and rebelled against—the story of Jesus' birth, public life, the Passion story, his Resurrection and Ascension. And finally, Hopkins' culminating version of the Incarnation story is the descent of the Holy Spirit, the beginning of the sacramental time of Pentecost. The story of the Incarnation, having been initiated in the beginning of the created world, having moved through the aeonian time zone into historical time, now lives on through the coming of the Holy Spirit in a kind of time paradox, its timeless presence in historical time that is sacramental time, Christ ever present in the "now" of the Holy Eucharist. Hopkins called his own narratizing of the Christian mythos as the story of Jesus,"The Great Sacrifice" (*Sermons* 107-115, Ch. Eight). Finally, it is significant that Hopkins opened his telling of the story of "The Great Sacrifice" in the language of figures: "Time has three dimensions and one positive pitch or direction. It is therefore not so much like a a river or any sea as like the Sea of Galilee, which has the Jordan running through it and giving a current to the whole"*(Sermons* 196).

We see here that Hopkins' approach to Christianity is the building of a narrative that becomes a "selving" Christed Event—a schemata of time and eternity, and in making that construction, opening up new reconfiguring insights for human "selving." Hopkins' retelling of the Christian story can be seen as an example of Ricoeur's hermeneutics of the religious imagination in action. What Hopkins did in his narrating the Creation story was to text the Christian mythos as his own "selving" narrative. Like Ricoeur, Hopkins deemed the life of Jesus as the paradigmatic story for all time, and like Ricoeur, he appropriated the Christ narrative, in its powerful figuration of sacrifice through love, as the most salient metaphor for "selving" the "passion for the possible" by finding a new way to-be-in-world.

Part of Hopkins' creative fire for writing redescriptions of Scripture in his spiritual writings and fusing them with the poetic heuristics of his own spiritual experience was fostered by his contemplating Ignatius' *Spiritual Exercises* throughout a lifetime. At the center of the Ignatian meditative process is the principle of narrative reflection.

What is unique about the Exercises is that they are not just an outlining sketch for the Bible stories. Rather the Exercises are a manual of directions for the exercitant to construct a highly personalized, transforming narrative encounter of the texts of Jesus' story in order to understand the character of his life and times, thereby appropriating Jesus' self-understanding to achieve a new knowledge of oneself. Ignatius presents imaginative ways for the exercitant to recreate Jesus' story as an interior realization of personal desires for a new possibility for his life in the world. This Ignatian narrative principle is elemental in all of Hopkins' spiritual writings, especially his religious poetry, in which he reexpresses the dramatic narratives of his "instressing the inscape" of the mystery of the Christ Event so deeply, that the self is startled into a new self-apprehension in relation to the "Great Sacrifice."

In order to see how Hopkins' religious imagination worked in reexpressing sacral texts as "selving" poetics, let us take a well known Hopkins sonnet, "God's Grandeur," and think of it as a miniature Christian religious narrative retold in three time zones, angelic, cosmic, and present reader's time. Moreover, let us sort out the poetic figures the poet used as symbolic touchstones of his integrated narrative depicting the Christian mysteries which he has redescribed in his building of his own poetic meditative narrative, in Hopkins' case, fashioned after the structure and the thematic design of the Ignatian *Exercises*.

The first line, "The world is charged with the grandeur of God," is a miniature telling of the story of Creation in one dramatic delcaration. The line affirms God, the Father, as Creator of the universe and the creation of the angelic and human time-worlds. The line corresponds to the opening text of *The Spiritual Exercises* which Ignatius called the "First Princple and Foundation" (12) that begins, "Man is created to praise."

The second line, "It will flame out like shining from shook foil," introduces in the antecedent of "it" the second Person of the Trinity. Christ, who, in Hopkins'commentary on the Ignatian theological narrative, is described as proceeding from the Father, first as the intrinsic processive manifestation of the Trinity in eternal time, and then he entered into angelic time, the first phase of the Incarnation, thereby revealing "that all creation from the first was in view of the Incarnation" (*Sermons* 111). Christ then become Jesus of Bethlehem in natural time producing his historical narrative, and now, in the duration of all time, remains the Christ of the Holy Eucharistic Spirit, the third personality of God, who "over the bent / World broods with warm breast and with ah! bright wings." "Flaming, "Shining," "shaking," and "brooding" are key narrative wordings of the archetypal figures in the sonnet elucidating the narrated meditative matters of Creation, the Incarnation, Christ, Lucifier, the Fall, Christ's Passion, Resurrection and Ascension, all disclosures of the Deity's hidden mysteries.

This sonnet can be read as a miniature of the crucial Christian narrative in the Old Testment and the New Testament. Further, these biblical poetic miniatures can be taken as Hopkins' imaginative redescriptions of his experiencing of the First Week of the *Exercises*, stressing (Hopkins would say "instressing") God as the Creator of the world, God Present in a our "selving" personalities, recollection of our human sins, and our realization of the responsibilities inplicit in God's gifts to us of our existence in a universe of being. These registers of natural and supernatural reality are the contemplative meditative centers of Ignatius' Contemplation he called "The Kingdom of Christ."

The next poetic line is a monumental narrative miniature: "It gathers to a greatness, like the ooze of oil / Crushed ." Again the "It," the flashing, shining, shaking Christ-grandeur, now in historical time, is poetically redescribed in all of the hidden powers of Jesus' Nativity, Public Life, Passion, and Crucifixion. In this one line, the Gospel tales about Jesus' times can be opened up in the present time of the redescribing meditator. All the spiritual paradoxes of Christology are unlocked in the words "greatness" and "Crushed." The Second Week of the *Exercises* is given over to contemplations of the life of Jesus, the focus being on what Ricoeur describes as redemptive reading, "refiguring the self" in Christ (*Time and Narrative* III 246). Ignatius' meditative devices he called "Composition of Place" and "The Application of Senses" are essentially imaginative ways to reconstruct the Jesus stories in an effort to make effective meditative acts. If such contemplations are spiritually productive, then the standard of Christ's lived spirituality becomes the basis of "electing" Christ in one's life, that is, transforming one's life to live according to Christ's principles of love. The line, "He gathers to a greatness like the ooze of oil / Crushed," might be read as stating the Christian norm of such an Ignatian "election, " imitating in one's life the Christ Spirit of the "Great Sacrifice," returning love through giving to others. In Ignatius' *Exercises*, the Second Week puts forth Christ as the principal standard and class level of making a new life. This is followed by The Third Week's contemplations on Christ's Passion, the Christed Event which is the ultimate model of achieving unconditional love in attempting to realize what Ricoeur calls the "passion for the possible."

The remainder of the octave, beginning, "Why do men then now not reck his rod" through the line, "Generations have trod," "all is seared."

"wears man's smudge," and "nor can foot feel," are the human tales in historical and personal existential time about the pervasive fallible misreadings or ignorance of the Gospel stories, a profound mystery about the human response to the gifting of the Christian faith. The passage is a marvelous instance of an Ignatian "composition of place" in the simple but effective imaging of historical time within the consciousness of eternity. The principal narrative focus is, of course, the Fall, with its consequent disorders in universal Nature and human nature, the "recking" mystery of human history and present time ("then now") with the most striking uses of sense language evocative of spoilage— "sear." "blear, "smear," "smudge," "man's smell," "bare," and wasted "feeling."

The narrative key to all of these figures is the diurnal dreary tales of human time as stories of repetitive human fallibility, "trodding" blindly everywhere, "trodding" on the central gift of Creation—the earth, other beings, one's own selfness; "trodding" on and on into the oblivion of Nature's ancient time cycle of change backgrounded contemporaneously by the Creator's own timeless creative intentions. Here the poet offers an instance of the complex state of contemplative Christed consciousness involving fusing, in the present tense of the self (kairos), a limit awareness of the Creator's intentionality (sacred time), all contextualized through the creative religious imagination, itself a "selving" discovery of the possibility of a transcendent hope for a human destiny beyond cosmic time. Such are the rich contemplative powers of the religious imagination poetically texting its spiritual reflections. In this rich contemplative complex, the poet has revealed to his readers how the narratives of the "selving" consciousness can find eternal signs in the flow of ordinary time.

The entire sestet of the sonnet is given over to the narrative of the Third Person of the Trinity, the Holy Spirit, whose story is that of a new manifestation of the Trinity into cosmic, hence historical and personal time. The central theme of the narrative is how the Jesus of time past is present as the perennial Christ of the Pentecost, the eternal now of the Christian kairos in the sacrament of Eucharistic love. Ignatius, in the Fourth Week of the *Exercises,* concentrated on asking the exercitant to focus on Christ's triumphs in his Resurrection and Ascension. This series of contemplations culminates in an ultimnate contemplation he called, "The Contemplation for Obtaining Love." Drawing from the progrssive contemplations of the previous Weeks, the intent of this last reflection is to energize the entire self to become a new self, a "selving" reconfiguration achieved by seizing the spiritually-graced possiblities for self-transformation through realizing the very coinherence of Christ in our very self-being. Ignatius, in this contemplation, stressed how God dwells in all Creation, especially in the human self, and in that indwelling "conserves" (*Exercises* 103) all existents as his Gifts. This indwelling force is the Holy Spirit bringing forth our Christed endowments.

For expressing this deific, ever loving goodness actively "seeping" everywhere, Ignatius used the figures of rays of light showering down over darkness and water constantly flowing into the parched earth. The traditional metaphor for the bringer of this perpetualizing renewal of love is the symbolic bird-spirit, the miraculous communicator of God to all that exists, expressing his omnipresence in the "selving" of everything In his Commenatary on Ignatius' meditative pattern for contemplatiing the presence of the Holy Spirit in time, Hopkins wrote, "God's power or Operation, which is attributed especailly to the Third Person, is put second, . . . because St. Ignatius is dwelling on the thought of communication, and the Holy Spirit is the communication of the communion of the Father and Son. It is by communication of this power that God operates the likeness of himself in things . . . ." Later in the same passage, he wrote, "it is the contemplation of the Holy Ghost sent to us through creatures. Observe then it is on love and the Holy Ghost is called Love . . . and the Holy Ghost as he is the bond and mutual love of the Father and Son, so of God and man; that the Holy ghost is uncreated Grace and the sharing by man of the divine nature and the bestowal of himself by God on man . . . . All things therefore are charged with love, are charged with God and if we know how to touch them, give off sparks and take fire, yield drops and flow, ring and tell of him" (*Sermons* 195).

In the octave of "God's Grandeur," Hopkins redescribed the story of the Christian mystery of the descent of the Holy Spirit to emphasize the timeless omnipresence of God in all existence: "nature is never spent" tells us of the unfathomable deepness of God's coinherence in Creation, a co-presence, we remember, that began in the second expression of divinity, the Incarnation of Christ. So "There lives the dearest freshness deep down things." Thus, despite all apparent evidences of dissolution, human and natural, "last lights on the black West," the charge of grandeur of the Father through the Son is still communicated ("give off sparks") through their divine bond and, therefore, "the Holy ghost broods with warm breast and with ah! bright wings."

The spiritual power of Christian hope, which this sonnet so brilliantly expresses, is what Ricoeur means by encountering the Gospel texts as the story of the "Passion for the Possible." In responding to the proclamation and testimony of the Christian story, each writer attests to the potential refiguration of the self in the appropriation of such texts, thereby connecting to their enabling and transforming capacities to bring to personal "selving" existence those very possibilities that the re-descriptive metaphors disclose.

The spiritual inspiration for this sonnet and all of Hopkins' religious poetry was his priestly life, a life dedicated to dying to a false self and receiving a new self, as Ignatius' *Spiritual Exercises* enjoin every Jesuit to try to achieve. It is accurate to say that Hopkins' religious poetry is a powerful literary version of the *Exercises*. The central focus of both is achieving personally an Incarnational consciousness which Paul Ricoeur so aptly described: "Hope, unconditional trust, would be empty if it did not rely on a constantly renewed interpretation of sign-events reported by writings such as the Exodus in the Old Testament and the Resurrection in the New Testament. These are events of deliverance which open and disclose the utmost possibilities of my own freedom and thus become for me the Word of God" (*Phil of Religion* 84-85).

Time and Story in the "Selving" Imagination

Ricoeur sees narrative as a form of mediation between individual actions in all of their complexity (incidents, accidents, characters, settings) and the shaping of events into holistic meanings through the "selving" poetic in a person's "I" positing hermeneutic process. Central to this mediation is, of course, language, especially the language of figuration, which opens up new insightful relationships affording levels of understanding which, we remember, Ricoeur called "reconfiguration" (*Time and Narrative* I, 66). For Hopkins, the same idea is expressed by his notion of "selving," by which he meant choosing the personality of the consciousness' "I." For both poet and philosopher, "reconfiguration" and "selving" essentially are acts of positing the "I" self through the hermeneutic mediation of Christian tests.

It is interesting to note that Hopkins used music as a symbol for narrating the Creation story. Starting with the idea that reality is a throng of things absolutely different from one another, yet "scaled" in the similarities of their differences, Creation is imagined as an archetypical choral composition. For Hopkins the universe is a magnificent song of beings singing the Creator's Being within themselves, the Creator's voice reincarnated in everything. Thus to Hopkins, what Creation means is this song, the orchestration of divine and natural voices out of which co-presence all beauty is made. God moves in Creation-time, then, through individualized creatures' "pitches," choired existence singing / "selving" harmonies as a unified chorus of praise. Intrinsic to the unified choral design of Creation is the harmonic ontic order (shared "is-ness" of beings and God's being).

The notion of harmonics in the hermeneutics of parallelism is fundamental in Hopkins' idea of human knowledge. The making of the "selving" word , whether transitional (concept) or contemplative (poetic), involves a hermeneutic matching of thing, image, feeling, idea, and being. Moreover, the kind of poetic knowing that Ricoeur emphasizes is for Hopkins a harmonic parallelism of images and thoughts brought to a unified clarity of splendid order through the dwelling, productive energies of poetic contemplation. (In his *Journals* (86-115) he wrote an elaborate Platonic-like dialogue about the parallelistic phenomenology of beauty.) Poetic harmonics overtake the difficulties of the differentiated universe as non-discursive by finding a higher harmonic "inscape" of being, a poetic hermeneutic which the "instressing" creativity of the poet's consciousness, in the flush of his expressive wording, harmonizes (Ricoeur's "reconfigures") the "inscapes" of the things he experiences in the utterances (word-scapes) of his poem.

The reconfiguring poetic text, then, reaches beyond the level of conception to a new level of unifying symbol ("unity of the whole") while retaining its connections to the concrete order of things. Recall Hopkins' notion of unifying esthetic form: "The further in anything, as a work of art, the organization is carried out, the deeper the form penetrates, the prepossession flushes the matter, the more effort will be required in apprehension, *the more power of comparision*, the more capacity for receiving that *synthesis* of (either successive or spatially distinct) impressions which give us the *unity* with the prepossession conveyed by it" (italics mine, *Journals* 126). This description of "selving" contemplative energy "inscaped" in art, a poem for example, is essentially the same hermeneutical principle on which Ricoeur centers his her-meneutic philosophy: "But when the reader actualizes the 'semantic virtualities' in the meaning by identifying with the signified mode of being so that the reader encounters a figure who represents 'I' as I *should be*, then we reach the stage of appropriation" (Klemm 148).

There is also a Ricoeurrian aspect to Hopkins' notion of productive poetic energy in the imagination. Ricoeur centers his hermeneutics on the productive energies of an activated imagination which mediates between the first level of language, concepts, and the second, symbols. Such formulations of intuitive possiblities, based upon perceived objects, produce a mediation that opens up "semantic innovation." Metaphoric language offers this mediation by predicating an emergent meaning to incongruent figural references, thereby transforming the meaning of literal reference: "Imagination mediates between literal absurdity and metaphorical suggestiveness to discern a new connection that is not part of the current lexicon" (Klemm 154). Congruent figuration produces a unifying icon based on incongruent images. In so doing metaphoric language generates a schemata for a redescription of reality as a synthesis at the upper level of language reference: "The imagination here mediates between the actuality of everyday life and the absence of the whole of things to synthesize the appearance of the redescribed and ontologically significant reference to new modes of being-in-the-world" (Klemm 155). It only remains to be added that Ricoeur holds that this imaginative mediation of metaphor reaches deeply into an affective and volitional attunement to an achieved understanding: "We feel *like* what we *should be*" (*"The Metaphoric Process"* 156).

In Hopkins the production of such creativity by the poetic consciousness correlates to the "selving" level of the poetry produced. He divided poetic language into three levels. The first level, the true level of "selving" poetics, he called "the language of inspiration" by which he meant "a mood of great, abnormal in fact, mental acuteness, either energetic or receptive, according as the thoughts which arise in it seem generated by stress . . . . Everybody of course has like moods, but not being poets what they then produce is not poetry." He called a second, lower level "Parnassian," the language of poets that "does not require the mood of mind in which the poetry of inspiration is written . . . that language which genius speaks as fitted to its exaltation and place among other genius, but does not sing." He noted such poetry is "not in the highest sense poetry. It does not require the mood of mind in which the poetry of inspiration is written. It is spoken *on and from the level* of the poet's mind, not, as in the other case, when the inspiration which is the gift of genius, raises him above himself " (*Further Letters* 216-219). He also discerned a middle level between Inspiration and Parnassian which he called Castalian, "the lowest kind of inspiration." For Hopkins the poetic level that "inscaped" the "selving I" is the poetry of inspiration, a poetry that is the product of the imaginative religious consciousness

Additionally Ricoeur's hermeneutic notion of a "limit experience" relates to Hopkins' "poetry of inspiration." As productions of the creative imagination, these kinds of mind energies have an expressive "reach" to them which carry powerful semantic forces that can alter consciousness. Some utterances are made that surcharge the mind so powerfully that they rearrange perceptions, transform affections, and reorder the "selving" consciousness into a new configuration, a new self-understanding and hence a possibility of living in the world on a different level of existence. This alteration of consciousness as a heighthening insight is akin to the "inscape" of inspired language produced by the energy of the "instressing" consciousness reaching for an inspired level of unified "selving" energy in and through producing or contemplating a unified, expressive, poetic form. The production and reception of texts are at the heart of Ricoeur's hermeneutics, for in his philosophic view, such texts possess the potential to change fundamentally the level of the self understanding its "I" selfness in the world. The poetry of inspiration, then, produces the "selving" "limit experience" that reconstitutes the "I am" of the self.

Further I wish to emphasize once more that such creative writing and reading concentrates on that mind energy which Hopkins designated contemplation. This energy he described in "Notes on Contemplation" as a kind of creative memory which, "when continued or kept on the strain the act of this faculty is attention, advertence, heed, the being *ware,* and its habit, knowledge, the being *aware.* Towards God it gives rise to reverence, it is the sense of the *presence* of God " (*Sermons* 174). Of course, primarily, though not exclusively, it is religious texts which respond most fully to such acts of contemplation, for the poetic dimensions of sacral texts are those which afford the consciousness-changing possibilities according to Ricoeur.

Again Hopkins' poetry of "inspiration," the kind of poetry that he mostly wrote, is composed in the language of the "limit experience," in his words the contemplative"awareness" of a radically different understanding of reality, the refiguring of personal experience through the symbolics of the story of Creation provoking in the "selving" consciousness most penetratingly "the sense of the presence of God." For both Hopkins and Ricoeur, the contemplative imagination is the way that knowledge of the eternal enters into time interacting with the pervasive human passion for new "selving" possiblity. Finally, for both Hopkins and Ricoeur, the actualizing narrative of this self-transcendence is the story of how Jesus of history can he read as the Christ-Event of consciousness. This narrative is a prime text for the hermeneutics of the sacramental word.

The Mind Battle: The Vanishing Self

The nightmare that continually haunts the self is its extinction. The "selving" effort to confront this dire awareness abiding in the consciousness is a kind of battle within which the self seeks with the greatest desires to find motivations to transcend this dreaded ending. Hopkins named these motivations in "selving" that energize religious consciousness to withstand this death battle within the self as "corresponding graces."

Any discussion of grace in Hopkins and Ricoeur must begin with two considerations. The first is the human predicament and the second is the phenomenology of selfness, the two angles of philosophic perspective from which arise the human order of "selving" being. Let us start with Ricoeur.

We recall that for Ricoeur, the hope for human meaning is confronted by limits (fallibility): time limits, natural limits, psychological limits, a movement towards mortality. The I-self, a powerful congeries of perceptive, reflective, affective, and expressive energies, is beset by a kind of interior hollowness in uncovering its selfness, an emptiness negating a hopeful, liberating self-understanding oriented to a fulfilling future. In asking what is ultimate human meaning, Ricoeur has developed an "assenting" philosophy of personal meaning, one that emphasizes the poetic imagination as a human power that can represent human meaning beyond finite existential limits by creating and reading narrative texts, cosmic and sacred, to open up new possiblities in being and living in the world. For Ricoeur, the central texts engaging the human passion for possibility are biblical, for they possess great kerygmatic powers for "refiguring" the self in the world. In the hermeneutic reflections of text-selving as self-positing, one exercises a changed self-interpretation as an effort to affirm the present self by uncovering an enduring subjectivity, a transfigured "I am." It must be emphasized that this transfiguration is accomplished through the hermeneutic powers of the consciousness interacting with primal "selving" texts. In this way the self enacts changes in the consciousness so that the "I-self" comes to be open to transcendent and enduring life possibilities.

Hopkins, in anticipating Ricoeur's general account of natural human fate, emphasized a distabilizing factor of "fallibility" in human beings which has profoundly shaped human destiny. Like Ricoeur, though from a greater emphasis scriptural and theological vantage point, Hopkins stressed in his concept the Incarnation the "distressing" rebellion of the angels in heaven and Adam and Eve in Eden (the Christian sacral myths of fallibility) as the shaping mythopoeic symbols of the dilemma of human meaning— the consciousness of obedience or disobedience in persuing human destiny. Like Ricoeur, Hopkins read Christian sacred narratives as revealing how the human will became involved in human fate. For Hopkins the essence of the Lucifer-Adam archeytpes in the human consciousness is that human volition became a freedom to either choose the good in the flush of the ego's powerful, vain desirabilities, or to degrade choice through a warfare between choice and desire, a kind of perpetual, internal, mind battle in parallel with its sacral mythic archetypes. The basic moral tension in this "war within" revolves around the consciousness of love, "selving" a "giving" love or a "taking" love.

What Hopkins has written about the mind battle of selfness is brief but astonishingly current with much general modern thinking regarding melancholia and depression. Consciousness philosophers, in thinking about the dynamics of selfness, dwell upon the pervasiveness of an opaqueness in the awareness of the "I," a consciousness as a kind of house of darkening selving-mirrors. Different explanations are offered regarding these phantoms. For Hopkins the "selving" shadow-cover is in the interiority of "I-ness" focusing on the "I's" lonely isolation because of delving into its unique separateness. Hopkins often used the word "self" as a sign for the "I" in the self, thus to a certain degree muddying verbally an essential distinction in his thinking. Nevertheless, it is clear that, in its highly "pitched" state, the "I" seemed to Hopkins incorrigibly absolute in its unique individuation; hence in all manifestations of the "I," what is evidential is its sharp "I" affirmations against all that is not the "I," resulting in a sort of warfare with everything other. This is the melancholy core of his famous "selving" description : "When I consider my selfbeing, my consciousness and feeling of myself . . . " (*Journals* 123).

For Hopkins the issue is, if each individual person is simply an abrupt "I-presence," and every one and thing else blankly unlike the "I" that is me, then how is this assertive floating "I"-ness posited in some mode of an authentic selving of the "I am" in the consciousness by its self-reflections on exterior experience? In his answer to this question, Hopkins defined differently from Ricoeur the structural fallibility inhibiting the "selving of I-ness" in affirming its "I am." The task of "selving," according to Hopkins, is subduing the tyrant "I-ness" that is the center and coinciding point of me-ness, thereby reconciling with the "I" all the otherness of everything around the "I." But if the "selving" utterances of the "I" self-identity are negative qualifying factors, which make any authentic naming of the "I" defective, then in what does the authentic positing of the "I" self consist? This "selving" dilemma suggests that the self's personality is an inadequate expression of that interior, positing energy that is the reality of the "I"; to Hopkins the " 'Self' objectifies somewhat the subject 'I' or 'me'" (Ong 30). For Hopkins, it seems, "selving" is a very imperfect reflective act, hence the instrinsic melancholia in his understanding of the self.

The deficiency in self-reflectiveness, it would seem according to Hopkins, is a fallibility in the very structure of the personality. The inward "I-ness," which each of us knows in some direct reflectiveness, is only partially expressive of the "I" self-consciousness; thus the "selving" consciousness, while to some extent an expression of self-identity, is always an erring specification of the "I." It follows that such positing diminishes the expressibility of the "I's" absolute distinctiveness. Accordingly, reflexive words such as "self," and "person" are insufficient expressions of the uniqueness of the "I" identity (Ong 29-32). No "I-ness," then, is truly knowable to any other "I-ness" or its own. Moreover, "I-ness" is open to a universal range of objectifications, wherever memory or imagination can project it, yet each and all of these are deficient either as identifications, names, analysis, or the presence of the "I." "The 'I' is defined by being self-referential, and our own 'I' snaps to attention and relates immediately, sensing the other as other, dead or alive, and identifying the 'other' as 'you'. . . . The self-referential 'I' defines itself in your work by relating 'you' to your own self referential 'I.' 'I' carries its own reference within it" (Ong 34).

Two aspects of Hopkins' concepts of "I-ness" stand out strongly. The first is the incommunicability factor of every "I." According to him, every "I" is an irrevocably solitary, utterly distinctive unity of energizing "I" selfness seeking out a "selving" response from various "I" self-reflections. Yet any encounter with an Other bears witness to the presence of the "I's" inscrutability. Unsurprisingly, then, the "stress" of each "I" is a powerful force seeking expression at shaping every chance for a self-identity in some way. Human beings especially have this driving towards "selving " power to self-reflexive expression. Here we meet a paradox, for while the "I" must divulge exteriorly its mysterious, distinctive interiority, it does so in inadequate expressive modes. The "I" drive for self-expression, so powerfully energized, remains inexpressible in any absolute sense, even though the "I" self-consciousness can interrelate with others as a way of some kind of self-reflection, a kind of self-giving and self-taking, but the "selving" is always less than fulfilling. This is the structural fallibilty, a kind of existential evil of finitude, in the human self as Hopkins understood it.

Another aspect is evident in the "wording" mode that self-expressions must take on, given the "I" 's abrupt decentering from all self-reflective consciousness. It is clear that the only language mode through which the "I" can even approach some self-clarifying identity is figurative language. For Hopkins, every self-expression is but a figure for the "I" 's distinctiveness. Each metaphor of the "I," whatever the genre of expression, is but a *discordia concors* parallelism, to be sure, plunged into self-scape by the potent energies of "I"-stress, but, nevertheless, a figurative union which intensifies the isolation of self-difference. This aspect of Hopkins' notion of the human personality is thus open to, must be open to, the hermeneutics of the "I"-self in that the "I" constantly seeks to be posited as much as possible in its "selving" acts. (The poetics of the positing "I" will be further developed in the next Chapter.)

How else do we even come close to some proximate self-identification? One noted contemporary philosopher, Bernard Lonergan, described exactly what Hopkins understood as the "selving I's" ambiguous participation in its consciousness: "What do I mean by 'I'? The answer is difficult to formulate, but strangely, in some obscure fashion, I know very well what it means without formulation, and by that obscure yet familiar awareness, I find fault with the various formulations of what is meant by 'I.' In other words, 'I' has a rudimentary meaning from consciousness and it invisages neither the multiplicity nor the diversity of contents and conscious acts but rather the unity that goes along with them. But if an 'I' has such rudimentary meaning from consciousness, then consciousness supplies the fulfillment of one element in the conditions for affirming that I am a knower" (*Insight* 328). On its own, the "I" must endure its "selving" limits within the consciousness. Thus there is a constant mind battle within the self. Moreover, such a conflict in the consciousness gives rise for the need for subduing the alert dictatorship of the "selving I" by confronting it in the reflective contents of consciousness in some way. Hopkins saw the solution to the "I's" positing tribulations through the aids called "graces." Failure to sudue the driving egoism of the "I" means that the agonies of the unsatisfied ego's self-serving drives will finally destruct the self. Grace beckons the self towards the possibility of a different "selving" solution, accepting willingly the grief of "selving" unfulfillment as an act of love. More about this loss to gain later.

It is instructive to juxtapose Hopkins' constantly attending "I-ness" with Ricoeur's reflective hermeneutics of the "I": "reflection is an effort to recomprehend the *ego* of the *ego cogito* in the mirror of its objects, its works, and ultimately its acts." Now, why must the positing of the ego be recomprehended through its acts? Precisely because the *ego* is not given in psychological evidence or in intellectual intuition or in mystical vision. A reflective philosophy is precisely the opposite of the philosophy of the immediate. The first truth—*I think, I am*—remains abstract and empty as it is unassailable. It must be 'mediated' by representations, actions, works, institutions, and monuments which objectify it; it is in these objects, in the largest sense of the word, that the *ego* must both lose itself and find itself" (*Conflict* 327). Thus, unlike Hopkins' notion, the "I" finds more possible "selving" identity in the consciousness according to Ricoeur, but like Hopkins the "I" must accept its "selving" limitations.

Ricoeur's approach to "selving the I" is in some ways comparable to Hopkins. Hopkins concentrated more on the pre-reflective "I," while Ricoeur focuses on the reflective articulations of the "I" self in various stages of the activating consciousness. Hopkins did assert that we cannot find the "I" directly and so does Ricoeur. And like Hopkins, Ricoeur asserts that the philosophy of immediate "selving" remains sterile because the "I" can only be pointed to or conceptualized—both approaches being axiomatic but end-stopped for further "selving" insight. Finally, both Hopkins and Ricoeur see the positing of the "I" as the internal driving force of "I-ness," which, in virtue of that unique "selving I-energy," produces representations that configure the "I" into some proximate meaningfulness, though Ricoeur seems to find a more adequate "selving" of the "I" in its self-reflective acts than does Hopkins.

Both Hopkins and Ricoeur take us beyond the suspicious meta-psychologies of Freud and Jung, for whom the anthropological "I" lies vampire-like, buried in the basements of the individual unconscious shadowing the conscious "selving I." In contrast, Hopkins' phenomenology of the "I," in parallel with Ricoeur's philosophy of the reflective consciousness, affirms that the perennial task of achieving self-meaning is a conscious self-realizing event. "Instress" is the self-reflecting "I" attempting to achieve its "self-scape," however imperfectly, as Ricoeur's positing of the "I"-self is focused on reaching, as far as possible, the identity of the "I" in the contents of the reflective consciousness, whatever the structural fallibilities in the self. Both temper the limit factor in the "selving" of the human personality.

A curious biographical side note must be added here. While it is evident that for Hopkins the achievement of "selving" involves a "selving" hermeneutic principle, given the figurative relationships between the "I" and its self-reflections in the personality, he seems to have spent a lifetime frustrating that constructive though limited mode of self-expression most congenial to his nature, that of a poet. It is unclear just why this was so. Can it all be put down to a narrowing "selving" scrupulosity? All his mentors affirmed the suitability of his "I-ness" and his human nature, but Hopkins tended strongly to see his poetic nature as dangerous to the moral integrity of his "I." He even tried to explain this in conceptual terms, but his analysis contradicts all of his mentors: Suarez, Scotus, and Ignatius Loyola. He argued that God endows selves, not necessarily with appropriate natures, but rather in a random fashion. Thus the "I" that best expressed his "selving" as a priest (choice) could be in conflict with his poetic nature (desire). For him his "I" and his personality were often at odds. What could he do but suffer the radical discordant affiliation he felt between his self and personality? Thus he endured the struggle of this psycho-strife all his days in trying to find those existential parallels, "selving" substitute reflections, of his "I-ness" in his priestly vocation while all the time being drawn to the poetic life where his affective nature responded more fulfillingly to his "I"-self with the greatest expressive compatibility. Hermeneutically, this "selving" dissension could be described as a battle of "selving" words, the figurations of the priest sometimes countering those of the poet. What in fact happened, of course, is that out of these parelleled "instressing / distressing" mind=battle tensions, he produced a powerful religious poetry of self-scape bearing the marks of the abrupt oddness and singularity of his "I-ness," both priest and poet vitalizing his "selving" metaphors in an implosive union of poetic "selving" (Downes, *The Ignatian Personality of Hopkins* 143-180). I think it is these powerful psychic "selving" tensions, which he captured so incisively in his poetry, that are so striking to modern readers.

The mind battle for both Hopkins and Ricoeur resides in their notions of fallibility. For each thinker the structural flaw in the self devolves basically around the will. For Hopkins, distinctive selfness has as its prime "instress" moral freedom. The power to choose is the most salient particularization of the "I" self-expression because choice reveals the "I" in its most accurate "selving" light: "What I do is me." What Hopkins meant by this is that choosing, "doing-be," asserts most trenchantly the personalizing distinctiveness of the "I." Such "doing" involves, in the moral wake of Adam, choosing badly, that is, choosing kinds of self-affirmations which often take little or no cognizance of the gift of being, Creation; the self observes no due reverence and praise for the "instress" of the Incarnation sacramentally present in the self and every other existent.

Hopkins spent considerable effort *(Sermons* Chapter Three) analysing the ethics of the making of the fallible personality. Following the traditional distinctions between the powers of volitional rationality, the interrelations of the energies of the elective will and the affective will, he asserted that the stress of choice in us is an implanted divine stress of volitional energy through which God could, and sometimes does, shape individual choices by influencing our affective wills. However, as a human differentiating element in his act of Creation, God enjoins persons to choose the utterance of their own personalities in virtue of endowing them with free natures. Moreover, at least for Hopkins, in consquence of the Fall, there is a continuing lack of parallelizing of the elective powers and the affective powers in the volitional consciousness so that choice, more often than not, expresses naked "I-ness" leading to expressions of solipsism or narcissism rather than a fruitful, volitional, Creational paralleling producing the elective desirablilty of the true "good." The "good," if chosen, is a confirming relation between creaturely proximate and ultimate ends; "doing this" acknowledges the God-centered purpose of all choices, loving and serving Him, by actually choosing this "good" rather than a lesser good, thereby achieving an integral personality consisting of the harmony of choice and desire reflecting the aboriginal harmony of Creation.

The all-powerful incline of the voluntary consciousness towards its own egoistic "I" is potentially disastrous: "In so far then as the desire or affection we entertain towards any object comes nearer our true selves or bare personality, in so far will it be the harder to change, and if it were ever the relation of mere self towards that object it would be necessary and unchangeable, though free; neither of course would the subject wish to change it. And in fact the lost do not wish, do not will at all events, if it were even possible, to repent and love God." *(Sermons* 153). This is to say that the "pitch" of voluntary consciousness works at a level of freely choosing its own ends as ultimate goods. Why? Because there is a confusion in about apparent "goods" and ultimate "Good" in the "I" in "selving" its personality As we have seen in Chapter 3, here lies the whole issue of the moral dilemma of the "selving" personality. The dilemma of moral alienation in the human volitional consciousness is central to Hopkins' focus on "selving" the "I" in the self.

Ricoeur also discloses a fatal-potential in the fallibility of the human self. His delineation is in hermeneutic terms, but, nevertheless, choosing in the sense of electing optimal human meaning ("reappropriating true selfness") out of the affectivity of hope and the condition of freedom is also prime in his thinking.

This is to say that for Ricoeur self-reflecting consciousness consists of acts of choice that transform alienation into new harmonious possibilities for human meaning at a transcendental level. Here too, as for Hopkins, ethics is a form of "I" positing conversion, for ethics' "goal is to grasp the side of the ego in its efforts to exist in its desire to be . . . . This effort is a desire because it is never satisfied; but conversely, this desire is an effort because it is the affirmation of a unique being, not simply a lack of being. Effort and desire are the two aspects of this positing of the self in the first truth: I am" (*Conflict* 329). It follows, then, that self-positing reflection is this "selving" volitional act of true moral appropriation; the hermeneutics of the "I am" is a moral state of consciousness in which the "I" is posited in possible ethical, self-renewing affirmations.

For both Hopkins and Ricoeur, given human ethical fraility, transforming the fallibility of human nature through moral freedom and refiguring beauty is a task that cannot be achieved alone. This brings us to explore further the subject of grace, hermeneutically understood as an alleviation of the pains of fallibility in the "selving" consciousness. As we have seen, for both Hopkins and Ricoeur, mankind is isolated in a kind of perpetual, solitary lockup; the "I" self is in some sense in a psychic prison, seemingly doomed to die in absurd anonymity doing ordinary time. Is there hopeful "selving" freedom anywhere for the self? The answer both give is yes: it is in the graced consciousness of faith that hope and freedom are disclosed in the revealing hermeneutics of the sacral powers of words. The volitional / reflective consciousness is the meeting place of Nature, self, and divinity—being / words / Word / God. This meeting place both writers call "grace," the power to be open to community and love.

"Grace," said Hopkins, "is any action, activity, on God's part by which, in creating or after creating, he carries the creature to or towards the end of its being, which is its self-sacrifice to God and its salvation" (*Sermons* 158). Hopkins named graces as awakening ("momentary" or "quickening"), sustaining ("continuous" or "correcting"), and transforming ("elevating" or "aspiring"), but intrinsic to each is the notion of some gifting on God's side and some correspondence on the human side: "For grace is any action, activity, on God's part; so that so far as this action or activity is God's it is divine stress, holy spirit, and, as all is done through Christ, Christ's spirit; so far as it is action, correspondence, on the creature's it is *actio salutaris*" (*Sermons* 154).

Ricoeur complements Hopkins' notion of grace. While Hopkins, focuses on the theology of grace, Ricoeur emphasizes more the hermeneutics of grace. It is in Ricoeur's working out of the correlatons of reflective consciousness and the dynamics of hermeneutical transformation—the power of any figurative, sacral text to refigure human meaning—that he affirms the grace event of self-being as a gift of Creation—the Word as the grace of gifting words (*Essays on Biblical Interpretation* 109-135). In this thankful awareness, Ricoeur argues, we come to realize that we are not of own self-making, but rely on the revelatory gifting ("selving wording") of Being itself—God. It is our poetic consciousness, our powers of the reflective imagination, which are open to be shaped by the creative wording of being, by the events of Creation, and by the Event of the Christed Word; while all are sacralizing texts, the prime constitutional, testimonial texts are the biblical narratives of the Incarnation, Passion and Resurrection of Jesus which, for both Hopkins and Ricoeur, are powerful grace sources of awakening to the actualizing freedom and hope in the self.

Such is the essence of the poetical hermeneutics of grace according to the philosopher of Christed hermeneutics and the poet of the Incarnation. Hope is the power of the "instress" of words and wording, and freedom is the refiguring potential actualizing in the transfigured "inscape" of the self-worded. Hopkins and Ricoeur both see Nature, God, and self worded in Christian sacral narrative through the Kerygma of the Word: "The grace of the imagination is conveyed through the sacrament of the word" (Vanhoozer 265). This is to say that the symbol that is the Christ Event is the hermeneutic center of "selving" the Christian consciousness

But the worded graces of the Christ Event will not happen in and through biblical or other texts alone. There must be, as has been noted, what Hopkins calls "correspondence," and Ricoeur the "passion for possibility" that arises from encountering texted "Testimony." Both notions are similar in that both place stress on "selving-activation," "electing" for Hopkins, "appropriating" for Ricoeur. In fact both "selving" modes are two parts of the same activity. Hopkins noted that grace enters ordinary time as freedom of choice in uplifting the self. Similarly, Ricoeur affirms that positing the "I" self involves the temporalizing of the reflective consciousness and the hermeneutic field as transformative narrative—

the remaking of the self through "selving" choices and acts. Both Christian writers stress that the textual sources releasing the "selving" kerygma of the "I" comes most hermeneutically powerful for them in encountering the Gospel narratives, the origin of the most imaginative altering possibilities of the event of "selving," especially the narrative of Jesus' Passion as Testimony to the true meaning of "Kingdom of God."

The parabolic Jesus story is the archetypic "limit-experience" for both Ricoeur and for Hopkins—"The Great Sacrifice." Here are worded the figurations of the mystery of the Jesus of history becoming the Christ of faith. I say "becoming" because this Event not only offers Testimony open to the hermeneutics of the "selving" reconfiguration of selfness, but also announces an alteration of ordinary time into a new holy time immanent in ordinary time—the Pentecostal time of the Holy Spirit—proclaiming the onset of the eternal present in the nowness of God's Kingdom abiding within the flow of ordinary time. It is conversion, in the sense of authentic assenting commitment, that introduces the self to the Pentecostal time of the Eucharist, a kind of perpetual narrative of the Holy Spirit. In its conversion to Eucharistic time, the self posits the "I am" of the self as in time (at battle) and out of time (peace). The battle of the mind is open to the spiritual conversion of a truce, a treaty of hope afffirming that the self will not disappear. Such real "selving" assent is the fruit of Testimony. (Though space does not allow a full-blown comparison, it is instructive to compare J. H. Newman's analysis of the kind of probate testimony involved in "selving"assent in his famous study, *The Grammar of Assent* (37, 87, 276-281: also see commentary by S. Prickett 274-277). Newman's approach focuses as well on what might be called the poetics of religious assent, the human capacity to be opened to the transforming "selving" possibility of a transcendent spiritual destiny through the operatons of special hermeneutic sensibilities.)

The Stress of Mystery in Christian Hermeneutics

The telling figurations of the "selving" mind battle are indelible in the consciousness. The words for this psychic travail of self-texting is Ricoeur's notion of "trial," and Hopkins' use of "wreck." As we have seen, for Ricoeur, the pain of "selving the I" of the self is a hermeneutic conflict of "selving" interpretations. In the context of faith, the center of the conflict lies in the mythopoeic mysteries of the sacral events in history whose recoverable spiritual meanings refigure the self. Ricoeur says yes to the possibility of positing the "selving I" through the foundation of events and words born out by authentic sacral Testimony. Ricoeur does not mean by authentic the empiricism of history; he means the kind of eventful and verbal witness in which individuals have revealed some contact with transcendent meaning, some confession in which the confessor's self is actually radically transformed by some encounter with absolute power and knowledge, which elevates the consciousness towards a transcendent destiny. This he calls the "criteriology of the divine." He finds such criteriology in the sacral narratives of the Old Testament and the Gospels in the New Testament. The authenticating criteria lies in both the recorded events, their narrative wording and their spiritual metaphors, all of which constitute authentic Testimony. Testimony involves a suffering witness carried to its ultimate in affirming transcendental spiritual principles, the absolute giving over of egoism, as an act of love, by abandoning the "I" of the self to the redeeming presence in the consciousness of an absolute Being . For Ricoeur this is the central theme told over and over again in the Bible, but especially in the story of the trial of Jesus, which, he asserts, embodies the arch-paradigm of authenticating Testimony (*Essays on Biblical Interpretation* 115). Jesus' life is the classic story in time liberating the "I" to achieve the potentiality of full and true "I-selfness"— the faith consciousness of hope and freedom.

Hopkins, we know, was deeply congnizant of the parallel between history and the testifying consciousness which he poeticized in his great ode, "The Wreck of the Deutschland." In this long narrative poem, he began quite consciously to envision grace as an actual "selving" event in ordinary time in the form of a Christed narrative. Indeed, "The Wreck" is about a real event in time and about an Event of grace that he envisioned as immanent in that tragic occurrence in natural time. This ode, his first major poem in his poetic maturity, is, in my reading, about what Ricoeur calls the event of "Testimony." Hopkins narrated the experience of the five nuns who were to die in this now famous shipwreck as being involved in a kergymatic event in ordinary time. The symbolization of this "selving" Event was, as Hopkins redescribed it, the act of one of the taller nuns, who stood on a table in the ship's saloon, so that she thrust herself through a skylight into the fury of the storm and was heard to call Christ to "come quickly!"

The religious poet construed the nun's spiritual heroism as a vital act of Testimony to the advent of some direct experiencing of God. It is just such an event in ordinary time revealing some immanent, transcendent meaning that constitutes Testimony. The persons involved, even and particularily at the moment of severity of their suffering, became "selving" Testimony in and through the "selving" events which authenticated and transformed them. The creative imagination of the poet worded ("inscaped") their Testimonial event, that is, "caught" the deep relgious meaning of such revelatory religious acts through his imaginative refiguration. The tall nun's act was poetically refigured in and through the poet's religious imagination so that the historical event is now worded as a refiguring "selving" event, so rich in spiritual meaning, that its resdescribed wording takes on hermeneutic powers to unleash in sympathetic readers similar personal "selving" reconfigurations.

Through Hopkins' ode, we too, as readers, can encounter "selving" graces in appropriating his poetic texting of the nuns' Testimonial Event and, thereby, begin to resolve the extremities of conflict in our own "selving" "wrecks." This use of the poetic religious imagination is the crux of Christian hermeneutics for both Hopkins and Ricoeur. Herein lies the mystery in the hermeneutics of "selving" faith: the "I" of the self must discover the spiritual meaning in its own "selving" thoughts and deeds as testamentory of the gift of divinity which is central to the Jesus' story. Hopkins wrote in his ode: "His mystery must be instressed, stressed; / For I greet him that days I meet him, and bless when I understand."

Much later, after Hopkins wrote his poem (1878), he came across the writings of a young French mystic, Marie Lataste (*Sermons* 109, Appendix I), who confirmed his sense of time and narrative as spiritual destiny, what he called two "strains" or intentions by which God moves in the world. One is the "creative" strain in which God works through things according to their natures, and the other, a "sacrificial, redemptive" strain—wrecks—through which God offers a traumatic "selving" shift in consciousness leading to radical transformation, both involving free choice as an opportunity for corresponding to God's bidding graces. Hopkins' life seemed to follow the second strain.

As for Hopkins, so for Ricoeur, the paralleling of the patterns of ordinary experience in natural time with the patterns of graces in supernatural time is the mysterious structure of the religious narrative of Testimony, the "great sacrifice," as expressed in the Christed narrative of the trial and death of Jesus. The texts of Christ's ultimate sacrifice best symbolize the mystery of the "selving" transforming "passion for the possible" in the consciousness. Again Hopkins never put his notion of such "selving" religious passion clearer than he did in a letter to his sometimes friend, Robert Bridges:

> Christ's life and character are such as appeal to all the world's admiration, but there is one insight St. Paul gives us [Philippians 2: 5-11] which is very secret and seems to me more touching and constraining than everything else is. This mind he says, was in Christ Jesus—he means as man: being in the form of God—that is, finding, as in the first instance of his incarnation he did, his human nature informed by the godhead—he thought it nevertheless no snatching-matter for him to be equal with God, but annihilated himself, taking the form of servant; that is, he could not but see what he was, God, but he would see it, and be it as if he were not and instead of snatching at once at what all the time was his, or was himself, he emptied or exhausted himself so far as that was possible, of godhead and behaved only as God's slave, as his creature, as man, which also he was, and then being in the guise of man humbled himself to death, the death of the cross. It is this holding himself back, and not snatching at the truest and highest good, the good that was his right, nay his possession from a past eternity in his other nature, his own being and self, which seems to me the root of all his holiness and the imitation of this the root of all moral good in other men" (*Letters to Bridges* 175).

This kenosis of self, so beautifully described by Hopkins from the story of Jesus is what Ricoeur means by the hermeneutics of the imaginative appropriation of Christian religious texts, the "great poem of existence" (Vanhoozer 258-263; Klemm 128). Encountering such sacral wordings can conjure up in the consciousness a sense of the gift of Creation, a graced appropriative act in which the ego submits itself to a "selving" reconstitution that is open to suffering the trials of transforming change. As one reader of Ricoeur wrote about the movement from life-denying despair to an affirming actuality of the freedom of hope in Ricoeur: "Imagination, as the metaphysical power that allows man to symbolize and therby create the new self in accordance with the promise and hope of redemption, is the means by which the soul can, and eventually does, come to live the resurrection of Christ in anticipation of his own resurrection" (quoted in Vanhoozer 250). One need only add that Hopkins felt he uttered the same conferring religious self-empowerment every time he recited the Eucharistic commemoration of Jesus' Passion in the ritual of the Christian mass: "This is my Body . . . This is my Blood." In a most fundamental sense, Hopkins and Ricoeur echo each other in the poetic hermeneutics of such "selving" sacramental words.

Chapter 5

Poems of Existence

The Achieving Self

We begin this chapter by summarizing some critical perspectives of Ricoeur and Hopkins' construction of the self. As for Hopkins, so for Ricoeur, the "I" of the consciousness is imperially present, radically distinct, and powerfully charged. The energy medium of the "I" is a congeries of sensation, feeling, and conception fused into the "I's" wording of experience, a "wording-bundle," whether idea or image, that is an incipient narrative of the "I" attempting to construct and reconstruct its selving identity. The nature of this wording is for both Hopkins and Ricoeur essentially metaphorical discourse, the most fully human utterance in which language becomes a harbinger of a different level of understanding selving experience, a new horizon of meaning beyond the plane of the practical. It is in and through metaphor that the "I" discovers new self-meaning, thus new possibility to achieve whole selfness.

This process of self-reflection for both Hopkins and Ricoeur affirms that the "I" of consciousness is unfinished, incomplete. Indeed, there is a feverish awareness that the "I" experiences itself as abandoned, lost, even condemned. Such felt awarenesses conflict the "selving" process, diminish the individual human possibility, narrow the meaning of self-existence. In combating these denying conflicts, the "I" must resort ever more energetically to selving language that is productive of the possibility of a new vision of self-meaning, metaphors of a new way of selving in the world. Metaphorical language does this by imaginatively creating new selving interactions between the "I" and its experiences, thereby posing new meanings to the conscious order of the things of one's life, new redescriptions of common reality which awakens the "I" to new selving meanings possible in a higher world order. The mode of such events of language is, of course, temporal, for the language of metaphor, like the language of literality, builds into a temporal unity whereby diversity is synthesized into patterns of meaning at different horizon levels. Narrative, then, is the wording of the temporal world of the "I" into differing possibilities of self-understanding, a new life plot, which opens up the option of choosing to "do" a reconstruction of the "I" into a newly possible self. At this point of self-awareness, for both Hopkins and Ricoeur, the poetics of the selving individual "I" must move beyond the play of possibility to the action of choice, the ethic of commitment to-be-in-the-world of temporal order at a new horizon of meaning opened up by and through the hermeneutic liberations of imaginative metaphor.

For the "I" to achieve a self-identity reconfigured into a discovery of hope and freedom to possess self-meaning, the subjectivity of the "I" must enter into the conflicts of interpretations of the language of selving. The language of selving is comprised of all the secret internal wordings of the "I" as well as all the wordings the "I" encounters as social discourse, historical discourse, and imaginative discourse, all time-framed in some way, all posing interpretative conflicts, yet all offering mimetic redescriptions of the "I's" experiences, uncovering heuristics as potential self-transformations for creating altered human meanings at different horizons of reality. In phenomenological terms, "selving" is an encounter with "texts" in which the "I" pursues the text from sense to meaning, a "reading" process by which the text's meanings become structured into the consciousness so that the identity of the "I" is reshaped into a new and different self-meaning.

Such a reshaping of the consciousness marks a crossing over from the interpretations of experience as a play of imaginative possibilities, possibility as the playful opening of the "I" to new ways of self-interpretation, to a movement from the poetic consciousness towards the kerygmatic consciousness. In poetry (and by extension all poetic uses of language), conversion takes place in the consciousness as an entering into a figurative world of enriched language from the narrowing word references of literality. Moreover, conversion as kerygma takes place when the creative possibilities of poetic language instill, not only a new vision of selving in the world, but also a capacity on the part of "I" to commit its self-identity to live the disclosing vision actively, that is, to seek communal activation of the commitment, and to attempt to connect all experience to an interpretation of the newly appropriated self-identity. In this way poetic consciousness becomes religious consciousness. Writings that produce this crossover in readers, Ricoeur called "poems of existence" and Hopkins the "poetry of inspiration."

The "word" centeredness of consciousness makes "reading," in the widest application of the term, critical to the selving of the "I." For both Hopkins and Ricoeur, in the deepest sense, subjectivity is a poetic state that, in the time-framed dynamics of the consciousness, operates as a narrative identity. The "I" of the self is "the pupil of all the works of art, works of literature, works of culture which I read, which I loved, which I understood. And therefore, it's a kind of deposit, a treasure of all these experiences" (Valdes 454). Reading begins the long process of self-reflection to create a new interpretation of the selving "I." Taken together, all our readings are in some manner opportunities to arrive at a narrative redescription of the "I" self. Reading, in this hermeneutical sense, is a gradual forging of an altering self-focus in that we learn to take in texts so completely that in a sense we become in and through the texts *the narrator of our own story* without completely becoming the author of our life." We follow the narrative voices of the literal authors so deeply that a transference takes place whereby the "I" variants of figurative consciousness result in a new self-understanding of the "I" selfness The authorial narrator becomes the "I" narrator of the reader's consciousness (*Ricoeur Reader* 437). Such a transference, it must be emphasized, avoids the front-loaded subjective persona of narrator, thus escaping from the potential narcissism of the "I," so common an indulgence in modern literature; rather precisely through the denial of such self-centered narcissism "poems of existence" present the opportunity to escape from self-enchantment to the creation of a new I-self open to reshaping horizons of self-meanings.

The remainder of this chapter is dedicated to my tracing the narrative of consciousness in Hopkins' poetry. I will attempt to put into practice the readership which Ricoeur so powerfully details in his linguistic hermeneutical philosophy. Indeed, many of the benchmarks of my reading approaches will clearly be sponsored by Ricoeur's hermemeutics. (Moreover, inevitably some recapitulation of the "selving" notions discussed in earlier chapters must be made to provide hermeneutic contexts for the readings I am making in this culminating chapter.) I will start reading Hopkins' poetry in the chronology of Norman MacKenzie's definitive Oxford edition. While I group poems which I think are the

center of my reading focus on any one facet of the lyric narrative I am
developing, I will usually concentrate in depth on one or two poems. I
will, now and again, refer to Robert Martin's biography to point out
pertinent biographical contexts; Norman White's new biography, yet to
be fully digested, can be counter-checked for biographical variation by
the reader. Both life-studies offer supplementary biographical evidence
underlying the reading context I am pursuing. As a life-long reader of
Hopkins, the overriding focus of my interpretation will be to describe,
elucidate, and generally share my appropriation of Hopkins' lyric narrative
of his selving consciousness.

Northrop Frye has described the character of such a reading:

> Literature is a technique of meditation, in the widest and most
> flexible sense. We journey through a narrative; then we stop and
> and confront what we have read as though it were objective. It
> is not objective, because it is already a part of ourselves. There
> is a further stage of response, however, where something like a
> journeying movement is resumed, a movement that may well take
> us far beyond the world's end, and yet is not journey (*Words With
> Power* 96).

The Lyric as Selving Consciousness

It is a common literary observation that the appearance of the lyric
form in culture marked the advent of the selving consciousness, a form
that has become more dominant in literary culture as consciousness has
become the subject of imaginative expression. It has been argued that the
modern understanding of self-consciousness began with the introduction
of the the sonnet form, the dominating form in Hopkins' canon.

If it is understood that all selving "wording" is time-framed, which
is to say that the "I" of consciousness narrates itself as a "temporal unity
out of a diversity of characters, events, goals, and causes" (Vanhoozer
89), then it follows that the stories of selving-consciousness are in effect
heuristic fictions. What gives these fictions transforming powers is their
mimetic action as a worded plot which, through figuration, redescribes
reality beyond literality. Mimesis is not a copy of the real but a
redescription of it. Mimesis thus offers possible disclosures of a new
horizon of ordered reality beyond the actual order. Such narrative

disclosures are activated through imaginative language, whatever their literary forms. For all literary forms are metaphorical in their expressive structures, narrated heuristic syntheses of a new sense and meaning of the chaos of raw experience: "It is this synthesis of the heterogeneous that brings narrative close to metaphor" *(Time and Narrative* I, ix).

Mimesis has not been understood as part of the imaginative action of lyric poetry, since its historical applications have been to drama and fiction. Mimesis, in these literary forms, is activated through extended dimensions of objective references underwriting their didactic qualities; however, lyric language is not shorn of selving reference. Lyric forms possess greater capacities for modeling the deeper structuring processing of the consciousness, for while lyric writing does not abandon exterior experience; it does not dwell in its expressiveness on outward forms, but rather concentrates its heuristic modeling on the interior interactions with sensations, feelings, and images in the recreation of the self. As Ricoeur has noted, "What is changed by poetic language is our way of dwelling in the world. From poetry we receive a new way of being in the world. Even if we say with Northrop Frye that poetic discourse gives articulation only to our moods, it is also true that moods as well as feelings have an ontological bearing. Through feeling we find ourselves already located in the world. In this way, by articulating a mood, each poem projects a new way of dwelling. It opens up a new way of being for us" *(Ricoeur Reader* 84-85).

This insight to the selving hermeneutics of the lyric coincides with a new understanding of consciousness in historical culture. Walter Ong has pointed out that the creation of the book took a different turn in the Age of Romanticism. Oratory, "the mover in human affairs," lost its dominance. The growing accumulation of written accounts of "public" knowledge, while heavily increased through the advent of printing, was gradually supplanted by writing that became ever more personal and private: "Books privatized intellectual activity of particulars as oratory once publicized it. In this new climate of privatized study of particulars, it is understandable that the private self should command detailed, analytic attention as never before. Consciousness had taken a new turn" (21).

Not surprisingly, scholars are beginning to be more attentive to the narrative configuration of lyrics in book forms (see Fraistat). Studies are now being made about the ordering of collections of lyrics based upon various critical perspectives—biographical, cultural, political, and esthetic. Implicit in these critical approaches is the notion that a collection of lyrics constitutes a narrative, more or less plotless depending upon the organizer. Devices of progression, recurrence, and sequentiality may dominate or be combined with biographical and / or thematic and figurative associations. Whatever the components, narrative integration is a reading dimension having hermeneutic implications for telling the story of the self (Miner in Freistat 18-44).

These historical and critical approaches have given rise to the hermeneutic concept of "Intertexuality," that is, a way of reading multiple texts as having interplaying meanings. There is a sense in which the term applies to all integrated texts as well.

The notion of"intertextuality," as we have seen, occurs in Ricoeur's hermeneutics, among other places, in his approach to reading the parables in the Gospels. For him the biblical imagination in the Gospels is most fully expressed in their larger intertextual framework, thus producing a"symbolic network." In this view, the parables form a constellation of stories which "intertextually" express the full meaning of the Kingdom of God. However "intertextuality" has another hermeneutic dimension. Readers of the Bible have the task of reconstituting the texts of the Old Testament and the New Testament into the time-frame of their own contemporary consciousness. Parable meaning through the work of the imaginative consciousness is appropriated as the reader's story, a level of intertextuality "where the Bible intersects the 'autobiographical' text or life of the reader, that biblical narrative figures and transfigures the reader's own historicity" (*The Conflict* 384-385; "Biblical Imagination" 65; Vanhoozer 199-204).

For Hopkins the notion of "intertextuality" is implicit in his use of parallelistic language. His use of a range of poetic techniques are all directed to the linguistic expansion of his texts. Indeed, the verbal power in his poetry arises from the terrific tension between the centrifugal intratextual energies in his poems and their centripetal textual energies. Moreover, as a writer of lyrics, Hopkins' poems form an intertextual collection which possesses calendrical, bio-spiritual, and liturgical meaning, if the texts are so recontextualized by the reader. Hopkins himself did not order his collection, as we know. His conviction that poetic creativity could make him liable to lapses into narcissistic egoism, thereby reducing his poetry to levels of ego-babel, however creative its linguistic form, may have inhibited the making of his poetic book. We do know that his conscience was very tender on the matter of his poetry and that he was very casual about the keeping of his poetic texts.

Poetry at its highest creativity is a poetry that recreates the consciousness sunk deeply into root human experience, the redescription of the I-self, the dilemmas of life such as guilt, sacrifice, love, forgiveness, and death, what Ricoeur has called "poems of existence." This is not to say that Hopkins could not have personally ordered his collection and, perhaps in so doing, provided his own intertextual dimensions of meaning. His reading of other poets makes clear that he was fully aware of the enlarging poetic contexts of the book form collection. Editors have from the beginning, I think quite rightly, organized Hopkins' poetry in their estimated chronological order of composition. Such an ordering allies natural time with psychic time out of which avid readers will reconstruct the narrative of Hopkins' poetic consciousness as a "plotted" meaning on the way to recontextualizing the poems into their contemporary situation. The readers' order will inevitably erect a new horizon of poetic meaning in a world of subjective human possibility. Out of this interpretative edifice emerges an heuristic of self-interpretive transformation. Such is the impact of "poems of existence."

Positing the I-Self

The first focus, and indeed the perennial focus, of the narratizing consciousness is the assumption and affirmation of the self. Most of us do this as simple self-enactment: the "I" in its subjectivity acts in and through its nature to become the experience of ourselves. At some point in the time-line of our experience, we more consciously begin to reflect on our I-self as something concrete within us, insistently present, different from anything else, deeply hidden somewhere in the density of our awareness, involved with mixing our thoughts with our feelings, somehow extensive with our bodies and most mysterious of all, bulging with a vast range of remembered past experiences, sometimes quiescent, other times in full intrusive surge.

Most of us endure the "I-ness" that we are without reflectively considering the immense personalizing implications of "selving." However, persons like the poet Hopkins and the philosopher Ricoeur, in their attempts to understand the hermeneutics of the positing of the self, astonish us into the apprehension that the narrative of "selving" is the vital center of self-consciousness. The first and quintessential truth of our self-existence is the positing of our selving "I."

We have seen earlier how Hopkins reflected on his "I-ness" as a plenitude, a "throng and stack of being, so rich, so distinctive," alone and apart from the outside world (*Sermons* 122). And we have noted that for Ricoeur the positing of the self is a thetic judgment which initiates, not psychoanalysis, but rather a process of reflection to recomprehend the "I's" identity as a concrete, living personality (*Conflict* 326-327).

As for most of us, if the story were written down, our early years could be described as discovering, exploring, and locating our selfness. In highly self-conscious personalities, as poets are, such a focus is intense, as was the case for Hopkins. Robert Bernard Martin titled the first chapter of his biography of Hopkins, "The Importance of Being Manley." Hopkins' early years were more reflective on the implications of his "I-ness," than is usual for youth, and later as a mature man, positing his "I-ness" became the center of his reflective attentions. Selving pervades all of his mature spiritual writings and is the empowering persona of all his poetry.

The fullest and most concentrated attention to "I-ness" is in Hopkins'sonnet, 'As kingfishers catch fire, dragonflies draw flame' (115), the poem to which all other poems are for me hermeneutically keyed. In this poem he sorted out his reflections on selving. In the octave, Hopkins, in his typical finely etched images, redescribes things "uttering" themselves. And what is the dynamic of this self-being? Some form of self-utterance: each thing "finds tongue" to assert its unique selfness. While the notion extends the concept of language to all being, it is not too much to say that everything that is has a "language" of self that discloses some feature of the uniqueness of each identity. So kingfisher birds "fire," dragonflies "flame," stones "ring," tucked strings "pitch," swung bells "clank." In everything, animate and inanimate, there is a form of ontic hermeneutic self-disclosure: "Each mortal thing does one thing and the same: / Deals out that being indoors each one dwells." The "I" of things is that "being indoors" where from flows expressions of each distinct nature: "Selves—goes its self; *myself* it speaks and spells, / Crying *What I do is me: for that I came.*"

But there is more to this utterance than self-utterance, it seems to me. The "selving speech" to the perceiver-poet represents more than other unique selves; they exist as participants in a dialectic of being, an exchange of self-utterance whereby difference through the hermeneutic exchange posits more than self-utterance. To the conscious perceiver-poet, the "Selves" uttering become "myself" speaking and spelling, and the cry is more than the cry of the individuality of everything; it is as well the cry of the poet-self "instressing the inscapes" of being. This reading suggests that while Nature is highly individual, all things are isolated in the identity of each selfness, yet in and through self-disclosure, there occurs not only self-assertion, but also some intimation of orders of reality and thus upper horizons of being. This is a besetting problem to the intelligent consciousness, because the cry of self is an authentic form of self-fulfillment. Each cry is one among thousands, hence it is a cry in a pluriverse of cries. In the natural order of things, these cries are finally plaintive, even profoundly sad, in their separating isolation. There is a funereal tone to be heard within the joy of "doing me." If ever there was a difficult turn in a sonnet, there is in this one, for octave closes quite fittingly "crying."

Ricoeur has stressed in his writings about selving the griefs of the "I." He has pointed out that there is an awareness in consciousness of a radical separation between what the "I" somehow was and now is. Time, space, distraction, and "some act of forgetting," well up into the consciousness disconnection: "I am lost, 'astray' among the objects of the world, separated from the center of my own existence, just as I am separated from others and, in some sense, the enemy of all. Whatever may be the secret of this separation, this diaspora, it signifies I do or originally possess that which I am" *(Conflict* 328-329). Out of this seemingly empty "absence from myself," selving reflection struggles to recover the completing "I am" of the lost "I."

The desire and effort to rebuild the "I am" is what Ricoeur calls appropriative reflection, the task of human life. This task is the unspoken middle between the octave and the sestet in Hopkins' famous selving sonnet. In a phenomenological sense, his entire canon is the consciousness-narrative sub-text of the turn in his sonnet. At issue are matters such as the awakening to selving, the awareness of being lost in the dark hole of self, the continuous anxiety of selving, the choice of whether seriously to search for one's true self, the discovery of the stories of hope in the building of the affirmation of the "I am," response to the testimony of hope, and the trial of the descent into the abyss as a journey of freeing hope. All of these elements are parts of the narrative of the selving-I which constitute the consciousness matter as a prologue to the sestet of the 'kingfisher" sonnet. We all are adrift in trying to make this turn.

The frame story for these middle matters, as Hopkins understood them, is the testimony of Creation. For Hopkins the frame story of selving appears at this horizon level of reflective consciousness. Indeed, his famous reflection beginning, "I find myself both as man and as myself something most determined and distinctive" (*Sermons* 122-122), is the cornerstone reflection of all selving. The master question then arises: "From what then do I with all my being and above all that of taste of self, come? Am I due (1) to chance? (2) to myself, as self-existent? (3) to some extrinsic power?" The key insight of this reflection is the meaning of Creation: all things act to purpose; that purpose is transcendental; everything, in its order of being, enacts the intentionality of a universal consciousness. The finest point of the frame story of Creation is the reflecting consciousness itself: "For(1) the universal being too most have its self, its distinctive being, and distinctive more than mine. For if this is what I find myself to have above all other things I see, except only my peers in nature, other men, this self, in its taste to me so distinctive, how much more this greater being" (*Sermons* 126).

On and out of this reflection on self and Creation (I have indicated here only the pattern of an elaborate selving-wording Hopkins made of this reflection), Hopkins derived his insight to the dilemma of the "lost" self, which William Barrett has described so accurately: "For eons of time, the universe existed without me, and will continue to exist for eons after I am gone; and measured now against time, rather than space, I am ever more poignantly aware of the brief finitude of my being. And yet this 'I' that will someday vanish must have for me a reality incomparable with any other. The thought of its finitude provokes me now to an uneasy sense of all my sins and shortcomings, misdeeds and omissions, failings and faintheartedness. And I am moved, once again, and even more intensely to ask, What meaning can this faltering moral existence of mine have? Not the 'meaning of life' as a universal formula, but *my* particular meaning" (*Death of the Soul* 13-14). Hopkins put it, speaking of the creative presence of the Universal Self, "I am compounded only with him and that by no choice of mine; if it is charity in him so to impart himself to all, that is not my case nor my merit either" (*Sermons* 127).

What or who, then, fills the gap between the "lost" self and the affirmed "I am"? How do we get to the first lines of the sestet, "I say more: the just man justices" and make any selving sense of them? Hopkins had, in his reflections of selfness of himself, posited his distinctive individuality, yet in so doing, he affirmed that his selfness is radically limited as to the source of his being, a "positive infinitesimal," still a personality with a nature as a field of selving, in and through which the self decides its destiny. The cunning mystery to this selving is, while the creating Universal Self is absolutely separate from all the selves generated in some way in its image, the issue of how this Master Self influences all self-being, especially those created selves most reflective of its horizon of being—intelligent consciousness. For the latter, in their donated mimetic reflections of the creating Master Self, are free, that is, have a personality at liberty to choose or not to choose to react to this influence, to respond to what is a discoverable pre-determinative disposition in the consciousness towards a transcendental destiny of ultimate self-affirmation. So the existence in which each individual finds him- or herself is a state of becoming, a process of selving fulfillment-seeking, the task of the reflective self, as Ricoeur put it.

This insight of Hopkins is not to say that human selves are defective; rather they are incomplete, the first and fundamental condition of the self. The second condition discoverable in self-reflection is that the self must freely choose to acknowledge its being-dependency upon an ultimate Self and, in this acknowledgement, to seek to-be-in-the-world according to this commitment. Selving, then, is a matter of finding the vital moral field of freedom in the personality whereby one decides one's horizon of destiny. This understanding, then, is the "justice" of self of which Hopkins speaks in the lines, "the just man justices," that is, sees plainly what is at issue in the reconstruction of the I-self—the options within and without the personality, and the horizons of destiny possible within the justice of Creation.

The beckoning "selving" paradigm is that discernment of a coming forth from the Universal Self and a mysterious returning. "What I do is me" is an incredible journey through which the self recovers direction and embarks on an everlasting self-realization. But it should be emphasized that the self must choose to take the trip. This choosing, "doing me," by the reflective consciousness, as the prime task of the self, means interpreting the self in and through the horizon of Creation. Here for both Hopkins and Ricoeur, the needed reflective consciousness must break through the barrier of the natural horizon with the aid of disclosing sacral metaphors to a new plane of awareness where explicitly the narrative of Jesus has vital bearing. Put plainly, the self in some reflective ascent discerns Christ as the perfection of created Nature issuing forth from the perfection of the Universal Self. In this transformation, the "I" glimpses a higher destiny. In virtue of this altered consciousness, appropriating the word / Word as the reflective mode of selving of the conceptual and sensuous soul, makes self-utterance the selving action of the self / soul opened to a new possibility of perfection of the "I am." At the very least there is the generation of a new freeing hope of this possibility. The word for this new selving spontaneity is "grace," that is, selving at this level of reflection "Keeps grace: that keeps all his goings grace" as the sestet declares in its opening lines.

And what is the power of "Grace"? Let us put it in Ricoeurrian terms first. How might Ricoeur interpret "Keeps grace"? In the context of his hermeneutics, "grace" means interpreting the events of sacral experience as an opening to self-deliverance. The capacity of the reflective consciousness to achieve this is a readiness to allow the "sign-events" of sacral experience to become an active reinterpretation of the self, a disposition requiring openness, humility, and submission. The name of this fundamental "grace" consciousness is faith, the trust in allowing the words of sacral experience to function as self-interpretation: "Faith is the attitude of one who accepts being interpreted at the same time that he interprets the world of the text. . . . Hope, unconditional trust, would be empty if it did not rely on a constantly renewed interpretation of sign-events by writings such as the Exodus in the OT and the Resurrection in the NT. These are the events of deliverance which open and disclose the utmost possibilities of my own freedom and thus become for me the the the Word of God" (*Philosophy of Religion* 84-85).

Here is the vital hermeneutic crossover between Hopkins and Ricoeur. For it is through the poetic "selving wording" of the "I" consciousness in the imaginative appropriation of the texts of the Christ-Event in the New Testament that opens up the possibility of the "new self" for Ricoeur, the inspiriting "Word" of God. Hopkins as well explained the breaking of the faith barrier as the action of a critical appropriation of a sacral text of St. Paul: "all those who from the first were known to him, he has destined from the first to be molded into the image of his Son, who is thus to become the eldest-born among many brethren" (Rom. viii, 29-30). Hopkins interpreted this passage as the key sign-event which St. Paul texted in all his own readings of the Christ-Event; "eldest-born" reveals that the first intention of the Creator was his Son, thus Christ's created nature is the active, prototypical pattern of all Creation, and hence Christ encloses all Creation as its finality. All Being will reach completion only in the fulfillment of some order of perfection in the created nature of Christ. (For an analysis of Hopkins' use of Duns Scotus in elucidating and affirming his notions of Creation, the Incarnation, Personality, and Grace, see Christopher Devlin's Appendix II in his edition of the *Sermons*.)

When St. Paul speaks of the Holy Spirit who "reaches our innermost being" (Ephesians iii, 16), Hopkins interpreted him to be speaking of Christ. "Innermost being" is the charge of the Christ-Spirit, the aboriginal mold of Creation, thus the grace of God's creative continuing powers. St. Paul in the same Chapter wrote, "May you be filled with all the completion God has to give" (19).Hopkins interpreted Creation as open-ended; Christ as the ultimate point of Creation's destiny is the active energy of the world of all possible being. To Hopkins this notion was especially applicable to human beings. Every person has an original pre-determination to the destiny of eternity in virtue of Creation, but achieving his destiny involves breaking the barrier that divides the subjectivity of the "I" into discovering the presence of God concretely in the self as the true corresponding identity of the selving "I," bringing the selving consciousness to an awareness horizon of God as the first principle of universal order.

In Ricoeurrian hermeneutic terms, the image of God as the sensible word must fuse with the concept of God as the intellective word, a fusion that becomes the Word. This hermeneutic process is the action of grace, in St. Paul's words the process of "completion," perfection of created nature coming out of uncreated being. But the barrier to the "justice" of Creation can only be broken by grace, freely given to "our innermost being" in virtue of the spirit of Christ, which each self must recognize, interpret, respond to, and testify that infinite being is human destiny. Once the self penetrates the wall of ego-desire and pride of mind, it is opened to be "lifted from one self to another,"as Hopkins put it. He expressed this insight in a figure most sympathetic to Ricoeur's understanding of the "selving" hermeneutic action of metaphor, the "grace" of language empowering the self.

Hopkins' figure for acknowledging the active presence of Christ in everything is "play," which connotes purity, innocence, openness, enjoyment, freedom, and creativity, all attributes of true "play" as the dramatic power to actualize the possibilities of the self. Indeed, In Hopkins' interpretation, Creation is Christ playing, that is, Christ being creatively portrayed in all existents, most especially in human personality. It follows that "selving" fulfillment means completion in and through Christed consciousness. St. Paul wrote: "We are his design; God has created us in Christ Jesus, pledged to such good actions as he has prepared beforehand, to be the employment of our lives" (Ephesians ii, 10). The "design" of Creation, as Hopkins interpreted St. Paul in the last line of his sonnet, is the preeminent actualizing sign for selving the "I": "For Christ plays in ten thousand places, / Lovely in limbs, and lovely in eyes not his / To the Father through the features of men's faces."

Such Christ "play," according to Hopkins, is the role humans must counter-play when they recognize the "justice" of Creation, for "the just man . . . / Acts in God's eye what in God's eye he is— / Christ. An explication of this line is in a prose passage in Hopkins' *Sermons*: grace is an activity on God's part, "divine stress, holy spirit, and, as all is done through Christ, Christ's spirit." The word / Word barrier, once crossed, becomes correspondence, "*actio salutaris*" from the human side, "in *esse quieto*" on Christ's. "It is as if a man said, That is Christ playing at me and me playing Christ, only that is no play but truth; That is Christ *being me* and me being Christ" (*Sermons* 154).

Selving in the Waste Land

As we have seen, for both the poet and philosopher, affirming the self is the central act of human existence; for both, there are structural barriers in the self's reaching beyond the horizon of naturality; for both, interpretation of historical, biographical, and sacral texts—the narrative of life—are the doors through which self-reflection must pass in recovering the "I am" through poetic reconfigurations of the self. For both, such reconfigurative self- reconstructions involve denying the narcissistic tendencies of the egoistic "I" in the full recognition that positing the self requires an external, constitutive, selving force, to which for both, there must be an opening within the self in finding and responding to the disclosed, newly possible, realizable ways to-be-in-the-world. And finally for both, the selving testimony of the Christ-Event is the prime sacral figuration which brings forth an empowering selving passion for a transforming self-realization.

If these statements are truly accurate expressions of the meanings of the texts of Ricoeur and Hopkins, what is their significance for me as a reader interpreter? I am first struck by the depth of self-reflection both authors convey through their writings, as I am impressed that their writings attempt to account for a real process that the consciousness undertakes. Each of us, however layered with the sediment of experience, is searching for an "I" affirmation in our selving. In this task, it is hard not to find one's own interiority shallow in comparison with their accounts. Yet encountering their texts sponsors much self-reflection on the character and process of one's own reflections. I find myself as reader paralleling the narrative of my selving with theirs. Remembering that their understanding of selving is the result of long, reflective distillations of the process helps with any sense of personal deficiency, while confidence in their phenomenological integrity is very strong.

In addition to the mentoring factor of integrity, there are other notable responses to reading Hopkins and Ricoeur, some contextual and some textual. On the contextual side, when one surveys the general contents of one's lifelong reading, especially for any person whose whole life has been dedicated to reading, how striking it is that so much writing, whatever the literary form, is so focussed on the self. Yet looking at these writings as a "selving"heuristic, we find much of the world's literature is limited to the horizon of the temporary and the pragmatic. I speak here of those writings which have primarily social, political, and ideological focuses. Reading such works which place such a heavy redescriptive emphasis on the naturalistic and cultural barriers to fulfilling self-identity underscores what Ricoeur has called the psychology of "suspicion" in human selving. Thematically, this is often the literature of hopelessness and servitude which forms a major canon in the world's literature. Reading such texts is to hear the story over and over again of the lost self.

Reading Hopkins and Ricoeur contextually in their cultural and literary milieus, we find the advent of selving consciousness very prominent in much artistic, humanistic, and sociological writings. Indeed "selving" in the sense of consciousness focus is the leading subject of most literary writing and much humanistic literature; such a focus has been especially strong for the past two centuries. Yet an inventory of reading responses to these writings finds decreasingly the advocacy of "selving" as a transcendent experience and increasingly the denigration of transforming personal selving. In the nineteenth century, the cultural seedbed of Modernism, the central importance of consciousness was located, only to see it anatomized into states of dislocation in the ensuing century under the headings of materialist idealism, scientific positivism, compromising pragmatism, and "no exit" existentialism. The subject of selving in modern culture is a grandly ironical one; by and large the direction of contemporary literate culture is to make its central subject disappear. It is not too much to say that modern literature is an heuristic of the disappearing self, what William Barrett has called the "death of the soul." To read William Wordsworth as the beginning of poetic literature of consciousness and Samuel Beckett as the endgame of consciousness is to see the sweeping boomeranging irony of the subject of selving in modern culture.

Of course, the weight of so much reading denying the possibility of transforming interiority is compounded by a greater and greater emphasis upon the sensate in culture, a phenomenon made world-wide through the advent of electronic media. This predicament has been largely underwritten in literate Modernist culture as behaviorist psychology, situational sociology, analytic philosophy, ideological history, and the reductionism of the literary imagination. Hopkins and Ricoeur, by contrast, come off as the true revolutionaries, that is, writers who assert with philosophical and poetic power the value and effort on the part of the self to affirm the hermeneutic path of self-consciousness that leads to new horizons of selving possibility. Both writers acknowledge that actual and central to becoming a full human being is a baseline spiritual factor in the selving consciousness: one cannot know oneself in any existential depth, nor can one take stock of one's place in the universe, without encountering the transforming reality of spiritual inspiration. According to Hopkins and Ricoeur, only the magnet of religious consciousness can arrest the spiritual dispersion that is disintegrating self and society in contemporary culture. There is therefore an envisionary challenge in reading Hopkins and Ricoeur, perhaps involving a recovery of the originary task of the foundation of Modernism— the Romantic search for transcendence. Hopkins acknowledged this in his remark to R. W. Dixon about Wordsworth's "Intimations Ode" in which the poet "saw something" that shocks us into a apprehension that causes us to tremble (*Letters to Dixon* 147-148).

The Search For Self

We have now some understanding of what is meant by the "achieved self." And we have some insight into the general phenomenological and hermeneutic activity that goes into the positing of the achieved self as the process has been explored by G. M. Hopkins and Paul Ricoeur. I think we are now ready to lay out what might be called the selving narrative pattern evident in the poetry of Hopkins. Since it is in poetic language that selving figurations are optimally revealed, I will be limiting my readings to the selving signs in Hopkins' poetry. Such an undertaking will both illustrate the phases of self-reflection which Ricoeur in his various writings has examined with such penetration as well as provide a poetic "objective correlative" to his philosophical hermeneutic of the imaginative consciousness. Reading Hopkins' poetry as a continuous lyric of the narrative of his selving will reveal that his poetry was indeed one of the elemental means through which he reconfigured his "I" into the selfness that he was to become. No critic has to my knowledge ever practically applied Ricoeur's hermeneutical notions to the reading of a major poet, nor has any critic read Hopkins' poetry as a selving hermeneutic.

Such an undertaking for an entire poetic canon, even one as limited as Hopkins', inevitably must be shortened. I can only lay out the pattern in his phase of selving by grouping some of the poems within each phase and discussing one or two in any depth. I also realize that some poems express more than one selving phase, and thus fitting these into one part of the narrative is arbitrary. In general, I want to gratefully acknowledge that I have followed the chronology of Norman MacKenzie's distinguished Clarendon edition of the poetry as have I made much use of his enriching commentary. What I have done is to provide a paradigm of the hermeneutics of selving in Hopkins' poetry as a supplementary commentary.

This initializing phase of selving begins in a kind of phenomenological darkness. Gradually as we emerge out of babyhood, we begin to recognize the persistent though elusive "I" that we are. And as well, we begin to encounter the layers of awareness within which the "I" abides. All of selfness is, of course, very dim, spasmodically encountered, and for the most part opaque to any continuous reflection on our part. Yet we increasingly begin to feel the self-concerns of the "I." In this self-concern, our selving begins. For most of us this initiating phase of selving is like walking down a nearly darkened path, a journey we remember more like a dream than an actuality. At some point, as we begin to self-reflect, we try to retrace the path of self awakening. The "I" self seems to become an identifiable power in the self-consciouosness Ricoeur as well begins his hermeneutic phenomenology of the self with sensing the object. We enter the levels of "selving" discourse—poetic, conceptual, and reflective— "by receiving it and determining it [the object]. Upon the thing it [he reflective self] apprehends the power of synthesis" (*Fallible Man* 28; Klemm 54, 159). "Selving" begins to happen consciously.

For Hopkins, a poet by nature, retracing his "selving" is particularly discernible in his earliest poetry. Looking at this juvenal poetry, we see several elements of his reflection. The first is his astonishment about the play of his senses. We see this in all his early poems. His youthful poem, "The Escorial" (1), for example, while written as an exhibition poem and thus full of skillful imitative poetic artifacts, nevertheless, exults in paralleling words with sensations, even as in this case, bookish ones:

No finish'd proof was this of Gothic grace
With flowing tracery engemming rays
Of colour in high casements face to face;
And foliag'd crownals (pointing how the ways
Of art best follow nature) in a maze
Of finish'd diapers, that fills the eye
And scarcely traces where one beauty strays
And melts amidst another . . .
This was no classic temple order'd round
With massy pillars of the Doric mood
Broad-fluted, nor with shafts acanthus-crown'd,
Pourtray'd along the frieze with Titan's brood
That battled Gods for heaven . . .

The same impulse of the awakening senses is notable in another
teenage poem, "A Vision of the Mermaids" (6), in which Hopkins
luxuriates in poeticizing the lushness of the senses in his depiction of the
mermaids :

Soon—as when Summer of his sister Spring
Crushes and tears the rare enjewelling,
And boasting 'I have fairer things than these'
Plashes amidst the billowy apple-trees
His lusty hands, in gust of scented wind
Swirling out bloom till all the air is blind
With rosy foam . . . a crowd
Of filmy globes and rosy floating cloud:—
So those Mermaids crowded to my rock . . .

Yet, even at this tender age, a new element enters into his selving
sensations, the element of transience:

And a sweet sadness dwelt on everyone;
I knew not why,—whether that they ring the knells
Of seaman whelm'd in chasms of the mid-main
As poets sing; or that it is a pain
To know the dusk depths of the ponderous sea . . .
I know the sadness but the cause know not.

The "Siren" song of the mermaids is the poetic figure of the desiring, dreaming "I," yearning for comprehension of a new song of self.

Even in poems such as "Winter with the Gulf Stream" (7), ostensibly a straight Nature poem about winter's expected harshness being abated, it was thought, by some a beneficent relieving river flowing in the tumult of the icy ocean, expresses melancholy. The dreariness of winter rains drench all around—hoarse leaves, choking brooks, and the "weak notes" of wet birds. The teenage poet feels mainly misery. Later the college student, in trying a scene for a romance, feels the torpor of things trying to find selving voice: "O what a silence is this wilderness" (65)!

With the passage of time, the awakening consciousness takes on more definition; reflection begins to feel its selving powers: "in my degree / I prove it." The youthful poet begins to acknowledge that the consciousness has limited powers of "fixing" beauty internally in "uncharted" memory, or externally in vanishing esthetic forms (painting or poetry), whether the beauty of things or persons: "Confirmed beauty will not bear a stress / Bright hues long look'd at thin, dissolve and fly . . . / The sweetest sonnet five or six times read / is tasteless nothing . . . . " (58). This plaintive note of sadness begins early in Hopkins' consciousness and grows throughout his lifetime. For so young a man, his self-reflections on his states of acedia are very intense: "See how Spring opens with disabling cold, / And hunting winds and the long-lying snow. / Is it a wonder if the buds are slow" (62)? Nature's hard tardiness has its counterpart in the consciousness, a blocked threshold to his own transformation (maybe Hopkins' conversion to Catholicism; see MacKenzie 276): "Therefore how bitter, and learnt late, the truth!"

If the universe of the Other is a mystery, then moreso is the "I" of the self. As a university student, this awareness of the enigma of perception becomes a very powerful self-reflection for Hopkins. There is a strongly felt sense that the "I" of the self is in charge, has strong powers (74): "The earth and Heaven, so little known, /Are measured outwards from my breast. / I am the midst of every zone / And justify the East and West." Yet there is a motion in all things which confronts the measuring consciousness both as the "lovely ease in change of place," and the uncertain stability of the apprehending "I":

> The unchanging register of change
> My all-accepting fix'd eye,
> While all things else may stir and range,
> All else may whirl or dive or fly.

The mystery of the selving "I" occurs in one of Hopkins' earliest extant poems (3), "Il Mystico." A youthful, longish poem (142 lines), in imitation of John Milton's "Il Penseroso," the beginning poet ruminates over rumination, using the figure of the rainbow as the figure for the upper horizon of the reflecting consciousness. The rainbow beckons for a search for a deeper meaning to the senses through the elevation of the reflecting consciousness to a contemplative state, portending Hopkins' later development of his understanding of the "instress" of being as a deeply interiorizing energy of the "I" to take in the deepest structure of things, what he called their "inscapes":

> My spirit hath a birth . . .
>
> Touch me and purify, and shew
> Some of the secrets I would know
>
>   Or, like a lark to glide aloof
> Under the cloud-festooned roof,
> That with a turning of the wings
> Light and darkness from him flings;
> To drift in air, the circled earth
> Spreading still its sunned girth;
> To hear the sheep-bells dimly die
> Till the lifted clouds were nigh,
> In breezy belts of upper air
> Melting into aether rare;
> And when the silent heights were won,
> And all in lone air stood the sun,
> To sing scarce heard, and singing fill
> The airy empire at his will; . . .
>
> Then may I upwards gaze and see
>   The deepening intensity
> Of air-blended diadem,
> All a sevenfold-single gem,
> Each hue so rarely wrought that where
> It melts, new lights arise as fair,
> Sapphire, jacinth, chrysolite
> The rim with ruby fringes dight,
> Ending in sweet uncertainty
> "Twixt real hue and phantasy. . .

That I may drink that ecstasy
Which to pure souls alone may be.

We must also remember that Hopkins' earliest diaries are filled with
these aspirations. There are hundreds of entries wherein he tries to look
on Nature with the freshest of perceptions and attempts to utter his sense
experiences in the most paralleled of wordings his creative powers
possessed, perceptive and linguistic powers, it might be added, which
were prodigiously expressive.

For all his strong aspirations to "gaze and see / The deepening
intensity / Of the air-blended diadem . . . / That I may drink that
ecstasy / Which to pure souls alone may be," he early on recognized
limitations in his selving consciousness. Why would the senses not hold?
Could not the lamp of self hold back the dark? The self increasingly
seemed a tangle tying the beholder and the beheld in mysterious knot of
subjectivity and apprehension: "The rainbow shines, but only in the
thought / Of him who looks. Yet not in that alone, / For who makes
rainbows by invention?" Everyone selves the world individually: "And
many standing around a waterfall / See one bow each, yet not the same to
all, / But each a hand's breadth further than the next." Sensation is a part
of objectivity and subjectivity. Here Hopkins, at a very young age,
recognizes selving involves interpretation: "The sun on the falling waters
writes the text / Which yet is in the eye or in the thought." From this
existential predicament of the self, he must acknowledge "It is a hard
thing to undo this knot" (24). If one is to posit the self as actualizable in
the real world, then the interpretative "knot" must be untied. This dilemma
sets up the theater of the mind-battle in the self, the conflict of
interpretations.

The conflict within the self is fronted by many self-denying forces.
The first, the most threatening, is the death of the self. Hopkins, even as
a high school boy, felt the threat of a dark ending just as his life was
urgently moving forward in the spring of his youth: "I had a dream. A
wondrous thing: / It seem'd an evening in the spring /—A little sickness
in the air / From too much fragrance everywhere:— /As I walk'd a stilly
wood, / Sudden, Death before me stood: . . . / 'Death' said I, 'what do
you here / At this Spring season of the year?' / 'I mark the flowers ere the
prime / Which I may tell at Autumn time.' "(8) The figure of Death is a
regular companion in the journey of Hopkins' selving poetic
consciousness, sometimes expressed as mockery as in his satires of tomb
epitaphs (28 and *Notebooks* 38). The shadow of Death could be seen in
the over-elaborate shows of grief in Victorian funerals: "Why should their

foolish bands, their hopeless hearse / Blot the perpetual festival of the day?/ Ravens, for prosperously-boded curses / Returning thanks, might offer such array" (22).

The death anxiety within the subjective consciousness is a tracer shooting though the entire Hopkins canon. Early poems such as, "I hear a noise of waters drawn away" (49), and "Summer Malison" (51), are precursors of more mature expressions of the death specter in the self, poems now well-known for their powerful expressions of the subject: "The Wreck of the Deutschland, Part The Second" (101), "The Loss of the Eurydice" (125), "Felix Randal" (142), "Spring and Fall" (144), and "On the Portrait of Two Beautiful Young People" (168). I have not listed all the poems Hopkins wrote which touch or center on death as sacrifice, poems which call up the fact and ritual of death in the Passion of Christ, surely the most elaborate treatment of the subject of death in the entire Hopkins canon. My interest here has been to see the subject of death as an early, then perennial, element in the positing of the self, that naked anxiety gnawing at the selving "I" in all of its searching subjectivity, what Hopkins expressed as the consuming darkness shrouding the self in, "The Lantern out of doors" (113): "Men go by me . . . / Death or distance soon consumes them: wind, / What most I eye after, be in at the end / I cannot, and out of sight is out of mind."

Death is the shadowing backdrop, then, in front of which the search to achieve the fullness of the "I-self" goes on. The story of this search, so evident in Hopkins' writing, has notable episodes of "selving" consciousness. One, of course, is the motive of the arduous task of selving: "I must hunt down the prize / where my heart lists. / Must see the eagle's bulk, render'd in mists, / Hang of a treble size." The climb up the mountain peak into the mists to get beyond the shadow-self is the task of the ascent into full selfness. In the face of such a life-long task, the self often wearies and asks surcease, the very theme of one of Hopkins' most successful youthful poems,"Heaven-Haven" (20): "I have desired to go / Where springs not fail, / To fields where flies no sharp or sided hail / And a few lilies blow."

Self-reflection of the kind which searches at the horizons of the self is costly in terms of absorbing all the human faculties. All too often, the self loses drive to come to its true destiny: "Trees by their yield / Are known; but I— / My sap is sealed, / My root is dry" (69). Such energy-less states often give over to episodic feelings of being betrayed or lost. Friends disappear, "Where are thou friend, whom I shall never see" (57, perhaps written over the death of Digby Dolben, see Martin Ch. V). The same spirit is discernible in the feigning poem of unrequited love: "What have I come across / That here will serve me for comparison? / The skeptic disappointment and the loss / A boy feels when the poet he pores upon / Grows less and less sweet to him and knows no cause" (59).

Lost in space and time, the self wanders about in a meaningless, indifferent universe. Whatever the dramatic context of the following passage (31), and whoever is speaking, the episode of expressed consciousness is clear; this is the voice of the forlorn self: "I am like a slip of comet, / Scarce worth discovery, in some corner seen / Bridging the slender difference of two stars, / Come out of space, or suddenly engerder'd / By heady element, for no man knows."

Frequently the next episode of consciousness is one of alienation. Just as feeling lost seems to never abate altogether in the self, neither does alienation. We see it early and late in Hopkins' writing. In a longish early poem (10) entitled, "Pilate," young Hopkins attempted to reflect imaginatively on the consciousness of Pilate's alienation after his betrayal of Christ, perhaps an archetype of human disconnection. The best and most introspective early poem on the spirit of self-desolation is "The Alchemist in the city" (60), a poem which draws on a long tradition of cultural reflection on the journey to attain the ultimate truths of existence along with the powerful fruits of such knowledge. Perhaps for the first time, Hopkins, who possessed the strongest sense of the possibilities of his own creative, expressive powers, envisaged the possibility that he might fail. And as we know, this specter of self-alienation was to become a frightful depth-charge to his selving, leaving him with the impotent "I" he later called "time's eunuch." The alchemist is an excellent figure for the search for the "real gold" of the self. (Writers have employed the alchemist figure time and again to voice the desperations encountered in the narrative of selving, in Hopkins' time the most notable being Robert Browning's "Paracelsus.") In his poetic rumination, Hopkins centers on the alchemist's creative failures, his loss of inspiration, and his resultant retreat to the margins of existence as an alien. Yet in the deep recesses of his consciousness, he finds hidden his original desire to transform and be transformed: "I mark the tower swallows run / Between the tower-top and the ground / Below me in the bearing air; / Then find in the horizon-round / One spot and hunger to be there.? / And then I hate the most that lore / That holds no promise of success." He is left, isolated, haunted, but still looking: "There on a long and squar'd height / After the sunset I would lie, / And pierce the yellow waxen light / With free long looking, ere I die."

It is not far from this episode of consciousness to a state of guilt. Surely one of the most powerful negative states of "I"-ness" is the consideration that the "I" is in some way evil. How can it be, the "I" of the self asks, that such deep awarenesses of being lost, incomplete, alienated, and exiled, states that swarm out of the backdrop of mortality, are not the result of some aboriginal calamity which has engulfed the self? Not surprisingly, Hopkins felt the burden of this question very early in his selving development. Moreover, such an issue comes to the forefront, not just as an internal dilemma, but also wrapped in the enigma of history, cosmic culture, and one's own deep sense of imperfection.For this reason, the self is baffled on many levels of self-reflection. Evil comes to be known directly, personally, and devastatingly.

Not always, and certainly not for everyone, what we call religious consciousness may become the formula by which consciousness tries to understand evil—cosmic, natural, and personal. As we have seen, both Hopkins and Ricoeur address this problem formally in their writings. Ricoeur is eloquent in his explanation of the way symbols are read in Nature, that first and elemental human sense of sacredness in the world. These insights are followed by the making of cosmic symbols into myths, hermeneutically, the building of a narrative interfusing natural and human signs, the time-frame of existence. Out of the phenomenology of myth the human consciousness raises the issue of the self before the sacred. The experience of evil results in this confrontation from which follows a sense of "fallenness," feelings which eventually encompass the experience of fault. External defilement becomes the guilty language of sin, the subject of the Garden of Eden story.

Hopkins, reflecting on the theological implications of the narrative of transgression in the Bible, interestingly interpreted the story of Lucifer as a destructive selving. Lucifer, the highest selved among the angels, becomes Satan because of his failure to accept his angelic status as second in rank to the Son of God. Hopkins, as we have seen, narrated Lucifer's story as the spiritual symbolization of willingly rebelling against God's extrinsic and intrinsic order of Creation, thereby becoming the serpent, Satan, the external cosmic principle of evil and the internal principle of sin. In this understanding of existential defilement, Hopkins and Ricoeur come together, for both explicate the self-reflexive symbols of fault in the self in light of communal complicity in the despoiling of the sacred order. And both see the narrative of the consciousness of fault as the origin of personal guilt, the impulse to confession, atonement, and forgiveness in the self. "These are the elements out of which religious consciousness in the self is constructed. Here cosmos and psyche come together: I express myself in expressing the world; I explore my own sacrality in deciphering that of the world" *(Symbolism of Evil* 18). Religious consciousness is not some rationalist or scientific analysis of the world, but selving experience to the horizon of the eternal, a selving that opens the self to transformation beyond the rot of the world.

The phenomenological complex that is the consciousness of fault is very evident in the poetic narration of the building of Hopkins' religious consciousness. As a very young man, he imaginatively explored the consciousness of religious denial in his depiction of "one of the spies left in the wilderness" (12), in the form of a soliloquy. The spy bespeaks the spirit of hard heartedness against God and Moses as recounted in the biblical Book of Numbers. As one of the spies who had lost the spiritual courage to seek the Promised Land and was left to die in the desert, he laments: "Go then: I am contented here to lie . . . / I sicken, I know not why. / And faint as tho' to die." Young Hopkins was clearly reflecting on spiritual courage.

Such courage is harder to maintain in the direct experience of personal fault. In a university poem, "Myself unholy" (61), Hopkins' consciousness has moved very considerably beyond external textual meditations. Here the experience of guilt is manifest, an early instance which viewed in context of his whole life seems excessive: "Myself unholy, from myself unholy / To the sweet living of my friends I look—." The poet's own expressibility seems distraught in this very imperfect poem. However, the tone of the self-revelation of guilt is strong and unmitigating. Notable also is the context of poems like this one. Hopkins was going to confession, keeping lists of his sins, and confiding to his diary his deep scrupulosity about his moral integrity. Such recurrent feelings of fault frequently cast him down into a deep melancholy which lasted all his life, a melancholy which surfaced frequently in his letters and even more intensely in private diaries and poems, especially his last so-called "dark sonnets" (Gerald Roberts 97-109). One of his first voicings occurs in "Myself unholy": "And they are purer, but alas! not solely / The unquestion'd readings of a blotless book. / And so my trust confusedly is shook / Yields to the sultry siege of melancholy. / He has a sin of mine, he its near brother; / Knowing them well I can but see the fall. . . / This fault in one I found, that in another: / And so, tho' each have one while I have all . . . ." In and through his own fault, he sees the complicity of universal human fault.

Such guilty reflections, if dwelt upon in all seriousness, become central to the mind-battle of "selving." How can the self find in its acts and works any purity as an "I am," if the self finds itself trapped in the personality of external fault and internal sin? Is there help anywhere? The "knot" of consciousness becomes even a harder thing to undo. If such experiences of fault generate reflections beyond the finiitude of the human horizon, then new voicings for help and understanding may happen, but not always fruitfully. A good example of what might be called an early mind-battle poem is "My prayers must meet a brazen heaven" (67).In this poem Hopkins declares that the penitential wordings of his plaintive spiritual aspirations lack connection. The horizon of heaven is felt as a metal battleworks deflecting the arrows of prayer that are sent to soar as pleas for some castle-master's help for forgiveness:

> My prayer must meet a brazen heaven
> And fail and scatter all away.
> Unclean and seeming unforgiven
> My prayers I scarcely call to pray.
> I cannot buoy my heart above;
> Above I cannot entrance win.
> I reckon precedents of love,
> But feel the long success of sin.

The images of battle are stressed in the second stanza, the brass of heaven and the iron of earth, which are intermixed with the self. Hopkins senses in the poem a kind of metal curtain which hangs between himself and any forgiving understanding beyond himself. The result is the experience of an existential hardening which seems to doom him: "Nor tears, nor tears this clay uncouth / Could mold, if any tears there were." Prayer is selving wording of the sacred. In expressing the self, the "I" hopes to find a new, purified consciousness for its "I am." Sacral uttering, then, is crucial to the reflections on the feelings of fault in the self. However, prayer can arise from the self only from the spiritual seed of self-transformation which is called hope. Until then, there is no relief from the mind-battle: "A warfare of my lips in truth, / Battling with God is now my prayer." The issue here is fundamental: Dare I express myself as forgivable before the powers-that-be? Can I mold myself and / or can I be molded from above? This poem looks ahead to those powerful passages of self-deprecations in the prose ("For if you are in sin you are God's enemy . . . "(*Sermons* 240), and those depreciative metaphors in the last poems such as the "rack" of guilt in "Spelt from Sibyl's Leaves"

(167), "Where, selfrung, selfstrung, sheathe—and shelterless, thoughts against thoughts in groans grind."

Hopkins' lyric narrative of selving, only a part of which have I reproduced, epitomizes the story of selving that Ricoeur elucidates in his hermeneutic philosophy. Here we find the throngs of feelings of being lost, of being alienated, even exiled, and finally, pangs of guilt, all hamstringing the self in divergent states of disconsolation. Such feelings, in the selving process, become words expressing the fractured self, words that are paralleled to the equivalent tragic-fated cosmic symbols of universal order, words that conjoin with the cultural words of myth retelling of origins, betrayals, transgressions, and defeat in the tragic drama of humanity. Such are the self-reflections at this stage of the positing of each individual self. It needs only to be added that the number of those human beings who remain "selfstrung" at this stage of selving their "I am" is incalculable, a human deficit which makes evident why the world is so full of human misery. However, sometimes it is from the pit of such self-reflection that each of us is brought to the recognition that hope and freedom depend upon our responding to those horizon mountain calls for recasting the self out of the elusiveness of the guilty narcissistic "I" to the new possibility of a transformed personality.

Finding the Passion for the Possible: Conversion

We now come to the next phase of selving, a phase that is central to the task of positing one's self. The building of the "I" self involves interpreting the "texts" of our lives in the context of the horizons of the universe, of human culture, and destiny. In effect, each of us builds in the consciousness a redescription of each of these narrative levels, more or less complete, nevertheless, a composite narration which offers to us the opportunities to reinterpret our selfness in these several narrative contexts and thus put our self-meaning, self-worth, and self-identity into a new existential place in our lives. Religious selving is a prime element of reconstructing consciousness. Such a consciousness, I must emphasize, is not the doctrinal consciousness, not the conceptual consciousness, not the constitutional consciousness. These states of awareness are the refining intellectual and communal configurations of consciousness that grow out of the shaping of the internal refigurations of selving the religious consciousness. This insight into religious subjectivity has been all but

lost at times in the secularlization of knowledge since the post-
Reformational era in the Christian West, a misunderstanding that is a
seismic crack in assessing the revisionary movements of all the world's
historical religious sects. The private horizon of interiority in the religious
self is often passed over by traditional religious institutions for intellectual
correctness, continuity of ritual, and institutional integrity. While these
are legitimate concerns of any religious culture, they are secondary to the
depth and breadth of interior spiritual passion for self-transformation.
The central question in any religious system is how can the individual "I"
self be reinterpreted, "converted" to a new horizon of selfness though the
personal spiritual ministrations of selving ?

For both Hopkins and Ricoeur, this question is the central issue in
the formation of personal religious culture. The world's writings are replete
with conversion stories. Central to every one is the issue of the converting
force which surcharged the self. The conversion state of consciousness
can be described as a conflation of experiences which reconstitutes the
self into a new self-possessed interiority. While the whole spectrum of
human faculties plays a part in this selving refiguration, both Hopkins
and Ricoeur, as we have seen, designate the imagination as main driving
psychic energy which represents reality in a new order of relationships,
an order that is expressed basically in a metaphorical frame. The
proximate horizon of literality is placed in sharp encounter with a remote
horizon of super-reality reorganized in a newly different, strongly
contrastive, but possible alignment of the order of the universe. The
expressed contrast sets at odds common sense and absurdist sense, a
tension that twists "what if" into possible reality and, hence, opens up the
consciousness to a transforming assent to change (convert) the self in
accordance to the meanings of this grasp of a new being-order.

The focus upon the imagination as the converting figurative
empowerment makes the linguistic mode of consciousness central to
achieving a changed selfness. More particularly, it is the poetic expressive
consciousness, in the broadest sense of the term poetic, which utters with
passion, through suasive semantic innovations, the world as a new
creation, thereby abolishing literal meaning and its sub-set of reference
and, in its place, positing a new level of meaning with a new sub-set of
reference. The self can now reinterpret its "I"-ness in accord with a
mode of being at a higher horizon level. From this perspective, self in the
natural world of experience is radically altered as to its interactions,
understanding, and self-reflections. Conversion, in it most general
phenomenological sense, comes down to reordering self-reflection
interiorly in positing the self and choosing to exteriorize this new inner

order of self-understanding in concordant behavioral acts. Conversion, then, is expressed through the "language" of the imagination which utters a newly selving transcendent order which is called religious consciousness. If we are to trace religious self-transformation, we must follow the path of poetic expression by and through which the self rebirths the "I" to follow a different self-destiny.

Poetry, as existential utterance, is the language of self-processing transformation. If we look at Hopkins' conversion poetry, we see some patterns of self-change which his poetry demarks. The first pattern is that of probing the discontented self to locate images and figures which offer new self-possibility. I see him exploring new self-meanings in his endless list of metaphors for his observations of Nature in his *Notebooks*, specially his many uses of star imagery, even when he was not writing about stars literally. And his early youthful Christian poems reveal similarly a going beyond any received biblical meaning, poems such as "Barnfloor and Winepress" (17), "New Readings" (18), and "He hath abolish'd the old drouth" (19). In these writings, Hopkins was interacting with the traditional language of religious consciousness, playing with his own poetical interpretation of biblical language. For Hopkins, raised as an Anglican (we must remember that much of Hopkins' religious selving has Anglican roots), conversion to Christianize himself gradually came to mean for him authenticating the meaning of the Holy Eucharist in the historical tradition of the Western Christian Church. While this dogma was his "outside" self-concern, inside was his need to find the passion for his self-realization of being in the world in accord with the selving vision of his own individualized Christian self-meaning. My concern is the "inside" pattern of conversion that I am sketching out (See Martin 116-155 and White 139-145 for recent biographical versions).

The second pattern of conversion, what I am calling "internal assent," is consenting to the possibility of a pervasive hope to achieve a transmortal destiny. Here again, we find in the early poetry Hopkins exploring what the self-transformation of his conversion might mean. Poems such as "A Voice from the World" (38), "Boughs pruned" (48), and "Let me be to Thee" (70), explore the nature of change in the self which Christian religious consciousness brings about. The latter poem, for example, records the visionary aspect of the horizon of religious consciousness invoked by the poetic image of flying: "Let me be to Thee as the circling bird, / Or bat with tender and air-crisping wings / That shapes in half-light his departing rings." In the second stanza the poet focuses upon the inner changes involved in the "I" self of religious consciousness, the new shaping of reality expressed as a figure of music wherein the beat, the

tones and chording (a dominant that resolves a minor) utters a new song
of the self:

> The authentic cadence was discovered late
> Which ends those only strains that I approve
> And other science all gone out of date
> And minor sweetness scarce made mention of:
> I have found the dominant of my range and state—
> Love, O My God, to call Thee Love and Love.

There are also icon poems in this pattern, reflections on saints whose
lives expressed hagiographically Christian religious consciousness at a
very high heuristic level of transformation. These poems explore as well
what might be called the mystery of such consciousness. The poet
redescribed the received imagery of such star-religious consciousnesses
with more than awe and reverence; he was engaged in parsing the religious
language of sainthood to find the self-passion for his own transforming
possibility. Such poems are "For a Picture of Saint Dorothea" (42), "The
Queen's Crowning" (46), and "St. Thecla" (52). The last poem is a good
example of the hermeneutics of religious consciousness as Hopkins
expressed it. He pictured Thecla sitting on a housetop listening to St.
Paul preaching: "Firm accents strike her fine and scroll'ed ear, /A man's
voice and a new voice speaking near." She heard from Paul of God and
the story of Christ, His son; then came those words which somehow altered
her self-meaning and charged her with a new passion: "But most (it seemed
his sense) / He praised the lovely lot of continence: / All over, some such
words as these, though dark, / *The world was saved by virgins*, made the
mark." The poet admits the opaqueness of the converting words, nor
does he try to plumb meaning out of the tensional absurdity of the lines .
He simply acknowledges that this utterance opened up a new sense of the
world, one that converted Thecla's self utterly. The narrative of Ikon
religious consciousness, of course, depicts religious constancy, a static
heuristic to inspire, confirm, and bolster the self in its life-long trans-
formational ascents to higher religious consciousness. Such was the case
for Hopkins as is evident in his later religious poems about the Blessed
Virgin, St. Winefred, Margaret Clitheroe, and St. Alphonsus Rodriguez.
In each of these poems, the poet tried to redescribe the distinctive attributes
of the exemplar religious consciousness of each saint, looking towards a
dispensing spiritual meaning that might become the elevating grace of
his conversion reflections.

The culminating phase of conversion is that of full "selving" assent. The self, now enlightened and strengthened, risks a reconfiguration of the "I" at a new level of self-being. The mediation of such profound internal affirmations is critical, yet in their detail are almost mysterious, even to the convert. One day, it seems, take C. S. Lewis, for example, after getting off a bus, he felt a change in himself, which, upon some self-scrutiny, he realized that he had been converted to Christianity. It just happened in such a casual way, but he knew then his life was changed forever. And it was. We have many poems written in the time-frame of Hopkins' conversion, none of which can with any confidence be called the "conversion" poem. In fact, in some sense, every religious poem that redescribes one's personal natural order at a new, transnatural existential horizon will express a passion for the possibility for a new, transcending self. If I had to designate an "election" poem among Hopkins' early poetry, it would be "The Habit of Perfection" (77), even though such poems as "Nondum" (78), "Easter" (79), "Rosa Mystica" (96), and "The Half-way House" (71) might be candidates.

I choose "The Habit of Perfection" because it expresses those predispositions of religious temper which are the psycho-spiritual underlayment of conversion. I speak here of the language of religious metaphor in the poem, expressing the paradox of self-transformation through denial of the narcissistic inclinations of the "I" of the self. The tension of discrediting the affective senses of the subjectivity, while asserting spiritual fulfillment as intrinsic to the very act of self-denial, results, in the resolution of the figuration, in a new meaning to selving. That new meaning centers on what "Love" means at the horizon of religious consciousness. In the self-transmigration beyond the natural senses, the figures reveal a new reality for him at that time of his religious development, divine love figured as a higher sensuousness. Perhaps such passion for affirming the appetites of the senses must precede any converted change of mind and heart. The open submission of the exteriorizing powers of the subjectivity to interior transformation is, of course, elemental to all religious aspiration:

> Elected Silence sing to me
> And beat upon my whorl'ed ear,
> Pipe me to pastures still and be
> The music that I care to hear.

*****

Shape nothing lips, be lovely dumb;
Be shell'ed eyes with double dark
That brings the uncreated light:

*****

Palate, the hutch of Life and Lust,
Wish now no tasty rinse of wine:

*****

Nostrils, that dainty breathing spend
On all the sire and keep of pride,

*****

O feel-of-primrose hands, O feet
That want the yield of plushy sward,

*****

And Poverty be thou the bride . . .

Part The First of "The Wreck of the Deutschland" (101) is often
construed as Hopkins' conversion poem. It is true that this part of the
ode addresses powerfully the consciousness of religious transformation.
However, by the time the poem was written, Hopkins had already become
a Roman Catholic; moreover, at the time of his writing, he had already
been introduced to the spiritual regime of St. Ignatius, in whose *Spiritual
Exercises* there are specially contrived patterns of contemplative activities
to enhance personal assent in the affirmation of a life-long vocation. While
the biographical components in the the poem are undoubtedly vital, true,
and real, their specific reference to events in Hopkins' life is impossible
to ascertain. Possibly, the autobiographical element in the poem reflects
either his intense struggle in coverting to Catholicism or maybe his poetic
recapitulation of some of his spiritual experiences during his entry period
in becoming a member of the Society of Jesus (Martin Ch. XIV; White
171-189). What is splendidly clear is the passion of Hopkins' conversion
at work in his poetic religious consciousness.

In this part of the ode, we find narrated those internal movements of spirit within the consciousness, the wording of which propels the most intense ardor of religious love. The entire poem is a complex unfolding narration of the episodes of transcending religious consciousness, in effect, the story announced in the first lines, "Thou mastering me / God!" In a later poem, Hopkins expressed the polarities of such passionate religious love: "Thee God, I come from, to thee go, / All day long I like a fountain flow / From thy hand out, swayed about / Mote-like in thy mighty glow" (161).

We have seen in the episode of selving conversion the pattern of religious experience that takes place. As a reader of Ricoeur's philosophic account of the positing of the self and Hopkins' poeticization of the grammar of religious consciousness, I am struck by the centrality of image, metaphor, and symbol in and through which religious feeling emanates. Focusing upon figurative language as the expressive key to produce transforming religious consciousness affirms what Ricoeur means by "appropriation," that imaginative process by which metaphor becomes, through its hermeneutic selving dynamics, self-reinterpretation. Moreover, it is the poetic energy of the text which provides the surcharge of passion to risk being in the world in, by, and through the reconstituted "I"-ness of religious consciousness. For the reader, spiritual symbol, concept and affect come together in reading such religious poetry. Hopkins poetic texts are narrative redescriptions of his own spiritual transformations, which for readers become a heuristic for their own selving reflections. Hopkins' poetic interpretations of his spiritual consciousness enters the reader's own reflective considerations, and by their entry the reader is forced, via such hermeneutic transfer, into a selving encounter which demands some kind of positive or negative selving response.

Such a hermeneutic predicament posed by the texts of the religious imagination is precisely what Ricoeur describes as the reading / hearing encounter of Jesus' parables in the New Testament. The bafflement of common sense that each parable asserts is overcome by the new, higher sense of a transcendent "what if." The reader of such texts must decide whether to accept a changed self-intepretation with all of its transrational, anti-egoistic, submissive changes in the subjectivity of the selving "I." As a poet Hopkins expressed conversion in selving patterns similar to Ricoeur: the positing "I" is called from within and without the self to "correspond" to a gifting of new selving possibility. To do so means a realignment of the interior self in radical ways, a transformation that needs converting consent. This is the personality of conversion. Hopkins summed up the personality of passionate conversion plainly and pointedly in his poem about shipwreck (one could read "self-wreck") when he wrote, "I did say yes / O at lightning and lashed rod; / Thou heardst me, truer than tongue, confess / Thy terror, O Christ, O God." As in the Gospels, so in religious poetry such as this, the demanding poetic power of the spiritual heuristic of conversion is clear: the "I" self is elevated to an active assent to reshape the positing possibilities of the selving consciousness.

Testimony: The Song of Hope

Ricoeur, as did J. H. Newman (*Grammar* 37, 87), argues that what founds religious assent is "testimony," by which he means that the truths revealed by the poetic religious consciousness are grounded in the actuality of such truths having truly illumined and transformed someone's life. Testimony, then, is contingent upon history and biography: "Only testimony that is singular in each instance confers the sanction of reality on ideas, ideals, and the ways of being that the symbols depicts to us and which we uncover as our ownmost possibilities" (*Essays on Biblical Interpretation* 11). Similarly Hopkins' emphasis, when discussing the elevation of the self, as we have seen, was on self-realization of the spiritual ideals beckoning the consciousness: "For there must be something which shall be truly the creature's in the work of corresponding with grace: this is the *arbitrium*, the verdict on God's side, saying Yes" (*Sermons* 154). Parallel to Hopkins' hermeneutics of grace is Ricoeur's hermeneutics of appropriation of the texts of testimony, the poetics of the will: "The term testimony should be applied to words, works, actions, and to lives which attest to an intention, an inspiration, an idea at the heart of experience and history which nonetheless transcends experience and history" (*Essays on Biblical Interpretation* 119-120). For both writers, among all the texts, sacred and secular, which might take self-reflection to the horizon of transcendent existence, it is the poetic textuality of the Bible which possesses the greatest powers of invoking passion for the positing of a new self through original reconstructive self-reflections. However there are other sacral texts affording ascendant religious selving.

In coming to the religious experience of testimony expressed in Hopkins' poetry, we come to his major canon. No religious poet since

John Donne has so exuberantly celebrated the internalization of sacral texts into the consciousness as does his poetry, nor does any poet explore the self in its spiritual transformation more deeply. To his readers, Hopkins' poetic power was his ability to plot out his spiritual drama and poeticize it with great verbal heightening powers. His poetic words are so creatively alive with grammatical, semantic, and poetic energies, that they activate an explosive selving hermeneutic through his redescriptions of religious experience, a poetics possessing a kind of hermeneutic megalinguistic surge.

So surcharged is the language heightened in Hopkins' metaphoric constructions with their ricocheting figurative references, they take on a glowing specificity, sometimes, it seems, too bright to see into. The heightened "as if" of such a metaphorized religious mode is matched by a paralleled heightening "as if" of the formal linguistic modes. Such a fusion in the poetics of image, word, symbol, and figure results in poetry that barely contains the balance of its centrifugal and centripetal powers of the words that are uttered. I speak here of his famous poems, "The Wreck" (101), especially Part the Second narrating the consciousness of the drowning, freezing nuns, "God's Grandeur" (111), "The Starlight Night" (112), "Spring" (117), and the famous sonnet, "The Windhover" (120). In each of these poems, the reader encounters the most graphic poetic etching of the senses, followed by a narration of the sublimation of the sensorium, which invokes a new horizon of self-awareness. At this passionate level of possibility, the poet bears celebratory witness to the positing testimony of his experience, the testimony of the Christ-event which confers "existential verification" (Vanhoozer 260) on the actualizing spiritual ideal invoked in the poem. Of all the mature canon, it is no wonder that "The Windhover" has received the greatest attention of readers, for it is the very cynosure of Hopkins' selving religious consciousness. The drama of the transforming self is played out with power, ecstasy, and resolution. This sonnet is what I think Ricoeur means by "poem of existence," namely, the "selving" understanding of faith energized by the passion for the possible conveyed through the sacralizing poetic word.

A plot pattern in the narration of the testifying religious consciousness is that of the intercessors of testimony. In other testamentary poems, besides their icon-like poetic "inscapings," there are aspirative invocations. I refer here to the saints that moved and shaped Hopkins' religious selving, especially the poems about the Virgin Mary. "The Blessed Virgin compared to the air we Breathe" (151) would be a prime example of a figure conferring on him intercessory reflections along with St. Winefred, Margaret Clitheroe, St. Alphonsus Rodriguez and other ikonic sainted consciousnesses. Of course, the image of Christ, whose figuration penetrates to every level of Hopkins' religious consciousness, is the prime exemplar of the testimonial passion in his poetry. Imaginative grace, as one of Ricoeur's fine exegetes notes, "is conveyed by the sacrament of word" (Vanhoozer 265).The word is transmuted into the Word, for, as Ricoeur asserts, what the Jesus-Event put newly into the human condition was the aboriginal power of unconditional love, whose symbol is the Christ-Spirit of the possibility of love, now and forever.

Another pattern in the experience of Ricoeurrian Testimony is the mystery of assent. While this pattern is an element in nearly all of Hopkins' central poems in his mature canon, it is more focalized in some poems than others. The mystery of religious assent lies in the insight that the natural world is a figuration symbolizing a spiritual truth at the horizon of existence: our ultimate self-meaning, and that of the whole universe, is a gifting above and beyond this material world. Out of this gift arises the human obligation to love the giver of this gift. This is the key reflection on the mystery of Testimonial assent according to both Hopkins and Ricoeur. In Hopkins' words, "the world of man, should after its own manner give God being in return for the being he has given it or should give him back that being he has given" (*Sermons* 129).

Hopkins expressed this wondrous and spontaneous "giving back being" in those poems which catch the tenderness of spiritual passion, poems like "Pied Beauty" (121), "The Handsome Heart" (134), and "The Bugler's First Communion" (137). The two most dramatic poetic expressions of the mystery of assent in the religious consciousness are, perhaps, his sonnet, "Hurrahing in Harvest" (124), and the latter half of "The Wreck," starting with Stanza 16. In the spiritually dramatic passages in these poems, Hopkins attempted to word the redescriptions of heightened religious assent with language that illuminates the mystery of self-transformation. In the "Hurrahing" sonnet, the ascent to a spiritual horizon just happens, like breathing in and out, stressing the naturality of elevating grace added to Nature. However, in "The Wreck," he pondered and pondered the nun's call, recognition, and affirmation of Christ coming to her and her sister nuns. Such is the mystery of this "incomprehensible certainty" that is the testimony of the Incarnation as he told Robert Bridges (*Letters to Bridges* 186). It is the Incarnation, the narrative of God made manifest in his Creation, that especially transfixed Hopkins' Christian poetic consciousness in this poem. In his shockingly-charged wording as he poetically reflected on this tormented event, we, his readers, are struck speechless at his wonder as are we elevated to the contemplation of the possible advent of Christ at the moment of our own deaths. Will we call, will we recognize, will we affirm? Will we give being back? "The majesty! what did she mean?" These stanzas of poetic self-reflection on the nun's testimony characterize the poet's spiritual challenge and response; his readers as well encounter the mystery of such self-transforming assent in their own religious consciousness, whatever their divine ideal.

For both Ricoeur and Hopkins, the interior mystery of the Christian hermeneutics of individual selving assent is allied to the sublime mystery of the Incarnation culminating in the Passion and Resurrection of Christ. Hopkins redescribed this mystery in his shipwreck ode (Stanzas 5-8). Speaking of Christ, he wrote: "Since, though he is under the world's splendour and wonder, / His mystery must be instressed, stressed . . . ." Hopkins held that Christ is God's selving of Himself as Creation, thus Christ is the ontic deep structure of all being, still, his co-presence to all things, especially human beings, is a mystery which must be uncovered. The Christ mystery is coterminous with the totality of the history of the universe; "it rides time like riding a river," and manifests itself as a datum in historical consciousness as the "Christ-Event":

> It dates from the day
> Of his going in Galilee;
> Warm-laid grave of a womb-life grey;
> Manger, maiden's knee;
> The dense and driven Passion, and frightful sweat:
> Thence the discharge of it, there its swelling to be,
> Though felt before, though in high flood yet—
> What none would have known of it, only the heart, being hard
> at bay,
>
> Is out with it! Oh,
> We lash with the best or worst
> Word last!

Here Hopkins redescribed the historical Incarnation as an heuristic for the mystery of self-appropriation, the transforming assent to the Event of Christ. His focus is on the way the mystery lives on in time, history, and consciousness, especially that hermeneutic translation from the word of historical narrative to the Word of Christian religious narrative. This is the very drama of the hermeneutics of religious consciousness which Ricoeur addresses. Creative words of sacral language inspirit what he called the hieratic meanings of "the events of deliverance which open up and disclose the utmost possibilities of my own freedom and thus become for me the Word of God" (*Philosophy of Religion* 84-85). Hopkins' word for this appropriation of the text of the Christ-Event which radically reinterprets the self is "lash," suggesting at once the selving torment of strife, whipping, pain, and the sweet reprieve of binding, gathering, a bursting into a great plenty. Such an interpretative encounter with classic sacral texts is no mere critical exercise; it is the imaginative taking into the depth of the self the implications of the horizon meanings of the Christ-figured heuristic of the text to such a level of contemplative reflection, that the "I" locates a newly operative "I am." Ricoeur restates the confronting option facing the transformed "I": "One must choose between the 'encipherment' of all things, and the Christian Incarnation" ("Jasper's Philosophy" 624). Such is the hermeneutic selving range of the entire Christ-Event. Hopkins appropriately reflected the hugeness of the human potential openable in the Christed-texts in the closing lines of the stanza: "Gush!—flush the man, the being with it, sour or sweet / Brim, in a flash, full!"

Of course, most religious life is lived in less dramatic circumstances though the election of Christed love is spiritually always an interior event of great personal drama as is all authentic religious conversion, whatever the Event of Faith The hope that Christian testimony undergirds must endure amid the charges and duties of daily living, what Hopkins called"Time's tasking." It is ordinary life that is the setting of Jesus' parables wherein he describes "the Kingdom of God, and within ordinary life that Christian spiritual transformation occurs. Hopkins and Ricoeur's focus on the climactic spiritual implications of the most dramatic of New Testament texts should not be taken as an exclusive focus upon which to appropriate Christian significance. Both are fully aware that the appropriation of the events of spiritual transformation in the biblical texts is a lived venture, what Ricoeur describes as a living narrative, Hopkins a selving journey. Both stress that spiritual transformation is a working out through time of one's religious destiny. In every case, Christian hope must be discerned amid individual daily "goings-on," a discernment that involves seeing the "real presence" of Christ in one's life and choosing to respond to his horizon perspective in living it.

There are significant examples of religious poetry Hopkins composed during the daily life of his parish years, 1878-1881. Among the most notable of some fifteen poems written in the fullness of his priestly poetic creativity, are "The Loss of the Eurydice" (125), another shipwreck poem, "Duns Scotus's Oxford" (129), a poem about his admiration for his medieval theological mentor, "Binsey Poplars" (130), an ecological poem, "Henry Purcell" (131), a poem celebrating the great English composer whose music Hopkins greatly appreciated, "The Bugler's First Communion (137), a poem about the Christ-self in a young soldier, "Felix Randal" (142), a poem full of pastoral sadness over the early death of a blacksmith, "Spring and Fall" (144), a poem about the whispers of mortality in the consciousness of a young girl, and "The Leaden Echo and the Golden Echo" (148), a poem full of Purcell-like verbal music in which Hopkins arranged two motifs: death that takes all away and hope that promises rescue. While each of these parish poems has its own specific subject which the poet "inscapes" with touches of great delicacy, in each there is the subtext of the Testimony of Christian faith resting on the felt presence of Christ subsisting in the subject, scene, and narrated event which gives rise to such affirmations as in "The Golden Echo": "Give beauty back, beauty, beauty, beauty, back to God beauty's self and beauty's giver." The song of Christian hope that arises in the "eminent" texts of the Bible, the song of selving transformation, must be resung again and again while standing at life's "random grim forge." Testimony is this selving story.

Trial in the Abyss

The "selving" faith which accepts with unconditional trust the sign-events expressed in the sacred texts, the Bible, for example, must involve a constant renewal of selving reinterpretations. The hermeneutics of such texts must be met with matching creative selving responses. This spiritual phenomenology is what is meant by the Christian notion of the Holy Spirit, the third personality of God, which binds us to a new order of self-being. The Holy Spirit, in its sacral texting, is another name for Love, whose image is the descending and ascending living fire of spiritual love. This is what, as Hopkins explained in one of his sermons, is meant by the Holy Spirit being a paraclete: "A Paraclete is one who encourages men, stirs them, or calls them on to do good." But the Paraclete is as well "a comforter or consoler" (*Sermons* 97). It is the Paraclete who provides the enabling spiritual energies to hold fast to the new possibilities of our selving; it is the Holy Spirit who is the love charge of the transformed self, the self that lives in the wonderment of the gift of Creation as the living fire of the Spirit: "All things are charged with God and if we know how to touch them give off sparks and take fire, yield drops and flow, ring and tell of him" (*Sermons* 195).

But often people lose the "selving" capacity to "touch" being at the horizon of eternality. When this happens, they can become cast down into a very low pit of depressive self-dread, self-pity, self-anger, ending in self-denigration. I stress "self" because I am not talking about brain disorders. Even brain philosophers and scientists acknowledge that they cannot really account for the mysterious polar movements of the "I" consciousness (Daniel Dennet's "Center of Narrative Gravity" is essentially a new attempt to offer a concept of brain physicality as the self, another of scientism's assumptions about the emptiness of self-reflection: " 'I'm me!' is not really informative" [426 in Ch 13]). When this experience of emptiness recurs in the self, it is different from that first experience of lostness in the phase of self-awakening. Here, we are talking about the "I" falling into a kind of black hole within the self. The ensuing struggle is fierce, because there is the awareness in self-reflection that the self has fallen down, slipped back, from a self-affirming high place in which the "I" self felt positively aware and lived in the hope and freedom of a fuller self-realization of its "I am."

Spiritual mentors in all the great religions acknowledge this state of disconsolation in the self. It is seen as a kind of divine withdrawal, a heavenly test, the active dispiriting of evil forces, the contest of just judgment, even a special elevating grace operating in the paradox of self-distress. All of these perspectives are incorporated in what St. Ignatius, Hopkins' spiritual mentor, called, "the discernment of Spirits" (*Spiritual Exercises* 313-337, 345-352). Ricoeur views such states as the effects of human fallibility. Like Ignatius and Hopkins, Ricoeur understands the body-character of the human condition as a limitation upon personality, a limitation that possesses its own mysterious associations. While ontic finitude is the human condition, it is not evil *per se*. Evil enters in the self in the dynamics of self-interpretation. In Ricoeurrian hermeneutic terms, evil is essentially a failure of imaginative powers in the consciousness to raise the self positively to appropriate suasively human possibility at a new and higher horizon of being. Why do we fail to interpret the "texts" of experience to the levels of liberating possibility? For Ricoeur, radical evil in the self "makes of freedom an impossible possibility" ("Hope and the Structure of Philosophical Systems" 68), a nice parallel to Hopkins' hope in the self generated by the "incomprehensible certainty" in the mystery of the Incarnation.

In its "selving" Christian positivity, the "selving" hermeneutics of the narrating self is linked to the Incarnational mystery story of Christ, a co-presence in the metaphoric consortium of the "selving I." Hopkins wrote about this mystery explaining to Robert Bridges the hermeneutical differences between mystery as "a interesting uncertainty," a conceptual conundrum, and religious mystery, which both Hopkins and Ricoeur are talking about. He noted that in mystery in general, "the source of interest . . . is the unknown, the reserve of truth beyond what the mind reaches and still feels to be behind." But religious mystery moves beyond curiosity to putting the answer to the mystery by placing it in the "most tantalizing statement of the problem and the truth you are to rest in the most pointed putting of the problem." Hopkins here described the selving appropriation of such mysteries in its most provocative hermeneutic formulation.

Hopkins illustrated his point about appropriating religious mystery (in his words "instressing the incape" of God) by discussing the mystery of the Trinity:

> To some people this is a 'dogma,' a word they almost chew, that is a equation in theology, the dull algebra of schoolman; to others it is news of their dearest friend or friends, leaving them all their lives balancing whether they have three heavenly friends or one—not that they have any doubt on the subject, but that their knowledge leaves their minds swinging; poised, but on the quiver. And this might be the ecstasy of interest, one would think. So too of the Incarnation. . . . Therefore we speak of the events of Christ's life as a mystery. . . . Otherwise birth and death are not mysteries, nor is it any great mystery that a just man should be crucified, but that God should fascinates— with interest of awe, of pity, of shame, of every harrowing feeling" (*Letters to Bridges*, 186-188).

Christian selving appropriation / "instressing" is thus the interfusion of the mystery of the Passion of Christ and the selving mystery of individual human passion that is the condition within which consent freely takes place. As Ricoeur notes, we must selve the "I" within the limits of these two mysteries of incarnation. In this difficult consent lies the possibility, through the empowering selving of the poetic consciousness, to actualize life with joy, hope and freedom: "Consent 'is the ultimate reconciliation of freedom and nature which both theoretically and practically appear to us torn apart'" (Vanhoozer 239-248). It is the self's "balancing," "swinging," that often becomes the inevitable "harrowing" that is the religious trial of the abyss in the consciousness. To some degree, such is the selving fate of every human being in the universe.

Hopkins, within the limitations of his own body and character, certainly suffered the ravages of the disconsolate consciousness intensely (See Roberts; also Martin 381-382, 394-396, 407-410; White 366-377, 392-397). The crisis of fear and self doubt, which he so frequently narrated in his letters, notebooks, and poems, constitutes a clear delineation of the hermeneutic experience of the selving trial of the abyss. Here are matchless instances of redescriptions of patterns of self-crisis, the "I am" of the "I" in deep torment. While the writings overlap, and no one expression can be confined exclusively to one selving pattern, sorting through them to see possible patterns reveals the deconstructing consciousness under the threat of the total disappearance of the self. Plumbing these harrowing poems of existence still goes on among Hopkins' readers because of their powerfully incisive expressiveness of the collapsing self. What I offer here is mainly the shape of the patterns, not in any necessary sequence or order, with only the barest attention to the in-depth selving reflections which any one poem posits, and limited reflections on my part in responding to the selving heuristic they deploy.

Perhaps the initiating pattern of deep trial in the consciousness is the seeming withdrawal of any consolation from within the self and from the world without. The experience of disconsolation is a perennial aspect of our faulted selves. Our inner divisions, which despoil our personalities, seem miniature self-mappings of the grotesqueries of the grand horrors of history. Evil seems to abound. Our poise is shaken, we loose sustaining inner selving balance, and we move from feelings of isolation: "To seem the stranger lies my lot, my life / Among strangers" (154), to the shock of loosing control: "No worst, there is none, Pitched past pitch of grief . . . / O the mind has mountains; cliffs of all / Frightful, sheer, no-man-fathomed" (157). In a sense, the "I"self seems lost within the consciousness, now felt as a bottomless chasm.

The regular effort to sustain the positing "I" now becomes itself a distress in the self. Now this basic selving pattern, a constant in all self-consciousness, becomes a struggle to retain basic sympathy within the self: confronting our acts, works, words, with reflections that posit possibility for the "I am" of the self has turned into a negative and destructive never-ending ordeal. Hopkins expressed the pain of this human "dispassion" of the self in "Patience, hard thing!" (162): "We hear our hearts grate on themselves: it kills / To bruise them dearer." And the yearning for relief is clearer and dearer in his sonnet, "Peace" (140), "When will you ever, Peace / . . . under be my boughs?"

This descent from an affirming level of selving religious consciousness makes rescuing reflections focus upon enduring such spells of selving as a kind of grace-testing. Selving feelings are imaged as spiritual contests, trials of lost elevations of the self, mysterious deprivations of former ascents, renewing possibilities, and the affirmations of hope, all of which had posited a spiritually transformed "I am" of the "I." Self-reflections on these as dejections soon become ethical, then moral, then finally accusative as the quandary of God's justice and the self's deserving or undeserving predicament. The basic pattern of the poetics of the will as the arbitrating consciousness is a constant of selving from the beginning, as Hopkins noted in his poem about the spontaneous selving consent of youth, "The Handsome Heart" (134). And it is at issue in our encounters with all being: "To what serves mortal beauty— dangerous" (158). But now in the disconsolate self, the selving "I" becomes dangerously divided between its volitional and its affective nature— choice and desire. Hopkins caught the agonizing stress of such a selving dilemma in his sonnet, "Thou are indeed just, Lord, if I contend / With thee; but, sir, so what I plead is just. . . . and why must / Disappointment all I endeavor end? / How wouldst thou worst, I wonder, than thou dost / Defeat, thwart me" (177)?

The symbols of evil, so deeply embedded in the self-consciousness from the beginning, now are experienced as horrific sins. The pattern of disconsolating reflection appears as the language of judgment and damnation. In Hopkins' poetic narrative of his experience of a frightfully disintegrating self-consciousness of sin and hell, these powerful poetic reflections are the most threatening of all. They are backgrounded in earlier poems like "The Caged Skylark" (122), in lines like "Man's mounting spirit in his bone-house, mean house, dwells," in the willful "meanness" of self-fault in the senseless destruction of Nature, "Binsey Poplars" (130): "O if we knew what we do / When we delve or hew— / Hack and rack the growing green!" Or in "The Candle Indoors" (133), there is the constant wonderment of the selving heightening gains or grim losses of people passing through or by our lives, which distress fastens the poet's attention to his own mind-battle: "What hinders? Are you beam-blind, yet to a fault / In a neighbourhood deft-handed? Are you that liar / And, castby conscience out, spendsavour salt?"

"Instressing" these bottoming experiences of the fright of absolute self-loss redescribed in the poetic imagination becomes the selving reflections that can be named the hermeneutics of the agonies of the abyss. Here in the reflecting religious imagination, the self staggers, falls, gets up, staggers and so on. In the Christian ritual of the Crucifixion, such torment is mirrored in Jesus' staggers and falls, as he carried the cross, a transcendent symbol of such suffering. What are the elements of such a devastating series of self-reflections? One is the constancy of the apparent loss of the self in the disappearance of the instrumenting body in death, which is what Hopkins redescribed in"The Wreck" (stanza 11): ". . . flame, / Fang, or flood goes Death on drum, and storms bugle his fame. . . . / Flesh falls within sight of us . . . there must / The sour scythe cringe, and the blear share come."

The Hopkins poem that opens the most telling reflection on strife between Nature and personality is "Spelt from Sibyl's Leaves" (167). The poet envisions the coming abyss that is the inevitable death-event of the body: "Our evening is over us; our night whelms, whelms, and will end us." And what will be the ending of each of our stories of our individual selving? Hopkins redescribed, in the sestet of this sonnet, the drama of escape or entrapment on the brink of the abyss as a story about self-dispersion: "Our tale, O our oracle!" His figure of the life-long selving consciousness in seeking the "I am" of the "I" is a spool, raveling or unraveling, depending upon whether the self is consenting to the ascending possibilities of love as the union of the highest desires with our elective choice of the good, or whether the self is fatally split over sublimating the narcissistic "I," finally submitting to its vain indulgences. The self is figured as a kind of self-narrating tapestry which, as we weave or unweave it, tells the story of our ascendance or our descendance—the heaven and hell of two kinds of love. Hopkins' reflections at this time of his life (Martin 382-389) are thronged with grinding groans. "The Leaden Echo" (148), "The Lantern out of doors" (113), and "The Sea and the Skylark" (118) are poems in which Hopkins redescribed the reflections wherein he expressed the self as breaking down; despair is dominant in the consciousness, and the self may disappear into the darkness of death: "Men go by me . . . till death or distance buys them quite. / Death or distance soon consumes them . . . out of sight is out of mind" (113).

While Hopkins had expressed clearly the true path of his selving the spiritually possible in his religious consciousness, he now in the last part of his life frequently felt at a loss to achieve and maintain an affirming state of consciousness. This frightening inability in his "I" selving to raise in his self a consciousness of hope occasioned powerful poetic reflections on his seemingly depraved faults in his personality. Disturbing poems such as the unfinished "To his Watch" (164) and "The shepherd's brow" (178) are redescriptions of selving as a disordered, disordering consciousness, failing, thus falling into shame, disgust, and oblivion: "But man—we scaffold of score brittle bones. . . . / He!, Hand to mouth he lives, and voids with shame; / And, blazoned in however bold the name, / Man Jack the man is, just; his mate a hussy."

The self, closed off to any positive passion for self-possibility, what Hopkins dubbed, speaking of himself, "Time's eunuch," now becomes desperate. Just where the line is between coming to and falling into the abyss of self-desolation cannot be precisely drawn. However, there is no doubt that Hopkins' poems, "I wake and feel" (155), "No worst, there is none" (157), and "Not, I'll not, carrion comfort" (159), are abyss poems. Reading these sonnets from a Ricoeurrian hermeneutical perspective, I find them more powerful self-reflections of the desolate self than my earlier readings. In the first poem, the combat with time, the harrowing punishment of nightmares, the wailing of uncontrollable cries deep in the heart of the self, the sense of being abandoned by someone who is pledged to be by your side, and finally, the self-denying demeaning of the consciousness through physicalizing images which depict the self as giving in to becoming like sour, rancid, acidic bile, giving rise to the image of making God sick: all of these redescriptions of the self in the abyss convey the ultimate spiritual damnation: "God's most deep decree / Bitter would have me taste: my taste was me."

No wonder, then, in such selving condemnation, the "I" loses the creative energy to go on in the task of selving achievement. The volitional self begins to incline to self-annihilation, which is the subject in Hopkins'scary sonnet, "carrion comfort." In such disconsolation, even the temporalizing energies of the consciousness break down. The time-frame of the narrative of selving suicide of the sonnet is complex. The struggling torment of life towards death is redescribed as deranged sequences of dire temptations to end all consciousness from the brink of which the self struggles back again and again from suicide. The octave opens uttering desperate but confused reflections in an effort to seize, through some kind of last grasping effort (whose? the poet asks), a new beginning to try to posit self stability in order to hold on to the selving energy of the "I" self. In the sestet the slim victory for going on, barely achieved in the octave, depicts one of many dire suicidal struggles that has been overcome, so many that they have run together as darkened years of night battles in which the self fights with the highest and the lowest motivations in positing its "I"-ness.

These images of the "selving" reflections are violent, brutal, murdering; indeed, what Hopkins, Christian poet and priest, has expressed is the figural equivalent in human passion to the Passion of Jesus. Jesus' cry in the sacred text, " My God, My God! Why have you forsaken me?" shrieks through the poem. Still, the self survives through consent to some gift of elevating grace. Nowhere in all his poetry does Hopkins sound the death song of the positing "I" more than in this doubly desperate poem: "cry *I can no more.* I can; / Can something, hope, wish day come, not choose not to be." This is the frightening scream of the "selfyeast of spirit" in the pit looking up at the Christ-scape on the horizon of existence. Could anyone find a more powerful poetic reflection which Ricoeur delineated as the poetics of volitional "selving"? "One must choose between the 'encipherment ' *of all things and the Christian Incarnation.*"

Whatever the episodic end of the torment of the abyss of the self, it must be characterized by forgiveness. Forgiveness is another name for unconditional love. The occurrence of it in the self is no less a mystery than the deprecatory effects in its absence. But forgiveness does mysteriously happen in the self, releasing new initiating powers of the "passion for the possible" in positing the "I" self. It seems to begin with a correspondence to some hopeful feeling in the inner self: "My own heart let me have some pity on; let / Me live to my sad self hereafter kind, / Charitable; not live this tormented mind . . . ." Forgiveness, as well, involves some volitional response to allow oneself be projected towards a world of possibility orienting the self towards a higher horizon of human possibility. This is to say that hope is manifested through some experience possessing kerygmatic content: "Say but the word and my soul will be healed." For Hopkins and Ricoeur, the texts of the Gospels contain such regenerative narrative forms; there are, of course, parallel sacral texts for others to selve the "I-self." The reflecting "I" must find some self-freeing possibility from some such source, if the "I am" is to be transformed to a hopeful self-positing.

Once more, the beginning of such freeing hope is forgiveness, a movement within the self that seems mysteriously an interior activation correspondent to an exterior shifting of the self to a higher plane, a shift that is described as a divine activity. Its gifting occurrence both as to timing and character is a problematic event, but if and when it happens, it must be acted upon if positive change is to take place. Forgiveness cannot be willed: "I cast for comfort I can no more get / By groping round my comfortless than blind / Eyes in their dark can day . . . ." Often for the forgiveness that begets arriving hope, one must often wait: "I do advise / You, jaded, let be; call off thoughts awhile / Elsewhere." In the pause within the exhausted self, not always, but often, there is a spark of joy:

"let joy size? / At God knows when to God knows what." Hopkins depicted this joy as a giant smile on the horizon which shows a path, "lights a lovely mile" (163). But, as he wrote in another poem, "The Golden Echo" (148), there must be a consent, a correspondence, to make that joy an igniting of a new passion for possibility in the self: "Come then, your ways and airs and looks . . . / Resign them, sign them, seal them, send them, motion them with breath, / And with sighs soaring, soaring sighs, deliver / Them . . . back to God." In and through such consent the self repossesses the power to create the possibility of a fully realized "I am" of the "I," life towards eternity.

This brief exploration of the narrative of Hopkins' dark selving as redescribed in his ending lyric narratives, again I note, amounts to only an outline of the episodes of such a disconsolate religious consciousness. His remarkable lyric narrative of such reflections has and will continue to startle us into much deeper revelations about the decipherment of the dark spirits in the human self. Reviewing them here again, and many readers' responses to them, I think too much emphasis has been made on the strangeness and particularity of these his self-reflections, as if a holy and devout priest would be immune from the pains of dread. Dread is the scrim of consciousness throughout everyone's life; each of us as a self constantly struggles with cosmic dreams of catastrophe, nightmares of tragedy, and the terrors, failings, imperfections, and sins of one's own personal history, perhaps, just as harrowing as anything Hopkins experienced, maybe even worse. And just as these selving torments were his test and trial, so we must look to find our selving possibility in the opaque origins of our beginnings, the beckoning promises of the working out of the middle plot of our life's narrative, and the rude predicament of discomforting blackout-ending. Whatever our sources of sacred kerygma, each of us must try to find and decipher the poetics of the religious imagination to see, either in the releasing parables of Jesus as Christ, or whatever are our mothering sacral texts, the tender words of passion that will be our passionate, loving, trustworthy possibility for transformation to a personal, transcending freedom. For himself, Hopkins expressed such selving salvific release as the Christ-Event which he salutes in the concluding lines of his great shipwreck ode; the poet here unfolds the rich selving Christed meanings in overflowing figures of affirmative hope that thronged his religious imagination: "Pride, rose, prince, hero of us, high priest, / Our heart's charity's hearth's fire, our thoughts' chivalry's throng's Lord."

Freedom as Hope

For Ricoeur, it is that power in the consciousness we call the imagination which is the inaugurator of hope. In the revelatory heuristics of the texts of life, we first imagine the new self through revelatory interpretation, and in that deeply realized self-interpretation, we become reinterpreted, transformed to-be-in-the-world at a new horizon. We come to see life in a new way and, thus, we take on enabling powers to change the orientation of the self to this new possibility. In this consent we existentially verify this new "I am" of the "I" in the self by making it a lived event in our existence.

As for Ricoeur, so for Hopkins, such a transformation rests on some sacralizing hermeneutics, historical and meta-historical, in encountering very personally the texts of the biblical narratives. It is such texts as these that have the hermeneutic powers to release us from our own egoistic incarnations to the recognition that our self-being is gifted, and in that gift we dismiss our own false egos. We are released from the bondage of the narcissistic "I am" of our "I" to a new self-interpretation through the kerygmatic words of Jesus' Passion and Resurrection, which is Ricoeur's hermeneutic application of what Rudolph Bultmann, calls "faith": "The new self-understanding which is bestowed with 'faith' is that of freedom, in which the believer gains life and thereby his own self" (Vanhoozer 229).

Christ is the selving symbol in these texts that empowers such a change in our self-understanding. The biblical theme of dying to self becomes in Ricoeur's philosophy the idea of the self's abandoning all pretensions to justify and give meaning to one's own existence. "Ricoeur's hermeneutic philosophy internalizes Jesus' maxim: whoever would save his life must first lose it. With this thought we approach the very core of Ricoeur's thought about human beings, texts, and interpretations" (Vanhoozer 261). At the center of this core is the symbol of the "wisdom of the Resurrection," whose hermeneutic powers convey in the context of faith what Ricoeur calls the "economy of superabundance, which we must decipher in daily life, in work and in leisure, in politics and universal history. To be free is to know that one belongs to this economy, to be 'at home' in this economy. The 'in spite of,' which holds us ready for disappointment, is only the reverse, the dark side, of the joyous 'how much more' by which freedom feels itself, knows itself, wills to conspire with the aspiration of the whole creation of redemption" (*Conflict* 410). This is freedom as hope in the religious consciousness, the achieved self in Ricoeur.

Such self-freeing as the passion of hope is the very reflection of one of the last great religious poems Hopkins wrote, significantly composed near the end of his life and amidst his last ferocious mind-battles: "That Nature is a Heraclitean Fire and of the comfort of the Resurrection" (174). This poem is indeed an "eminent" text in Hopkins' canon, so frequent reference to it is made. Let us read it from a Ricoeurrian hermeneutic perspective The sonnet time-set is a day after a storm. The poet narrates the process in Nature by which fire becomes ether. It is notable that there is a downward surge of the elements preceding an upward movement. There is implied a purification, a refinement, that emerges out of the storm of the cosmos. Mankind undergoes a parallel process in body, and in virtue of the flesh as the instrument of the consciousness, the poet faces the implication that in Nature, human nature is drowned, dried up, blown away as so much earthly dust in the winds that move the clouds. This diurnal course, which Nature follows, is its processing of change and renewal: "Million-fuel`ed, nature's bonfire burns on."

And what of the fate of the selving "I"-consciousness of human beings in this drama of decay and renewal? Fastened to the body, does it suffer the same fate of Nature's material transformation? On the horizon of natural existence, it seems to be the case: "Man, how fast his firedint, his mark on mind, is gone.!" Each splendid "I"-self-consciousness in bodily form is plunged into the whirling, reductive atomization that is the grinding process of the elements: "Both are in an unfathomable, all is in an enormous dark / Drowned." What can the poet say about such a natural tragedy? He cries, "O pity and indignation ! " "Pity" is the cry because the highest is reduced to the lowest; "indignation" because hopeful aspiration has been discovered as finally futile. At this consciousness horizon of personal existence, there is only consternation: "Manshape, that shone / Sheer off, disseveral, a star, death blots black out; nor mark / Is any of him at all . . . ."

It is here, at this tragic moment of awareness of natural destiny, that the consciousness of hope is inspirited through the promises of the Event of Christ. In the sacral narratives of his acts and words, for Christians, there is engendered his Christed Spirit, which lifts the self to a hopeful transcendent horizon of human possibility, a freeing intimation in the consciousness of divine destiny. This coming of the spirit of the Event of Christ is a deeply interior awakening, for, from the beginning, there is the realization that Christ is the gifting source of all being, the meaning of the symbol of the Incarnation, God present in all Creation. If the selving "I" recognizes the meaning of the Christ Event and responds to its meaning as a gifting of a co-presence to the "I am" of the self, the selving "I" consents to the possibilities of this love by offering its selfness in return, then the "I"-self is changed utterly, freed into the consciousness of transforming hope that there is personal destiny in the ultimate meaningfulness of human existence. Christ either lives or dies in the vortex of this spiritual crisis in the consciousness. This powerful poem is just what the Ricoeur meant by the hermeneutics of the religious imagination, the word / Word profoundly selved in the consciousness. Hopkins in this poem redescribed the moment of Christian selving assent, his ultimate "poem of existence," affirming the hope and freedom of the achieved self:

> Enough! the Resurrection,
> A heart's clarion! Away grief's gasping, joyless days, dejection.
> Across my foundering deck shone
> A beacon, an eternal beam. Flesh fade, and mortal trash
> Fall to the residuary worm; world's wildfire, leave but ash:
> In a flash, at a trumpet crash,
> I am all at once what Christ is, since he was what I am, and
> This Jack, joke, poor potsherd, patch, matchwood, immortal
> diamond,
> Is immortal diamond.

Postscript

The Poetics of Redemption

1

Before pursuing some broader implications of this study, some concluding remarks are in order about the correspondence between the linguistic philosophy of Paul Ricoeur and the philosophy of poetic consciousness in the writings of Gerard Manley Hopkins.

Starting with Ricoeur, I submit that he has developed a provocative philosophic account of the hermeneutical making of religious consciousness which powerfully mediates how human meaning can be established beyond the "life towards death" consciousness that has so dominated the humanist culture of this century. In accomplishing this remarkable reorientation to posit "yes" to human existence, he has examined the philosophic design of the modern world as mapped by the consciousness philosophers of Modernism and found them useful in turning their often deconstructive account of the self as absurd into an account that asserts that there is meaning to human existence. Perhaps Ricoeur's capacities to achieve this mediation is the most remarkable feature of his hermeneutic philosophy.

In accomplishing this mediation, Ricoeur has made two major contributions toward restoring the powers of the human consciousness. First, he has incisively uncovered what many serious productions in humanist philosophic thinking have taken for granted, the creative, expressive powers of the human imagination. At the core of all speculative thinking is this imaginative power to reconstruct the various registers of consciousness intellection and volition into new configurations of orders and meanings, along with coordinating the subjectivity of the creating of the "I" self with these new perceptions. Ricoeur has shown that to restrict human meaning to the conceptual consciousness is to destructively dissect the self.

The second significant contribution, sorely needed today in modern consciousness philosophy, is Ricoeur's deep insights to self-understanding as the hermeneutical "graces" of language. Words are the best gift of human consciousness, for by them and through them we are and become what we will be. Indeed, words are the selving imagination constructively revealed. As such, Ricoeur explains, words connect the self and interconnect the self with the universe. Short or long distance, language is the dialing system by which the "I" of the self becomes an "I am" in the world. Words are the only means by which to get through to this affirming self-positing existence Speaking of the figurative imagination expressed in words, Ricoeur affirms, "Texts speak of possible worlds and possible ways of orientating oneself in those worlds. In that way disclosure becomes the equivalent for written texts of ostensive reference for spoken language. And interpretation becomes the grasping of the world-propositions opened up by the non-ostensive references of the text" (A Ricoeur Reader 314)). Such is the innovative discourse of the imagination in building new worlds of self-understanding.

There are all kinds of language registers, verbal and non-verbal , of course, but the ones that convey self-understanding, our most precious words, are poetic words, because such words open up the fullest range of "selving" possibility, enlarge the scope of human meaning, and uncover unknown horizons of existing. In doing this, Ricoeur has shown how poetic words can inspire the possibility of hope beyond any despair, for they move us to say "yes" to our human existence in the promise of a transcendent vision of our selving destiny. In fact, Ricoeur argues that in and through the poetic consciousness of existence touching a cosmic horizon, we can move from the consciousness of suspicion and anxiety to a perennial affirmation of human meaning as a "passion for possibility." Such selving nourishment lies in the hermeneutics of metaphoric words, in narrative words, and all those paralleling words which posit the self affirmatively in what we call "the real world." If suspicion and despair are consciousness states of self-hate and world-hate, then faith, hope, and love of our and the world's existence are counterpointing states of passionate possibility. These two accounts of self and the world divide existence into light and darkness. Ricoeur provocatively chooses the "selving" story of light over darkness, meaning over absurdity, hope over despair, transcendence over descendence, "yes" rather than "no" to ourselves and everything else.

Turning to Hopkins, I think insufficient attention has been paid to his own poetic and philosophic explorations of "selving." There is a remarkable philosophical account of the "selving" process in Hopkins' piecemeal writings—diaries, notebooks, and letters. In fact, perhaps the most fully worked out parts of Hopkins' prose are his writings on the religious self in his spiritual commentaries and notes. This is the writing that has struck me as so essential to studying and reading Hopkins. These writings are, I judge, amazing anticipations of modern thinking about the making of the human consciousness. Still Hopkins did not work out a full analysis of the selving process, so far as we know. Therefore, to bring out the hidden implications of Hopkins' remarkably contemporary understanding of human consciousness, I needed a current consciousness philosopher who has fully and richly developed a hermeneutics of selving that might be shown to be parallel with Hopkins' thinking. Moreover, a truly apt philosophical contemporary account of selfness was needed in making a true parallel to Hopkins' selving insights. Such a hermeneutic philosophy had to possess the speculative courage to address, explain, and confirm the selving role of religious consciousness in constructing the self as well as to employ the hermeneutics of the poetic imagination in positing the selving "I." The writings of Paul Ricoeur fully suit these necessities.

Only after thinking through the many direct parallels between Hopkins and Ricoeur did I realize that, as valuable as is Hopkins's prose statements about "selving," his most remarkable account of the self was his "selving" account in his poetry. Read in a Ricoeurrian context, Hopkins' canon is an extraordinary expression of the creative consciousness poetizing his self-reflecting "I" as he sought to find and affirm the "I am" of his selfness.

This is the incredible story of his poetry, incredible because, unlike almost all poets whose poems become entangled with the egoism of public authorship and the narcissism of fame and posterity, Hopkins' poetry was written, for the most part, as the private discourse of his own selving experience, poems to himself about himself.

This situation did not mean that his poetry did not possess the artistic security of public attention, nor did he as a poet in any way let his poetic writing become merely subjective intercourse. Perhaps anticipating entering into the artistic discourse of public readership, one of the most powerful aspects of Hopkins' poetics is its forensic powers. Though in hiding, he wrote to be read. Nevertheless, in his lifetime, as he wrote, he had almost no readership to interact with, and therefore, his compositions occurred almost solely, and mainly, through a very personalizing poetic consciousness, poetry created in and out of a hermetic setting. Limiting as this was to his literary progress, attention, and productivity, perhaps largely negative elements in his public authorship, the conditions of his poetic creatorship offered something very rare: a powerful poetic consciousness, highly self-aware of the creative hermeneutics of his own selving, free to be moved to poetize only those dramatically high and low moments in which he discerned and deciphered significant changes in his selving personality, all without hysterics of his texts being put on a public stage. This is, I say again, a rare occurrence in the annals of poetic production. The result is a canon of poetry that expresses with the greatest honesty, with the most individualized selving clarity, the hermeneutic path of selving his own self-consciousness drama, perhaps, one of the most astonishing instances in literary history of a poet's narrative about selving his "I am."

Hopkins' "selving" is, to my mind, the story of his poetry. His poems form a unique account of positing self-meaning. The general character and pattern of this especially unique human phenomenology is at the center of this study. However, I hasten to note that episodes of the narrative of Hopkins' positing of his selfness needs to be further worked out in more specific detail, especially the selving reconstructive figurations in individual poems in the context of a general hermeneutics of personality as I have suggested in this study. Critical readings of Hopkins would then move from doctrinal to psycho-linguistic focuses which would provide pertinent intertextual contexts for reading the poetry directly as a powerful lyric narration of achieving an "I" self, a "selving" story of the "passion for the possible," full of "the ecstasy of interest" in the making of selfness.

I am suggesting here new approaches to reading Hopkins. First, we must be aware that Hopkins as a poet was not in critical or creative isolation from the new spirit of consciousness that began to emerge in British Romantic culture. Indeed, Hopkins, through the creativity of his own genius, developed notions of selving and wrote poetry incorporating them that anticipate contemporary understandings of the making of the human self. While Victorian in many of the cultural features of his poetry, arguably Hopkins took Romantic consciousness further towards twentieth-century thinking about selfness than any other nineteenth-century British writer. Moreover, Hopkins was able to accomplish this development generally within the religious and moral traditions of Western culture, an intellectual and creative feat no other philosopher-poet in his immediate literary cultural heritage did so manage with such constancy of pervasive originality.

Second, I have attempted in this book to offer a different manner of responding to Hopkins' poetry. While not wishing to dismiss other reading approaches, I suggest that we read Hopkins at the ground level of our own efforts to achieve the fullness of our selving "I." I mean by this that we find in Hopkins' writings those passages wherein he expressed those vital stages of selving his own consciousness and, using them as a heuristic for our own selving development, uncover the "passion for the possible" in his texts and appropriate from them that vital energy for transforming our own ways of being in the world. I am saying that Hopkins deserves such deep reading and will offer selving rewards in approaching his "eminent" texts. If Ricoeur is right about the "grace' of poetic words conferring change in the self, and I think he is, then I urge that we correspond with that "grace" in encountering some of the most powerful "selving" poetry written in this or the last century. In reading Hopkins this way, we need not get distracted by circumstances in his personal life, his Catholicism, or his priesthood. These are but the correlates to the facets of his selving predicaments. In regarding his Christed sense of the self, every reader can admire the deep sincerity of his spiritual aspirations as expressed in his poetic songs of religious love. Hopkins' poetic words are full of the "passion for the possible" in achieving selfness. His poetry calls us to respond with a matching passion and offers to take us to the horizon potential of its poetic powers.

I urge this having no doubt that his poetry produces among readers the deepest selving reflections. This is what grasps Hopkins' perennial readers. One of these, a common gardener, told me that he finds himself mowing grass and clipping bushes while reciting Hopkins' lines to himself. As another one of these reader reciters, we agreed that it is not only Hopkins' splendid poetic powers, not just the elevating sublimity of his uttered poetic inspirations—the wonder of his words; rather, what jars and shakes such readers' consciousnesses is the plain and naked encounters in the poetry with himself, with his mind-battles, with his prodigious talents and gifts, with his vocations, with his body, and, of course, with his Christed consciousness—all their exhilarating joys and scorching painfulness. His explosive writings describing these transforming moments in his selving consciousness are poetic dramas whose plots enact the deepest ranges of desire, exaltation, and despair.

What we experience is the poetic drama of the rarest "selving I" searching for the passion of his most possible "I am." Such a venture touches deep into the life of every self-reflective reader. Whatever the horizon of our readership, if we come to Hopkins' writings truly open and ready to plunge into their hermeneutic richness, we are awed by such selving energy, however convinced or unconvinced we are about his particular path to the most hopeful future of his selving destiny.

Astute readers of Hopkins might react to this summary of Hopkins' poetic efforts as a dazzling creation of the selving "I" by stating that he never attributed such heuristic capacities to his poems; in fact, he rejected his poetry as a bar to the fullness of his selving religious consciousness. Did not Hopkins follow what W. H. Auden so powerfully asserted in his prose and poetry, that "poetry makes nothing happen"? For Auden writing poetry was "more like having a million . . . readers, unaware of each other's existence (McDiarmid 45)."

I think that basically Hopkins would have agreed with Auden's attitude towards the cultural uses of art and beauty. But I deny that in either poet there is no powerful heuristic enablement in their poetry. If there are dramatic selving redescriptions in the poetry, they will out as heuristics to a reader who appropriates the texts deeply. But this issue of poetic intentionality deserves exploration. Let us take Auden first because he made the vanity of the poem such a moral scandal and second, Hopkins' so-called denial of his poetic self.

The central issue with which Auden struggled was: Is there any spirituality in the utterances of the poetic imagination? He came to believe that texting the self created a barrier between the poet and divinity (McDiarmid 6). It follows that, if a poet seeks some transcendent destiny gifted by that super-self we call God, then pardon is in order for being a poet: "God may reduce you / on Judgment Day / to tears of shame, / reciting by heart / the poems you would have written, / had your life been good" (quoted in McDiarmid 7 from Auden's *About the House* 13). It seems that, in his early career, Auden felt that there could be love in poetry, thus some hopeful powers of transformation, but later in his poems and his essays, he denied "art's spirituality," claiming that "Love, or truth in any serious sense' is a 'reticence,' the unarticulated worth that exists, if at all, outside of words on the page" (McDiarmid 8).

Auden's stringent denials of any intrinsic spirituality residing in poetry is based upon a conviction that became very strong in him, that religion and culture should not be interfused. In effect, what Auden was saying was a correction of the Romanticism that he and other writers inherited from the nineteenth century, namely, a confusion of religion and culture. This emphasis is a much needed distinction in that it asserts what, I think, is true: the intentionality of poems is not the intentionality of prayers. Auden, in his own poetry, especially after his slow but deepening Christian conversion, and in his reading of the poetry of others, could see the moral collision between exercising his creative expressive powers as the utterances of the narcissistic "I," a dancing about in a stagy play of words with no intention but to flaunt "I-ness" for its own sake, not using his poetic creativity to make his poetic texting go "outside" towards evoking a horizon beyond human expressive powers. After all, he was, as we are, surrounded by mounds and mounds of poetic mania babble, signifying the emptiness of the sputtering dazzle of literary culture. Auden saw clearly that such literary works were the artifacts of secular culture, time glosses in transit: "For a poet brought up in a Christian society it is perfectly possible to write a poem on a Christian theme, but when he does so he is concerned with it as an aspect of a religion—that is to say, a human cultural fact, like other facts—not as matter of faith" (quoted in McDiarmid 10).

What, then, is the border between culture and religion? Auden is firm in his demarcation: "To be a Christian . . . both art and science are secular activities, that is to say, small beer . . . . There can only be a Christian spirit in which an artist, a scientist, works or does not work . . . . Culture is one of Caesar's things" (quoted in McDiarmid 11). "Spirit" brings us back to poetic intentionality where the vital distinction lies. An artist who creates out of the principal intention of redescribing the "tumbling" of the selving "I," may indeed make beauty but nothing more. And the world's museums and libraries are filled with such works. But there is a further consideration. If, in the intentionality of the making, the artist invests in the work the presumption of expressing "goodness" through some expressive means, in virtue of the powers of "self creativity," then a prideful presumption may enter in. The poem, novel, or visual piece attempts to take on a magnitude it cannot possess—an expressive creatorship rivaling the divine. Such intentionality, carried out or not, from a Christian point of view, can only be called the sin of pride at its most grave register. I offer the example of James Joyce as a prime example of such a prideful intentionality. As a reader, I do not find any "pardon" in his writing, only self "plaudite." From a Christian perspective, while there is in Joyce's writing all the artifacts of Christian consciousness, including the elaborate mimicking of Christian selving, there is a limited upper horizon of transcendency in his works. For me, the writings of

Joyce express resentment towards all orders of existence, a resentment powerfully expressed in grand tropes of ironical laughter—creation / Creation as an existential joke. No wonder, then, he is lionized as the star of the Modernist dispersion of the self. No writer has more creatively, perhaps finally, expressed the self as the best joke in existence and made a literary hero of the teller of that joke.

Auden insisted that because there is the "Joycean" intentionality in the imaginative proclivities of the poetic self, all artistic texting is in some sense vanity, that is, asserts self without asking pardon for the prideful evil in the assertion. McDiarmid offers a quote from Auden most pertinent here: "Every beautiful poem presents an analogy to the forgiveness of sins; not an imitation, because it is not evil intentions which are represented and pardoned but contradictory feelings which the poet surrenders to the poem in which they are reconciled." These "contradictory feelings" are the double-bind of creative intentionality— expressing the selving of the "I" for one's own sake, as if it were self-gifted, and expressing the selving of the "I" as an humbling admission, in the recognition that the "I"'s existence is a gift and thus owes any selving to the Gift-giver. This distinction is of huge importance to the religious consciousness in the recognition that, in the intentionality of the creative imagination, there is present in the "I" self the element of sinful pride. The work of art may reconcile this contention between the egoism of making something beautiful and intentially giving beauty back, thereby diminishing pride in one's creations, but, as Auden asserts, this is only an analogy to the forgiveness of sins.

Auden accepts this concession: "The effect of beauty, therefore, is good to a degree that . . . the possibility of regaining paradise through repentance and forgiveness is recognized. Its effect is evil to the degree that beauty is taken, not as analogous to, but identical with goodness, so that the artist regards himself or is regarded by others as God, the pleasure of beauty for the joy of Paradise, and the conclusion drawn that, since all is well in the work of art, all is well in history. But all is not well there" (19). By "history" Auden means the real stories of the moral state of each self in time. Auden here is trying to move art beyond mere vain ego-selving to some "outside" possibility for positing transformation, but he is careful to distinguish, as McDiarmid delineates, pardon (true religious change) and "pardon" (the feigning of forgiveness managed through text-play resolutions) (Chapter One).

Hopkins addressed the same issue of the dangers of beauty in one of his last sonnets. He shied away as a young man from developing his painterly skills partly because he felt as a young man their attractions threatening to his moral life. And even before any considerations of his priestly vocation, Hopkins saw in himself capacities to indulge himself in his visual and verbal sensibility to obsessive egoistic levels. His love of the beautiful was, indeed, so absorbing, that it seemed quite possible for him to make of it his religion. Walter Pater's tutelage at Oxford must have been one of his severest temptations because of Pater's attitude towards living for beauty alone, above all else. It may not be too much to say that Hopkins tried nearly the whole of his life to temper his love of beauty to complement the desire of his religious consciousness.

It is not surprising, then, that among his last poems (158) is one about dealing with the moral integrity of the attractions of beauty: "To what serves mortal beauty—dangerous . . . ?" He thought of the powerful attractions of musical beauty when "instressing" the melodious beauty of a "Purcell tune," his favorite composer. He gives beauty its due. Beauty makes us aware of the selfness of being, its rightful existence as a created thing, whose "inscape" mastered, can afford us a grasp of the very identity of a thing. And in that grasp, we discover the very creative energy put there by the Creator: "See, it does this: keeps warm / Men's wits to the things that are; what good means—where a glance / Master more may than gaze, gaze out of countenance."

Hopkins then took up human beauty, using the Venerable Bede's story of how Gregory, later Pope, seeing the physical beauty of young Yorkshire slaves, remarked about their angelic faces, and later would send St.Augustine to convert England. Hopkins used this story to further illustrate what he meant by "warm / Men's wits" and "what good means." But there is a greater implication. The "good" attribute that the beauty of a thing is has as its highest purpose the most attractive expression of the Creator's intentionality—to share Himself throughout all Creation, especially the beauty of human beings. So the warming of "Men's wits" to beauty's beautifying "gaze out of countenance" should not lead to "worship block or barren stone" as art or religion. Art and religion as culture are, after all, but artifacts of the selving self in human culture, and while we may admire and appreciate both, we should only love its makers who create through the gifts of the Maker: "Our law says: Love what are love's worthiest, were all known; / World's loveliest—men's selves." And what in men's selves? Hopkins, in accord with his own phenomenology of self and parallel to Ricoeur's hermeneutic of selving reflection, sums up in six words the whole subject of this book: "Self flashes off frame and face." This is to say that each being, in its own order of existence, but particularly the existential order of human being, utters its unique "I-ness" in the selving task of positing its "I am." Such is the reflexive "flash" of the Creator in the "self-flashes" of Creation, especially "men's selves."

"What do then? how meet beauty?" Hopkins asked. He answered his question with more equanimity than did Auden, yet their views are not greatly far apart. Both acknowledge beauty, both see its dangers, and both insist that, in the greater scheme of things, beauty in itself is but a placing of an object of desire before the consciousness in order to transform the self to desire beauty's Maker. This is the only way to take beauty deep into the heart. So less suspiciously than Auden, but just as guarded, Hopkins advised: "Merely meet it; own, / Home at heart, heaven's sweet gift; then leave, let that alone." Finally, he says, treat beauty as an opportunity for corresponding to an elevating grace; at least be open to this selving transformation: "Yea, wish that though, wish all, God's better beauty, grace."

We see, then, for Hopkins there is a powerful spiritual meaning possible in the beautiful, and therefore spiritual meaning possible in artistic beauty. I think it significant that this poem on beauty was written two years (1885) after his physical and spiritual disequilibrium began, when he began to feel disinherited from the beauty of the earth, alienated from the creative possibilities of his "I"-ness, and disdainful of "dear and dogged man" (149). He, on his clearest days, could keep beauty balanced in the scheme of selving. Moreover, unlike Auden, who sees a kind of intrinsic moral corruption in the intentionality of the maker of art, a corruption that may well corrupt its appreciator as well, Hopkins, while acknowledging the moral dangers of beauty and art, is able to see art and beauty as a means to a love at a higher spiritual horizon. We should also remember that artistic expression is a double mediation— those of the maker-utterer and those of the reutterer-reader. Either intentionality is susceptible to corruptions of all kinds. Thus the enacted intentionality of one may well effect a very different esthetic / spiritual meaning for the other. The conflict of interpretations is always a factor in any selving experience. A poet, then, says Hopkins in his last "dark" sonnets (1885), may express powerfully what Ricoeur calls a "limit experience," that is, a powerful expression of human meaning at the level of the horizon of eternity, but the transforming "selving" interpretation may fail to crossover to the numinous for the poet, though his poem may be for the reader a metaphor of altering transcendence.

In the above analysis, we now can see why Hopkins rejected his poetry. As Auden did later, he discerned, in himself especially, and in the literary persona of other artists, the powerful play of the egoistic "I." As a priest of God, he judged that, given his strong drives to exercise publicly his poetic nature, he would undoubtedly fall into such artistic pride. Indeed, as we know, he was troubled life-long over the matter (Martin 164-165, 174, 229, 232-3, 247, 335-336, 346-347; White 117, 159, 221, 348, 370, 392-94, 440, 443, 448, 460). In his effort to develop his religious consciousness, his poetic desires in the "selving" of his "I" became central to his spiritual advancement. And, as we know, he both won and lost this struggle. He lost in that he finally let go of his poems, despite the terrible painfulness of giving them up, for him a hurtful kind of self-crucifixion in which he seemingly went against his human nature. And he won in that in his *retractatio*, he finally gifted them to God's Providence for whatever spiritual elevation such an act might bring him: "Also in some meditation today I earnestly asked our Lord to watch over my compositions, not to preserve them from being lost or coming to nothing, for that I am very willing they should be, but they might do me no harm through enmity or imprudence of any man or my own; that he should have them as his own and employ or not employ them as he should see fit. And this I believe is heard" (*Sermons* 232-233).

Auden could get art no closer to divinity than the forgiveness of the artist and his artifact. For Hopkins, grace is beckoned through the imagination. Both wanted the imagination in some way to be a vehicle of religious transformation through its creations. What is intriguing in this comparison is that Hopkins behaved towards his poetic personality in full accord with Auden's view, yet wrote poetry that regularly belied this attitude. Both, in the fullest recognition of the vanity of poetic wishes, in the last analysis, are *retractatio* poets. Perhaps this is why their works are so often charged with powerful spiritual meaning.

2

The broader issue here is the dilemma of religious consciousness in the contemporary world. This dilemma is easily stated, though its formulation in history is vast and complicated (Taylor). The evolution of the cosmos, as best as we can discern, has been and is towards greater consciousness (Edwards), yet the world that has been expressed as "contemporary" is a universe that is a vast machine indifferent to any deeply human purpose (Barrett). This elemental alienation is directly contrary to the interior life of every human person. Therefore, twentieth century human culture has been, and is filled, with anxiety, grief, and pain. There is no need to document here how such a radical conflict has produced a century filled with the many horrors of human destruction. As no culture has, we have documented these tragedies.

Despite that our times have been so convulsively disordered, we do know what the essence of our historical "modernness" is, namely, the destiny of consciousness. Moreover, we do posit a "selving" inwardness that reveals the presence of a selving "I"-ness, that in and through our inwardness each self is the key element of any advancing human culture, and at the center of our "selving" is a moral core. However infinitesimal the contemporary scientistic mentality makes us feel within the unbounding expanse of the universe, within our interiority, we regularly experience a call to significant choices that define our selfness, dignify our being, and answer our desires for a higher destiny. Contemporary intellectual, political, and economic culture constantly denies this moral center of the self, tries to explain away as psychosis, the outrage of our alienation with Nature and its overlay by historical human culture, and offers an apparent anodyne through the gratification of sensate egoism (see Taylor on modernist heresies, Chapter 24). But each of us, in choosing to become our unique selves, is that moralist Immanuel Kant so accurately described: "Granted that the pure moral law inexorably binds every man as a command (not as a rule of prudence), the righteous man may say: I will that there be a God, that my existence in this world would be also an existence in a pure world of the understanding outside the system of natural connections, and finally that my duration is endless. I stand by this and will not give up this belief . . ." (quoted in Barrett 101).

This "selving" righteousness is our deepest human, self-concern. While we as persons exist in the most particular state of selfness, the horizon of our existence is within the totality of the cosmos. It is exactly in this enduring, existential quandary that the question of God arises and hence the center of human selving activity is what we call the religious consciousness. It is notable that much of modern thinking, scientific and philosophic, either negates this deep moral core of human selving interiority or analyzes it to the point of dismissal. The immense vitality of this human aspiration is made irrelevant. Religious culture and the sacral texts along with their traditions are studied as historical cross-anthropology and archaeology. The abounding human depression that pervades enormous numbers of human beings in society is treated as communal and personal disorder somehow unconsciously entrapping each self, whose remedy is a recognition that we are culturally sick and need brain-altering drugs to assuage our bad fates. No wonder that, as William Barrett has shown, the direction of the mentors of the modern world has been to explain "modernity" as the dispersion of any spiritual horizon within the self and, in consequence, the deconstruction of the significance of the self as possessing any ultimately essential human meaning.

Against this raging holocaust of the self at every level of contemporarylife, every "selving" person is searching for human meaning at every horizon of existence, but especially at the horizon of ultimate meaning. No amount of erudite philosophizing or scientizing, if the human subjectivity enters the argument, can obviate the reality of this existential fact, that this search is at the very center, in some way, of every human self. Self-concern not only exists in the core of the consciousness, but it is the deepest, most pervasive passion in the human personality. It is this selfness that we are, this selfness that we must experience, this selfness that we must abide. Each human subjectivity is made up of this selving consciousness-task to become the "I am" of our hope.

But, as we have seen, each "selving" consciousness, through its memorial powers, operates as a history-maker, that is, a builder of the story of the past that was and a future that may be. Unless consciousness is the change factor of history, history is only a boring list of dated repetitions. What makes history a story with meaning is the enacted and enacting passion for human meaning in the historical story. For a long time, consciousness in history, particularly ordinary consciousness, received little attention, but beginning with the culture of Modernity, whose roots reach back two centuries (Taylor Chapter 17), the story of the existence of and story of the common self began to be explicated so as to become the historical "realism" of the "mode of life-narration" in literate culture. Curiously this contemporary attention to what is called "social history" has made the historical necessities of "selving" meaning more manifest while, in many instances, leaving out the crucial factor that history is basically the narration of the spiritual aspirations of the consciousness. So many cultural historians, even some of the best such as Charles Taylor, become so overwrought with the failures of human religious culture (519) that they become shut off from the human passion for spiritual meaning. Even the brightest few are caught up in the alienation of the many, which Pascal stated so trenchantly: "The eternal silence of those infinite spaces frightens me" (quoted in Barrett 90).

It is in this emptiness that Hopkins finds the "grandeur of God" and Ricoeur uncovers "the passion for the possible." This book is about using their words to help us raise "selving" passion to the horizon of hope and finally freedom, even joy.

Works Cited and Consulted

Hopkins

The Correspondence of Gerard Manley Hopkins and Richard Watson Dixon. Ed. C. C. Abbott. London: Oxford University Press, 1955.

Further Letters of Gerard Manley Hopkins. Ed. C. C. Abbott. 2nd. Ed. London: Oxford University Press, 1956.

The Journals and Papers of Gerard Manley Hopkins. Eds. Humphrey House and Graham Storey. 2nd. Ed. London: Oxford University Press, 1959.

The Journals and Papers of Gerard Manley Hopkins. Eds. Humphrey House and Graham Storey. 2nd. Ed. London: Oxford University Press, 1959.

The Letters of Gerard Manley Hopkins to Robert Bridges. Ed. C. C. Abbott London: Oxford University Press, 1955.

The Poetic Works of Gerard Manley Hopkins. Ed. Norman MacKenzie. Oxford: Clarendon University Press, 1990.

The Sermons and Devotional Writings of Gerard Manley Hopkins. Ed. Christopher Devlin. London: Oxford University Press, 1959.

About Hopkins

Bump, Jerome. "Reader-Centered Criticism and Bibliotherapy: Hopkins and Selving." *Renascence: Essays on Values in Literature* XLII (Fall 1989 (Winter 1990): 65-86.

A Concordance to the English Poetry of Gerard Manley Hopkins. Comp. Robert J. Dilligan and Todd K. Bender. Madison: University of Wisconsin Press, 1970).

Downes, David Anthony. *The Ignatian Personality of Gerard Manley Hopkins.* Lanham, Maryland: University Press of America, 1990.

Emmons, Jeanne. "The Cloven Pomegranate: Metaphor in the Poetry of Gerard Manley Hopkins." *The Hopkins Quarterly* XVIII (3) (October 1990): 85-101.

Ellis, Virginia Ridley. *Gerard Manley Hopkins and the Language of Mystery.* Columbia: University of Missouri Press, 1991.

Ellsberg, Margaret R. *Created To Praise: The Language of Gerard Manley Hopkins.* New York: Oxford University Press, 1987.

Ferlita, Ernest. *The Uttermost Mark: The Dramatic Criticism of Gerard Manley Hopkins.* Lanham, Maryland: University Press of America, 1990.

Fulweiler, Howard W. *Letters from the Darkling Plan: Language and the Ground of Knowledge in the Poetry of Arnold and Hopkins.* Columbia: Univ. of Missouri Press, 1972.

Gerard Manley Hopkins: Early Poetic Manuscripts and Notebooks in Facsimile. Ed. Norman H. MacKenzie. New York: Garland Publishing, Inc., 1989.

The Later Poetic Manuscripts of Gerard Manley Hopkins in Facsimile. Ed. Norman H. MacKenzie. New York: Garland Publishing, Inc., 1992.

Lichtmann, Maria R. *The Contemplative Poetry of Gerard Manley Hopkins.* Princeton: Princeton University Press, 1989.

MacKenzie, Norman. *A Reader's Guide to Gerard Manley Hopkins.* Ithaca: Cornell University Press, 1981.

Martin, Robert Bernard. *Gerard Manley Hopkins: a Very Private Life.* New York: G. P. Putnam, 1991.

Miller, J. HIllis. "The Creation of the Self in Gerard Manley Hopkins." *ELH,* 22, (1955): 293-319.

_____. . *The Disappearance of God.* Cambridge: Harvard University Press, 1963.

_____. *The Linguistic Moment.* Princeton: Princeton University Press, 1985.

Milroy, James. *The Language of Gerard Manley Hopkins.* London: Andre Deutsch, 1977.

Ong. Walter. *Hopkins, The Self, And God.* Toronto: Toronto University Press, 1986.

Phillips, Catherine. "The Mixed Emotions of Hopkins' 'Portrait of Two Beautiful Young People.'" *The Hopkins Quarterly* XVI (4): 137-147.

Plotkin, Cary H. *The Tenth Muse: Victorian Philology and the Genesis of the Poetic Language of Gerard Manley Hopkins.* Carbondale: Southern Illinois Press, 1989.

Roberts, Gerald. "'I know the sadness, but the cause know not.'" *The Hopkins Quarterly.* XVIII (3): 97-111.

_____.Ed. *Gerard Manley Hopkins: The Critical Heritage.* London: Routledge and Kegan Paul, 1987

Robinson, John. *In Extremity: A Study of Gerard Manley Hopkins.* Cambridge: Cambridge University Press, 1978.

White, Norman. *Hopkins: A Literary Biography.* Oxford: Clarendon Press, 1992.

Ricoeur

"Biblical Hermeneutics." *Semeia* 4 (1975): 29-148.

"The Bible and the Imagination." *The Bible as a Document of the University.* Ed. Hans Dieter Betz. Chico, Ca.: Scholar's Press, 1981. 49-75.

The Conflict of Interpretations: Essays in Hermeneutics. Ed. Don Ihde. Evanston: Northwestern University Press, 1974.

Essays in Biblical Interpretation. Ed. Lewis Mudge. Philadelphia: Fortress Press, 1980.

Freud and Philosophy: An Essay on Interpretation. New Haven: Yale University Press, 1970.

"Hermeneutic of the Idea Revelation." *The Center for Hermeneutical Studies.* Ed. W. Wellner. Feb. (1977): 1-22.

"History and Hermeneutics." *The Journal of Philosophy*. 73: 683-695.

"Hope and the Structure of Philosophical Systems." *Proceedings of the American Catholic Association* 64 (1970): 55-69.

Interpretation Theory: Discourse and the Surplus of Meaning. Fort Worth: Christian University Press, 1976.

"The Metaphorical Process as Cognition, Imagination and Feeling." *Critical Inquiry* 5 (1978): 143-159.

"The Narrative Function." *Semeia* 13 (1978): 177-202.

Oneself As Another. Tr. Kathleen Blamey. Chicago: University of Chicago Press, 1992.

"Philosophical Hermeneutics and Theological Hermeneutics." *Studies in Religion* 5 (1975-1976): 14-33.

The Philosophy of Paul Ricoeur: An Anthology of his Works. Ed. Charles E. Reagan and David Stewart. Boston: Beacon Press, 1978.

A Ricoeur Reader: Reflection and the Imagination. Ed. Maria J. Valdes. Toronto: University of Toronto Press, 1991.

The Rule of Metaphor. London: Routledge & Kegan Paul, 1978.

The Symbolism of Evil. Boston: Beacon Press, 1969.

Time and Narrative. 3 Vols. Chicago: University of Chicago Press, 1984-1988.

About Ricoeur

Dornisch, Loretta. *Faith and Philosophy in the Writings of Paul Ricoeur.* Lewiston: The Edwin Mellen Press, 1990.

Kearney, Richard. *Dialogues with Contemporary Continental Thinkers.* Manchester: Manchester University Press, 1984.

Klemm, David E. *The Hermeneutical Theory of Paul Ricoeur.* Lewisburg: Bucknell University Press, 1983.

Lowe, William James. *Mystery and the Unconscious: A Study in the Thought of Paul Ricoeur.* Metuchen, N. J.: The Scarecrow Press, 1977.

Vanhoozer, Kevin J. *Biblical Narrative in the Philosophy of Paul Ricoeur.* Cambridge: Cambridge University Press, 1990.

Wood, David. *On Paul Ricoeur: Narrative and Interpretation.* London: Routledge: Press, 1991.

Selving, Hermeneutics, and Religious Consciousness

Barrett, William. *Death of the Soul: From Descartes to the Computer.* New York: Doubleday Anchor, 1986.

Bruns, Gerald L. *Hermeneutics: Ancient and Modern.* New Haven. Yale University Press, 1992.

Capon, Robert Farrar. *The Parables of Judgment.* Grand Rapids: William B. Erdmans, 1989.

Caraman, S. J., Philip. *Ignatius Loyola.* New York: Harper and Row, 1990.

Carter, Robert E. *God, The Self and Nothingness: Reflections: Eastern and Western.* New York: Paragon House, 1990.

Collins, Christopher. *The Poetics of the Mind's Eye: Literature and the Psychology of Imagination.* Philadelphia: Univ. of Penn. Press, 1991.

Dennett, Daniel C. *Consciousness Explained.* Boston: Little Brown, 1991.

Edinger, Edward. *Ego and Archetype.* New York: G.P. Putnam, 1972.

Gerhart, Mary and Russell, Alan. *Metaphoric Process: The Creation of Scientific and Religious Understanding.* Forth Worth: Texas Christian University, 1984.

Guerriere, Daniel, Ed. *Phenomenology of the Truth Proper to Religion.* Albany: State University of New York Press, 1990.

Ignatius Loyola. *The Spiritual Exercises: A New Translation.* Tr. Louis J, Puhl, S. J. Westminster, Maryland: The Newman Press, 1953.

Jay, Paul. *Being in the Text: Self-Representation from Wordsworth to Roland Barthes.* Ithaca: Cornell University Press, 1984.

Ker, Ian. *Oxford Lives: John Henry Newman.* Oxford: Oxford University Press, 1990.

Lonergan, Bernard. *Collection.* Ed. F. E. Crowe, S. J. New York: Herder and Herder, 1967.

_____. *Grace and Freedom: Operative Grace In the Thought of St. Thomas Aquinas.* Ed. J. Pectorit Burns, S. J. New York: Herder and Herder, 1971.

_____. *Insight: A Study of Human Understanding.* 3rd.. Ed. New York: Philosophical Library, 1970.

_____. *Method in Theology.* New York: Herder and Herder, 1972. *Lonergan's Hermeneutics: Its Development and Application.* Eds. Sean E. McEvenue and Ben F. Meyer. Wash. D. C. : The Catholic University of America Press, 1989.

McCormick, Peter J. *Fictions, Philosophies, and the Problems of Poetics.* Ithaca: Cornell University Press, 1988.

Moore, Michael D. "Newman and the Motif of Intellectual Pain in Hopkins' 'Terrible Sonnets,'" *Mosaic* 12 (1979): 29-46.

Newman, John Henry, *Essays Critical and Historical.* Vol 1. New Work: Longmans, Green, 1910.

_____.. *Grammar of Assent.* Intro. Etienne Gilson. New York: Doubleday Image Books, 1955.

Nichols, Ashton. *The Poetics of Epiphany: Nineteenth Century Origins of the Modern Literary Movement.* Tuscaloosa: The University of Alabama Press, 1987.

Nixon, Jude V. *Gerard Manley Hopkins and His Contemporaries: Liddon, Newman, Darwin, and Pater.* New York: Garland Publishing, Inc., 1994.

_____ "The Kindly Light: A Reappraisal of the Influence of Newman on Hopkins," *Texas Studies in Literature and Language* 31 (Spring 1989): 66-85.

Ormiston, Gayle L. and Schrift, Alan D. *The Hermeneutic Tradition.* Albany: State University of New York Press, 1990.

_____. *Transforming the Hermeneutic Context.* Albany: State University of New York Press, 1990.

Patterson, David. *The Affirming Flame: Religion, Language, Literature.* Norman: University of Oklahoma Press, 1982.

Prickett, Stephen. "Newman: The Physiognomy of Development." *Christianity and Literature.* 40 (Spring 1991): 267-277.

Privateer, Paul Michael. *Identity and Ideology: Romantic Voices in British Poetry—1789-1850.* Athens: The University of Georgian Press, 1991.

Raine, Kathleen. *The Hopkins Society: The Third Annual Lecture.* Worcester: Stanbrook Abbey Press, 1972.

Shea, Eugene. *The Immortal "I": Toward a Fourth Psychology of Being / Loving / Knowing.* Lanham, Maryland: University Press of America, 1991.

Slinn, E. Warwick. *The Discourse of Self In Victorian Poetry.* Charlottsville: University of Virginia Press, 1991.

Stone, Jerome A. *The Minimalist Vision of Transcendence.* Albany: The State University of New York Press, 1992.

Sulloway, Alison G. *Gerard Manley Hopkins and the Victorian Temper.* London: Routledge and Kegan Paul, 1972.

Taylor, Charles. *Sources of the Self: The Making of Modern Identity.* Cambridge: Harvard University Press, 1989.

Tennyson, G. B. *Victorian Devotional Poetry: The Tractarian Mode.* Cambridge: Harvard University Press, 1981.

Tracy, David. *The Analogical Imagination: Christian Theology and the Culture of Pluralism.* New York: Crossroad, 1986.

Ward, Bernadette. "Newman's *Grammar of Assent* and the Poetry of Gerard Manley Hopkins." *Renascence* XLIII (1-2 Fall / 1990/Winter / 1991): 105-121.

Webb, Eugene. *Philosophers of Consciousness: Polanyi, Lonergan, Voegelin, Ricoeur, Girard, Kierkegaard.* Seattle: University of Washington Press, 1988.

_____. *The Self Between: From Freud to the New Social Psychology of France.* Seattle: University of Washington Press, 1993.

White, Stephen L. *The Unity of the Self.* Cambridge: The MIT Press, 1991.

Cosmos, Consciousness, and Poetics

Donoghue, Denis. *The Old Moderns: Essay on Literature and Theory.* New York: Alfred A. Knopf, 1994.

Duns Scotus on Will and Morality. Tr. Allan B. Wolter. Washington, D. C.: The Catholic University of America Press, 1986.

Edwards, Denis. *Jesus and the Cosmos.* New York: Paulist Press,1991.

Egan, Desmond. *The Death of Metaphor.* Savage, Maryland: Barnes and Noble Books, 1990.

Fraistat, Neil. *The Poem and the Book: Interpreting Collections of Romantic Poetry.* Chapel Hill: The University of North Carolina Press, 1985.

_____, Ed. *Poems in Their Place.* Chapel Hill: The University of North Carolina Press, 1986.

Frye, Northrop. *Words with Power: Being a Second Study of the Bible and Literature.* New York: Harcourt Brace Jovanovich,1990.

Goodman, Nelson. *Languages of Art: An Approach to a Theory of Symbols.* Indianapolis: Hackett Publishing Co. Inc., 1976.

Hart, Kevin. *The Trespass of the Sign: Deconstruction, Theology and Philosophy.* Cambridge: Cambridge University Press, 1989.

McDiarmid, Lucy. *Auden's Apologies For Poetry.* Princeton: Princeton University Press, 1990.

Meisel, Perry. *The Myth of the Modern: A Study in British Literature and Criticism after 1850.* New Haven: Yale University Press, 1987.

Mitchell, Ed., W. J. T. *On Narrative.* Chicago: The University of Chicago Press, 1980.

Moore, Stephen D. *Literary Criticism and the Gospels: The Theoretical Challenge.* New Haven: Yale University Press, 1989.

Parmenides of Elea. Ed. by David Gallop. Toronto: University of Toronto Press, 1991.

Polkinghorne, John. *One World: The Interaction of Science and Theology.* Princeton: Princeton University Press, 1986.

Prickett, Stephen. *Words and The Word: Language, Poetics, and Biblical Interpretation.* Cambridge: Cambridge University Press, 1986.

Sass, Louis A. *Madness and Modernism.* New York: Basic Books, Harper and Collins Press, 1992.

Searle, John. *The Rediscovery of the Mind.* Cambridge, Mass.: The MIT Press, 1992.

Smith, Curtis, D. *Jung's Quest for Wholeness: A Religious and Historical Perspective.* Albany: State University of New York Press, 1990.

Index

WITHDRAWN